Old Masters, New Subjects
Early Modern and Poststructuralist Theories of Will

୬

DOLORA A. WOJCIEHOWSKI

Old Masters, New Subjects

Early Modern and Poststructuralist Theories of Will

STANFORD UNIVERSITY PRESS, STANFORD, CALIFORNIA

1995

©1995 by the Board of Trustees of the Leland Stanford Junior University
Printed in the United States of America

CIP data are at the end of the book

Stanford University Press publications are distributed exclusively by
Stanford University Press within the United States, Canada, Mexico, and Central
America; they are distributed exclusively by Cambridge University Press
throughout the rest of the world.

To my aunts,
Mary Eileen Cotter (1904–1986) and
Zita Marie Cotter, S.C.L. (1921–1993)

Acknowledgments

∾∙

There are many friends and associates who helped bring this book into being; for their constructive criticisms, their suggestions, and their moral support I am deeply grateful. First of all, I would like to thank my colleagues at the Department of English at the University of Texas. Among these are Professors John Rumrich, Eric Mallin, David Wallace, Beth Hedrick, Walter Reed, Bill Worthen, Kurt Heinzelman, and Wayne Rebhorn—present and former members of the department who talked over ideas with me, suggested bibliographical resources, read portions of the manuscript, and offered invaluable advice. I would like to thank all of these colleagues for their assistance and input. Most especially I would like to thank Professor Leah Marcus, also of the Department of English, for her particular contribution to this endeavor. Her superb critical and editorial insight, together with her helpful mode of encouragement, were of enormous benefit to me.

I would also like to thank certain colleagues in other departments at the University of Texas for their support. Professors David Peterson and Bruce Hunt of the Department of History read Chapters 2 and 4 respectively. Their critical commentary and empirical counsel were highly beneficial and greatly appreciated. In addition, I would like to thank Professor Katie Arens of Germanic Languages for her reading of Chapter 4 and for her energetic discussions of various related issues. Also, I thank my colleagues in Comparative Literature at the University of Texas for their support and interest in this project—especially Professor Sidney Monas, also of Slavic Languages, for his kind and supportive advice over the years. Some mention should be made, too, of the Early Modern Interest Group at the University of Texas, who heard a version of Chapter 4 and provided many useful ideas and criticisms. They were a much-appreciated audience.

There are other friends and colleagues around the country (indeed, around the globe) whose valuable advice and thoughtful criticisms I would like to acknowledge here. Professor Albert Ascoli of the Departments of Italian and Comparative Literature at Northwestern University provided essential editorial and scholarly advice for the entire manuscript; I owe him a special debt of gratitude. Professor Marilyn Migiel of the Department of Romance Languages at Cornell University has been a supportive friend and colleague; under her editorship a segment of the Galileo chapter was published in the *Stanford Italian Review*. Her advice on that and other portions of the manuscript was greatly appreciated. Professor Krystyna Kurawinska-Courtney of the Department of English at the University of Lodz, Poland, read the introduction and Chapter 1 and offered useful criticisms and bibliography; she also provided much-needed moral support at a critical time in the production of this manuscript. To my long-time friend Cathy Caruth, professor of English and comparative literature at Emory University, I would like to offer special thanks, no less for her readings of the first two chapters of the manuscript and for our discussions of ideas treated therein than for the encouragement, advice, and good humor she has offered over the years.

Professor Michael Cahn, of the University of Constance, Germany, co-organized with me a University of Texas symposium on literary theory, science, and relativisms in 1988, which was germinal to the writing of the Galileo chapter. Professor James Bono of the State University of New York, Buffalo, generously offered his advice and expertise in a reading of that same chapter. Professor Craig Kallendorf of the Department of English at Texas A & M University provided excellent paleographical advice concerning the Petrarch chapter, for which I am grateful. Professor Bud Fairlamb of the Department of Humanities at the University of Houston–Victoria offered an excellent critical reading of several chapters of the manuscript. To each of them I offer my thanks.

I would like to thank my students for their insights into these and related texts. I would especially like to acknowledge John Zuern, of the Comparative Literature Program at the University of Texas, for his work on Martin Luther; Elizabeth Beckmann, former graduate student in the Department of English, for her reading of Teresa of Avila's *Libro de la vida*; and Emilio Medina, former undergraduate at the University of Texas, now of Emory University, for his ideas on literary theory. To these and many other students I am extremely grateful; they have made my job worthwhile.

I would also like to acknowledge the University Research Institute at the University of Texas. The Institute granted me a Summer Research Award, which was extremely useful at the early stages of the production of this book.

I am also grateful to Professors Rita Copeland and David Wallace, formerly of the University of Texas, now of the University of Minnesota, who offered very important guidance and support for the publication of this manuscript. Helen Tartar, Humanities Editor of Stanford University Press, and Lynn Stewart, Associate Editor for the Press, have been a delight to work with on this project. I thank the *Stanford Italian Review*, as well, for allowing me to include a much-extended version of "Galileo's Two Chief Word Systems" (10, no. 1 [1991]: 61–80) as Chapter 4 of this book.

Professors Thomas Greene of Yale University and Margaret Ferguson of the University of Colorado, Boulder, directed my dissertation on confessional autobiography some years ago. For their advice and criticism during that phase of my training I am indebted.

Last but not least, I would like to thank my friends and family for all their help during the completion of this book. Liz and Fred Asnes, Janice Inskeep, Cheryl Johnson, Brad Nelson, Mary Ellen and Ken Pon, and Russ Quinn were very supportive at various stages of this work, as were Professors Margot Backus, Lydia Bernstein, Shoshanah and Frank Dietz, David Guenther, Beth Kolko, and Helena Woodard—all of whom have been very special friends to me. I thank my parents, James and Betty Wojciehowski; my aunt and uncle, Dody and Jack Cotter; and my brothers and sisters—Jim, Bart,

Dana, and Kati. Finally I thank Ben Moss for his rigorous reading of the manuscript and suggestions for its organization, his invaluable insight into the fundamental issues of this research, and his patient and loving support over the years of its writing. Without him, and indeed, without all of these people, this work would not have been possible; I remain very much indebted to each of them.

Contents

◦

Abbreviations

&

A   *The Autobiography of St. Ignatius Loyola.* Trans. Joseph
F. O'Callaghan. Ed. John C. Olin. New York: Harper and
Row, 1974.

D   Galilei, Galileo. *Dialogue Concerning the Two Chief World
Systems.* 2d rev. ed. Ed. and trans. Stillman Drake. Berkeley: University of California Press, 1967 [1953].

ES   *Sancti Ignatii de Loyola Exercitia Spiritualia.* Ed. Joseph
Calveras, S.J., and Candido de Dalmases, S.J. Monumenta
Historica Societatis Iesu, no. 100. Monumenta Ignatiana,
2d ser., vol. 1. Rome: Institutum Historicum Societatis
Iesu, 1969.

FN   *Fontes narrativi de S. Ignatio de Loyola et de Societatis
Iesu initiis.* Vol. 1, *Acta Patris Ignatii scripta a P. Lud.
Gonzalez de Camara 1553/1555.* Ed. D. F. Zapico, S.J.,
and C. de Dalmases, S.J., with P. Leturia, S.J. Narrationes
scriptae ante annum 1557. Monumenta Historica Societatis Iesu, no. 66. Monumenta Ignatiana, 4th ser., Scripta
de S. Ignatio, vol. 1. Rome: Institutum Historicum Societatis Iesu, 1943.

LT   *The Life of Teresa of Jesus.* Ed. and trans. E. Allison Peers.
Garden City, N.Y.: Image Books, 1960 [1944].

LV   Teresa of Avila. *Libro de la vida.* In *Obras completas*, ed.

Efrén de la Madre de Dios, O.C.D., and Otger Steggink,
O. Carm. Madrid: Católica, 1962.

LW *Luther's Works.* 55 vols. Ed. Jaroslav Pelikan, vols. 1–30,
and Helmut T. Lehmann, vols. 31–55. St. Louis: Concordia Publishing House, and Philadelphia: Fortress Press,
1955–76.

OL *Opere latine di Francesco Petrarca.* 2 vols. Ed. Antonietta
Bufano. Turin: UTET, 1975.

Opere *Le Opere di Galileo Galilei.* 20 vols. Ed. Antonio Favaro.
Edizione Nazionale. Florence: G. Barbèra Editore, 1933
[1890–99].

S *Petrarch's "Secretum" with Introduction, Notes, and Critical Anthology.* Ed. Davy Carozza. Ed. and trans. H.
James Shey. American University Studies, no. 17. Classical Languages and Literature, no. 7. New York: Peter
Lang, 1989.

SE *The Spiritual Exercises of St. Ignatius.* Trans. Anthony
Mottola. Garden City, N.Y.: Image Books, 1964.

WA *D. Martin Luthers Werke: Kritische Gesamtausgabe.* 65
vols. Weimar: Hermann Böhlaus Nachfolger, 1883–.

It is certainly not the least charm of a theory that it is refutable; it is precisely thereby that it attracts subtle minds. It seems that the hundred-times refuted theory of a "free will" owes its persistence to this charm alone; again and again someone comes along who feels he is strong enough to refute it.

F. Nietzsche, *Beyond Good and Evil*

Old Masters, New Subjects
Early Modern and Poststructuralist
Theories of Will

ॐ

Introduction

⌖

A Portrait of the Artist

A master is an overlord, a victor, a teacher; an "old master" is a cultural icon, an emblem of present regard for past masteries. The phrase "old masters" evokes a self-conscious and grandiose view of the world and one's power in it. It suggests a past, Renaissance or Baroque, when mastery was not only possible, but de rigueur. Names like Leonardo, Michelangelo, and Rembrandt spring to mind, men whose vision, versatility, and humanity have been revered as marks of a bygone age of extraordinary accomplishment. In a broader sense, "Old Mastery" connotes not just painterly skill, the power to create a mirror of the world in remarkable detail, but also the virtuosic mastery of many knowledges—music, statecraft, science, philosophy, literature, mathematics—ascribed to that prodigy known as the Renaissance Man.[1] Central to this conception of mastery is the proverbial iron will of the "complete men" of the Renaissance, men lionized by historian Jacob Burckhardt and his successors. By the end of the thirteenth century, Burckhardt declared, "Italy began to swarm with individuality," once the medieval veil of "faith, illusion, and childish prepossession" had been torn away. What Burckhardt created was less a history of the Renaissance than a theory of the self, the origins of which he located in an idealized past. Characteristic of this self was an "impulse to the highest individual development," plus a "powerful and varied nature, which had mastered all the elements of the culture of the age." Burckhardt called this masterful individual the "all-sided man"—*l'uomo universale*.[2]

This traditional view of Renaissance mastery is founded on the belief that individualism, as both a concept and a behavior, emerged during the early modern age. Regardless of how historians and critics have valued Renaissance selfhood and Old Mastery, the coupling of emergent individualism with the early modern period persists to this day.[3] "Subjectivity," the philosopher Fred Dallmayr asserts, "has served as cornerstone of modern philosophy since the Renaissance. . . . Modern subjectivity has tended to foster a distinctive type of individualism: one which treats the ego as the center not only of theoretical cognition but of social-political action and interaction."[4] Similarly, new historicist Stephen Greenblatt has argued that "there is in the early modern period a change in the intellectual, social, psychological, and aesthetic structures that govern the generation of identities,"[5] a thesis that also serves as the starting point for William Kerrigan and Gordon Braden's recent, more conservative study of Renaissance individualism.[6]

Perhaps more than anything else (nascent capitalism or the rise of the nation-state, for example), it is the rhetoric of voluntarism in early modern texts, the exaltation of human will, that gives rise to the idea of the Renaissance as the age of self-conscious individualism. One encounters such voluntarism throughout the canon of Renaissance writings, particularly in humanist texts, where freedom and necessity are debated regularly; indeed, these arguments constitute a rather prominent genre of philosophical and theological writing.[7] In his famous and infamous assertion of human will, Giovanni Pico della Mirandola offered what was to become the central topos of Renaissance voluntarism: Man is free, he said, to determine his own position in the hierarchy of creation. In the *De hominis dignitate* (1486), the exuberant Pico envisions God's saying to Adam:

In conformity with thy free judgment, in whose hands I have placed thee, thou art confined by no bounds; and thou wilt fix limits of nature for thyself. I have placed thee at the center of the world, that from there thou mayest more conveniently look around and see whatsoever is in the world. Neither heavenly nor earthly, neither mortal nor immortal have We made thee. Thou, like a judge appointed for being honorable, art the molder and maker of thyself; thou mayest sculpt thyself into whatever shape thou dost prefer. Thou canst grow downward into the lower natures which are brutes. Thou canst again grow upward from thy soul's reason into the higher natures which are divine.[8]

For Pico, man is a slippery creature, capable of angelic as well as bestial behavior. Man is his own work of art, a being in control of his own destiny. Certainly this creature controls the destinies of others as well. As Lauro Martines and Anthony Grafton and Lisa Jardine have argued, Pico and several of his contemporaries couched their extreme voluntarism in a rhetoric of heroic, humanist domination—a rhetoric legitimating, not coincidentally, the political programs of fifteenth-century Italian urban elites.[9] This powerful ideology of human freedom, of man's ability to master everything from his baser instincts to dead languages, was widespread in humanist writings of the fifteenth and sixteenth centuries. The humanist rhetoric of "the dignity of man" and the freedom of the will spread westward across Europe, disseminated in particular by intellectuals in the service of, or in search of, powerful patrons.

In *Il principe* (1513), Niccolò Machiavelli reveals more clearly than does Pico the political expedience of voluntarist rhetoric. Machiavelli advises the would-be prince never to succumb to a sense of fatalism, but rather to take control of his destiny by beating Fortune into submission. "Fortune is a woman [La fortuna è donna]," he writes, "and it is necessary, if one wants to hold her down, to beat her and strike her down. And one sees that she lets herself be won more by the impetuous than by those who proceed coldly" (p. 101). Machiavelli's misogynistic voluntarism is complicated by the fact that Lady Fortuna can be raped by the strong but can never be completely mastered by anyone.[10] Yet though Machiavelli does not resolve the conflict between human will and fate, the message he preaches is one of becoming, by force or cunning, the master of one's own destiny, and of others' as well.

The Renaissance rhetoric of free will surfaced in a variety of discourses, depending on what the humanist sought to valorize: philosophy (as in the case of Pico), philology, politics, poetry, or science, for example. Nearly a century after Pico composed his oration, Philip Sidney, in his *Defence of Poetry* (1583), described in Neoplatonic terms the ennobling and liberating qualities of learning: "This purifying of wit—this enriching of memory, enabling of judgment, and enlarging of conceit—which commonly we call learning, under what name soever it come forth, or to what immediate end soever it be directed, the final end is to lead and draw us to as high a perfection as our degenerate souls, made worse by their clayey lodgings, can be capable of" (p. 28). Sidney asserts that one transcends bodily limitations to arrive at a higher, spiritual perfection by means of various forms of intellectual mastery—that is, by means of the will. A few decades later Shakespeare's Hamlet announces man's quasi divinity, his transcendent willfulness, presumably in a more ironic vein: "What a piece of work is a man, how noble in reason, how infinite in faculties" (*Hamlet*, II.2.303–4). Though clearly for different purposes, both Sidney and Shakespeare allude to humanist commonplaces about the freedom and dignity of man, ideas still circulating in their own time.

Writing in the early seventeenth century, Galileo Galilei found the voluntarism of his humanist precursors still serviceable. In his *Dialogue Concerning the Two Chief World Systems* (Dialogo sopra i due massimi sistemi del mondo) (1632), Galileo defended the god-like powers of man's intellect, arguing that although the capacity of the human mind is only a fraction of that of the divine, nevertheless, what men do know, they know divinely: "But with regard to those few [propositions] which the human intellect does understand, I believe that its knowledge equals the Divine in objective certainty, for here it succeeds in understanding necessity, beyond which there can be no greater sureness" (*D*, p. 103). In asserting the power, not so much of all human knowledge, but specifically of his brand of mathematical science, Galileo helped invent an ideology of scientific mastery still very much alive today—namely, the popular notion that science is the truest and most objective discipline, capable of giving humans the greatest power and control over the natural world.[11]

The Idea of the Renaissance

As the preceding passages suggest, certain early modern discourses—humanism, voluntarist philosophy, and emergent scientific rationalism, to name a few—seem to contain in crystalline form those notions of mastery, of the will to power, that Burckhardt, precursor of Nietzsche, took to be characteristically Renaissance. Yet Renaissance analyses of the will invariably took into account not only the possibility of freedom, but also the complex limitations imposed on the human will by external forces identified as Providence, fate, or fortune. Renaissance voluntarism has often been contrasted to Reformation determinism, but as Charles Trinkaus has argued, this opposition is extremely problematic. Trinkaus emphasizes the convergence within Renaissance and Reformation thought of distinct notions of the failure of the will within one or more spheres of human existence. There is, in other words, no Renaissance philosophy of pure voluntarism.[12]

We might think of Old Mastery, then, as the rhetoric of will and freedom found in the writings of Pico, Machiavelli, Galileo, and numerous other early modern figures, a rhetoric that, in turn, was valorized as a still more radical voluntarism by Burckhardt and by the tradition of Renaissance studies he fostered. In addition, Old Mastery is an emblem for an *idea* of the Renaissance, an interpretation of that era based on the selective reading of certain voluntarist aspects of Renaissance thought. Certainly a rhetoric of freedom gained currency in the early modern period, and it was on this rhetoric that Burckhardt and many successors chose to focus, generally to the exclusion both of concurrent theories of determinism and of the self-undermining aspects of that rhetoric itself.

Today the rhetoric of free will, individualism, and mastery continues to thrive within many discourses, but that of Renaissance / early modern studies is not necessarily one of them. Although Burckhardt's glorifications of will and individualism held sway within Renaissance studies for over a century, the ideas of Old Mastery central to that tradition have gradually fallen out of fashion over the past several decades. Instead, recent investigations tend to challenge or revalue the Old Mastery once ascribed to that age. Significantly, the period name "Renaissance" has given way to the less golden "early modern," although the former term is still widely used, even in conjunction with the newer one, possibly because there is some confusion or ambivalence about their connotations, or possibly for semantic variety. Leah Marcus has argued that whereas the older nomenclature suggested rebirth, renewal, human freedom, high art, and high class, the newer term implies not only a broader temporal frame of reference, but also a rejection of the earlier historiography and its valuations.[13] Whereas "Renaissance" evokes a vision that valorizes a certain past as the age of mastery, "early modern" calls up a view that questions or rejects that mastery—in other words, that reflects the preoccupations of poststructuralism. Marcus explains: "To look at the Renaissance through a lens called early modern is to see the concerns of modernism and postmodernism in embryo— alienation, a disjunction from origins, profound skepticism about the possibility for objectivity (in literary studies or anywhere else), an emphasis on textual indeterminacy as opposed to textual closure and stability, and an interest in intertextuality instead of filiation."[14] This shift in period concept, attested to by various "rewritings" of the Renaissance, is due in large part, though not exclusively, to the encounters of recent generations of critics and historians with post-structuralist theory.[15]

It is precisely this encounter—or conflict, perhaps—between post-structuralism and traditional Renaissance studies, or, more specifically, between recent theory and an idea of the Renaissance, that occasions this book.[16] At stake is the notion of the individual, or subject. "Subject," however, is no more a synonym for "individual" than "early modern" is for "Renaissance." Whereas earlier (pre-poststructuralist) thinkers tended to see the individual as a unified, centered, autonomous, and free being—a creature, in short, not unrelated to the "universal man" or old master of Burckhardtian fame—poststructuralists see the subject as the antithesis of that individual. The poststructuralist subject, far from being autonomous, fully conscious, and freely willing, is a product or function of some broader, determining category—for example, language, social class and ideology, or the hidden forces of the unconscious. The post-structuralist subject is, in short, a determined subject. Our starting point, then, is this apparent opposition between old master and new subject.

New Subjects

In *Twilight of Subjectivity*, Fred Dallmayr describes a theory of subjectivity that he calls, after Jacques Derrida, "the end of man."[17] Dallmayr argues that this late-twentieth-century rejection of "the conception of man as a self-centered and self-directing agency" is actually the most recent and pronounced phase of an antihumanist and antisubjectivist trend that can be traced back at least as far as the mid-nineteenth century. This interdisciplinary movement to redefine the subject reflects "a steadily deepening dissatisfaction with basic premises of Western thought as they are evident in traditional philosophy (with its reliance on consciousness and the thinking subject) as well as in traditional social theory and practice (with a focus . . . on individual initiative and human autonomy)" (p. 21). Poststructuralism, then, represents the culmination of a movement that has questioned or rejected traditional definitions of subjecthood, wherever they existed in the past or still exist today.

The term "subject" continues to be used in various and sometimes mutually exclusive ways, as Paul Smith points out in his analysis of poststructuralist theories of subjectivity. Within some traditional theoretical contexts, "subject" still refers to the concept of the "individual" or the "person." Within psychoanalytic discourse, however, "subject" often refers to "the unconsciously structured illusion of plenitude which we usually call 'the self.' " In other contexts, such as the marxist, the term "subject" denotes "the specifically subjected *object* of social and historical forces and determinations."[18]

In general, poststructuralist theory takes the first of these senses of "subject" as the false or problematic one. In their discussion of "the category of 'subject,' " neo-marxists Ernesto Laclau and Chantal Mouffe define the traditional rationalist and empiricist constructions of "man" as based on three distinct notions: "the view of the subject as an agent both rational and transparent to itself; the supposed unity and homogeneity of the ensemble of its positions; and the conception of the subject as origin and basis of social relations."[19] The notions of the individual as self-conscious, self-contained, and self-directed (autonomous and freely willing), then, are the three "conceptual targets" of poststructuralist theories of subjectivity.

Smith, like Laclau and Mouffe, directs his critique not simply at what he takes to be the traditional voluntarist accounts of the subject, but also at poststructuralist revisions thereof. These critics argue that the problem with much poststructuralist thought—deconstruction in particular—is that it "lacks a theory of subjectivity and

agency"; current theories that "privilege the *subjected* state or status of the 'subject,' or [that] construe an abstract or cerned notion
of subjectivity, tend to foreclose upon the possibility of resistance."[20]
Thus it is the poststructuralist subject's apparent lack of freedom or
autonomy that causes Smith concern, for activism of any sort does
not mesh easily with the determinist models of human activity suggested by deconstruction, by marxist philosophies such as Althusser's, and by some psychoanalytic theory. Recent critics' discomfort with such modern determinisms has resulted in the negotiation of a theoretical third course somewhere between traditional,
voluntarist notions of the subject and poststructuralist determinisms.
It is this third course—the pursuit of a more enabling or empowering notion of human agency in the face of various determinist mot-
toes of poststructuralism ("it's all language"; "everything is ideology"; "it's just the linguistically structured unconscious")[21]—that
marks the contemporary theoretical agenda as *post*-poststructuralist.

    We will analyze the freedom/necessity dialectic within contem-
porary critical theory in the next chapter. For now, though, let us
say that Jacob Burckhardt and poststructuralist theorists would
agree on exactly one point about the preceding discussion: that
"mastery" is predicated on the concepts of individualism, of the autonomy of the thinking and willing subject, and of the liberating
power of human knowledge and creative expression—in short, on
ideas of freedom, dignity, and control customarily (though not exclusively) identified as Renaissance. For the latter group, though,
mastery is an empty category against which recent theories of non-
mastery exist differentially. Indeed, one implicit and explicit assumption of deconstruction, of marxist and post-marxist criticism, of
psychoanalysis, and of psychoanalytically shaped feminisms is that
there *is* an opposition between old master and new subject, between
earlier voluntarist and recent determinist models of subjecthood. In
other words, the idea of the Renaissance, now largely defunct within
Renaissance studies, has played a key role in poststructuralist
thought as the antithesis of contemporary theories of subjectivity.

    It is important to note, however, that the subject of the Renais-
sance, in both senses, rarely emerges overtly within poststructuralist criticism. Instead, the philosophical inheritance most often cri-

tiqued is that of Descartes, Kant, Hegel, Husserl, and Sartre, central to whose writings are various notions of self-presence or self-consciousness.[22] However, as discussed above, "humanism," "individualism," "mastery," and related concepts often invoked by poststructuralist critics point back beyond the more recent past to the early modern period. Indeed, the inheritance of poststructuralism (the metaphysics of presence) has been traced beyond the early modern period back to classical and/or medieval times. However, to the extent that the notions of humanism and of individualism are generally linked to the early modern age, emergent capitalism, and the rise of the nation state, it is important to examine the largely unexplored connection between late-twentieth-century theory and the idea of the Renaissance. For the idea of the Renaissance, that Burckhardtian glorification of the individual and of the will, is in key ways the subtext of poststructuralist debates on the subject.

The Ransoming of the Will

This book has a double purpose: to analyze early modern theories of will and subjecthood, and to explore their relation to poststructuralist thought. The title tropes on a history of veneration by making new subjects of old masters. By offering new readings of canonical early modern figures, the book analyzes discussions of will as framed by "masters" Francis Petrarch, Martin Luther, Ignatius Loyola, Teresa of Avila, and Galileo Galilei. All of these texts are in some sense autobiographical in that they display certain conventional markers of self-referential discourse. Some are confessional autobiographies in the Augustinian mode; others are letters, treatises, or debates composed in the first person; still others are dialogues with fictitious characters that were nevertheless read (for example, by the Inquisition) as autobiographical. Collectively these texts offer a variety of representations of early modern subjectivity, understood both as personal point of view and as an expression of the conditions and boundaries of personal identity as they were once understood.

Moreover, the works of each of these writers embody a paradigmatic early modern discourse on will: humanism, the Renaissance philosophy of man par excellence; sixteenth-century predestinarian and voluntarist theologies of the will; or the emergent discourse of scientific rationalism. All of these discourses are structured by a tension between the desire for mastery and the acknowledgment of the impossibility of that desire. The following chapters explore the conflicts on will within each of these texts, together with the resolutions attempted by their authors. Also common to these discourses is a distinct rhetorical strategy—the use of a rhetoric of authority, of voluntarism, to deny or compensate for the various forms of predestinarian bondage of the will experienced by the writers. I call this strategy the "ransoming of the will." Ironically, to assert some form of freedom requires that one simultaneously admit servitude or non-freedom, the condition from which one would ransom oneself by the payment of a certain argument. The expenditure of reason, will, or words is a mode of procurement, but it is arguably never an entirely cost-effective procedure.

This argument brings poststructuralist theory to bear on the Renaissance, and vice versa, by focusing on mastery—that is, on certain ideologies of human power long believed to have originated in the early modern age—and on the ideologies of non-mastery that recur in poststructuralist criticism: the problems of knowing, the unreliability of the signifying process, the decenteredness of the human subject, and the political ramifications of the self's illusions of mastery and control. By reproblematizing the early modern notions of mastery that poststructuralism constructs as its antithesis and rejects, this book also offers recent theory a new subject—itself—by holding up an early modern mirror of its own conflicted views of mastery.

This book argues that the dominant critical paradigms of the late twentieth century recast, in numerous unacknowledged ways, earlier discussions of freedom and power. Early modern theories of will bear a striking resemblance to contemporary theories of the limitations of will, subjecthood, and linguistic expression, in that both sets of approaches attempt in various ways to ransom the will from some form of determinism. Though early modern proponents of humanism (Petrarch), the freedom of the will (Loyola), the "freedom of the Christian" (Luther), the freedom of women to write (Teresa), and the new science (Galileo) each assert one sort of mastery or other, they are deeply anxious about the myriad external forces that undermine their desires for freedom, power, and autonomy. Likewise, poststructuralist thought, while insisting on its own lack of anxiety in the face of "predestined" modes of nonclosure, perhaps responds to a similar dilemma—namely, how to understand and cope with these limitations on human power and intellect. Arguably, the denial of anxiety is the central trope of mastery at the heart of poststructuralism. Furthermore, the "reconstruction" of the subject during the past decade of post-poststructuralist ("ethical") criticism attests to quite open anxiety provoked by deconstruction and related non-masteries.[23]

Chapter 1 provides an overview of several poststructuralist theories of the subject, then analyzes the backlash against such "determinisms." Recent theory (post-poststructuralism) has sought in various ways to recuperate the subject position, the notion of agency, and/or some concept of the individual, while also claiming categorically that the rehabilitated notions of subjecthood do not resemble the subject ideologies of yore. This chapter analyzes these antinomic views on subjectivity within the theoretical debates of the last several decades and also explores the rhetoric of anxiety and of mastery within this modern dialectic of will.

The central chapters of the book move from the contemporary free will / necessity debate to precursor analyses of will and subjectivity in the early modern period. Chapter 2 analyzes the rhetoric of will, freedom, and "fortuna" in the writings of Francis Petrarch, particularly the *Secretum*, an autobiographical dialogue often thought to depict a religious or philosophical crisis on the part of this "first modern man," in whose psyche Renaissance humanism was supposedly pitted against medieval notions of piety and virtue. This chapter concentrates on a political dimension of the *Secretum* by linking that dialogue to what was for Petrarch the most pressing crisis of 1347—namely, the populist uprising of Cola di Rienzo in the city of Rome. Petrarch's debate on freedom and determinism in the *Secretum* and other writings can be read as an expression of an early modern humanist's desire to master the volatile class relations of early modern Europe.

Chapter 3 moves from humanist to theological debates on freedom and determinism, exploring works by Martin Luther, Ignatius Loyola, and Teresa of Avila. In many ways these figures espouse radically differing views on will: Luther's outwardly predestinarian theology contrasts with Loyola's post-Tridentine voluntarism, and Teresa's mystical theology stands apart from both, precisely because freedom and fate had different connotations for a sixteenth-century woman of *converso* origins. Yet there are also common features within the writings of Luther, Loyola, and Teresa, especially within their autobiographies, where they recount their conversions to a deeper level of religious commitment. Those common features include a rhetoric, if not a theology, of the will, for the rhetoric of spiritual conversion is necessarily the rhetoric of mastery, a representation of the writer's will as ransomed from one or more forms of predestinarian bondage. This rhetoric of mastery, together with concomitant theories of human nonfreedom, has interesting implications for the debate on determinism and subjecthood now under way in critical theory.

Chapter 4 focuses on another early modern rhetoric of mastery: the scientific method as developed by Galileo Galilei in the early seventeenth century and reflected in his *Dialogue Concerning the Two Chief World Systems*. Galileo's desire for access to the true meaning of physical reality (the book of Nature) and his uneasy acknowledgment of the profound limits of his hermeneutic method constitute another version of the free will / predestination debate. Early modern science, like the discourses of humanism and theology, contains its own paradoxes of freedom and predestination, as the writings of Galileo suggest.

In the Afterword I summarize the rhetorical forms of early modern mastery and then point out a number of twentieth-century discourses where such rhetoric is still in use. Finally, I suggest some reasons (in addition to those given by contemporary theorists) for the poststructuralist questioning or rejection of mastery, and for the repetition of the dialectic of will in a most unlikely place—that is, in contemporary theory.

CHAPTER I

The Metamorphoses of the Subject in Critical Theory

~

The Contemporary Freedom/Necessity Dialectic

Old Mastery as an ideology of human will and authority continues to flourish in a variety of contemporary settings. The rhetorics of science (man's control over nature), of the liberal arts (intellectual pursuit of one's full humanity), of many organized religions (free will and moral responsibility), of capitalism ("democratic self-determination"), and of made-for-television movies (the individual's triumph over adversity) provide a few examples of Old Mastery revisited. The rhetoric of free will, of individualism, of self-consciousness and self-control has not gone out of style in the last five hundred years, although its contexts have shifted somewhat. Indeed, these ideas of mastery still motivate contemporary social and political practices in the West. Old Mastery has enjoyed a minor renaissance in the last decade, as neo-individualist guardians have promoted their conservative political agenda in defending assorted monuments of unaging intellect.[1]

Simultaneously, however, assorted critics and theoreticians of authority have explained the problems, the impossibilities, the brutalities of each mythology of mastery. We have also seen throughout the twentieth century, and particularly in the last 25 years, a sustained critique of the ideologies of mastery, both as they supposedly existed in the past and as they exist today. Indeed, non-mastery might be considered the key trope of late-twentieth-century thought, and certainly of poststructuralist thought. The revolutionary theories of deconstruction, feminism, neo-marxism, and much psychoanalytic and cultural criticism have critiqued traditional ideologies of mastery. Their analyses of logocentrism, phallogocentrism, and all other "centrisms" permeating western culture aim to dismantle the still widespread ideologies of power/mastery and to subvert various powerful masters within western culture. Decentering critiques of both the hard sciences and the social sciences are widespread; the works of Paul Feyerabend, Steve Woolgar, Bruno Latour, Carolyn Merchant, Nigel Gilbert, Michael Mulkay, Evelyn Keller, Pierre Bourdieu, and Jean Baudrillard, to name a few,[2] offer critiques of mastery that are in many ways analogous to those put forward concerning philosophy and literary theory. Indeed, poststructuralist thought in every discipline has emphasized above all the problems of knowing, the unreliability of the signifying process, the decenteredness of the human subject, and the political ramifications of the self's fictions of mastery and control.

In the context of the poststructuralist theory that has relentlessly critiqued it, "mastery" refers to a set of assumptions about human power and will, assumptions central to a theory of identity that might be called Old Mastery. This theory entails a vision of the human subject as fully self-conscious, rational, and autonomous, revealed to itself through the Cartesian cogito. The autonomous subject is a masterful subject, in control of a variety of psychic, intellectual, and social operations. This "centered subject" is endowed with the ability to say what he means, to know what he desires, to will freely, and to know the "outside" world.[3]

Clearly recent theory has radically challenged these assumptions about human power and identity. Poststructuralist critics have argued that mastery is the locus of an impossibility, a set of ideologies that confers only the illusion of authority. Each school has focused on a different register of non-mastery. Deconstruction, for example, asks whether it is possible to control the linguistic medium—that is, to say what one means. Lacanian psychoanalytic theory asks a related question: can one ever really say what one wants? Lacan gives

Freudian theory a linguistic turn, linking the order of speech and language (what one says) to the order of desire (what one wants to say). Post-marxists ask (as did Marx himself) whether it is possible for the subject to act individually; in general marxisms question the notion of personal freedom, which is the ideological underpinning of its economic correlative, the capitalist free market. Feminists have questioned the prevailing definitions of gender, asking whether it is ever possible to ascribe essential meanings to sexual difference, often cited as the ground for patriarchal notions of mastery. Last, these and other poststructuralists question the belief in the closure presumed possible of rational inquiry, the faith in human power to know the world through the force of reason. Epistemological critiques scarcely originated with deconstruction and poststructuralism, but they achieved a radical popularity after the New Criticism.

Also assumed in the ideologies of selfhood critiqued by poststructuralism are all the traditional definitions of what a master is—for example, "a man having control over the action of another or others"; "the owner of a slave or an animal"; "the man who serves as the head of a household."[4] It is precisely these patriarchal, feudal, and capitalist definitions of master as powerful agent that poststructuralist theories, particularly recent feminisms and other types of political criticism, have challenged.

The questioning of mastery in its various forms seems to demand the denial or erasure of the subject, at least as it was conceived of within earlier critical models. Poststructuralist theory has insisted upon the fictional status of the centered subject, wherever that subject supposedly existed in the metaphysics of the past or can still be spotted in the humanisms and political economies of the present. Theorists in the late twentieth century feel obliged, for various reasons, to contest the masteries of earlier doctrines of selfhood, partly because those ideologies of mastery are continually evoked and given currency by the political rivals of poststructuralists today.

To the majority of contemporary theorists, the discourses of mastery in western culture entwine Old Mastery (the stereotype of humanist omnipotence, for example, and other supposedly premodern theories of autonomous selfhood) and current ideologies of mastery (such as phallogocentric justifications for economic and political privilege). Various forms of poststructuralism have placed into question both the theories of identity and power throughout history and their current embodiment in the political economies of the West. It has become increasingly evident to these theorists that it is one thing to assert within academia that the subject is "decentered" and another to convince the chairman of the Republican National Committee or the president of General Motors of that fact.

Thus a double strategy for dealing with masteries and "new masters" has developed—a provisional reinvention of the subject and of mastery together with a continual acknowledgment that those categories are "under erasure."[5] This double strategy, which we may take as characteristically post-poststructuralist, is an activist response not only to the disturbing reality of the as-yet-undeconstructed sector of patriarchal capitalist culture, but also, just as importantly, to the unnerving "determinisms" of poststructuralism itself. It is this aspect of the current freedom/necessity dialectic—the anxiety in some quarters over the loss of the subject, and the concomitant desire to reinvent the subject (in nonhumanist, nonindividualist terms, of course)—that will be analyzed below. As we shall see, the paradox of such criticism is that while it relentlessly challenges earlier notions of the subject as master and individual, it is often undertaken in the spirit, though certainly not in the name, of a vestigial humanism, which is a response both to the dominant culture and to the perceived disempowerments of deconstruction and its kindred critical movements.

Deconstructive Non-Mastery

As the negative hermeneutic par excellence of the late twentieth century, deconstruction offers the clearest (and most thorough) example of poststructuralist non-mastery. In his essay "The Resistance to Theory," Paul de Man offers a critique of the most basic assumption of mastery within academia—namely, the authority of the teacher/interpreter—by arguing that the foundationalist claims on which traditional pedagogy is based cannot be reconciled with theory (that is, with deconstruction). "It is better to fail in teaching what should not be taught than to succeed in teaching what is not true," he writes provocatively (p. 4). In other words, if one cannot know in the ways that scholars have always claimed to know, then surely one cannot teach this non-knowledge, this fiction of understanding— not in the name of truth, anyway, though perhaps in the name of morality, discipline, communal values, and other contingencies.

De Man asserts that until recently few had dreamed of questioning the basic feasibility of literary studies (not to mention that of every other discipline). "Literary history, even when considered at the furthest remove from the platitudes of positivistic historicism, is still the history of an understanding of which the possibility is taken for granted" (p. 7). But why, he asks, should one accept the notion that it is possible to move from language to some description of the "outside world," spatial or temporal? Without a doubt, it is convenient to do so; the world has generally understood such fundamental concepts as meaning and value to depend on that correspondence. Nevertheless, expedience does not constitute a right or even establish a possibility.

According to de Man, "what we call ideology is precisely the confusion of linguistic with natural reality, of reference with phenomenalism" (p. 11). In a wry decentering of marxist theory, de Man redefines ideology as language—not the supposedly stable medium of philosophical, historical, or scientific discourse, but rhetoric. Linguistic reality is no avenue to an understanding of the dialectical processes of history; it cannot be assumed to point beyond itself to the mecca of the real world. Thus one cannot avoid the inevitable ambiguities of the "tropological dimension of language" (p. 17), though all pedagogues (that is, nontheorists) have a stake in believing that one can.[6]

De Man extends an invitation to readers different from the conventional one of foundationalist discourses; in its stead he offers what some consider a different essentialism. Of deconstructive practice he writes:

Technically correct rhetorical readings may be boring, monotonous, predictable and unpleasant, but they are irrefutable. They are also totalizing (and potentially totalitarian) for since the structures and functions they expose do not lead to the knowledge of an entity (such as language) but are an unreliable process of knowledge production that prevents all entities, including linguistic entities, from coming into discourse as such, they are indeed universals, consistently defective models of language's impossibility to be a model language. . . . They are theory and not theory at the same time, the universal theory of the impossibility of theory. (p. 20)

Demanian gnosis consists not of the predictable claim to interpret and understand meaning, either inside or outside the text, but rather of the impossibility of knowing or definitively deciding what anything means. The rhetorical reader remains suspended among possibilities of meaning and positing, trapped within a "whirligig" of indeterminacies.[7] Such a reader is rewarded not by Truth, but certainly by the true (the "technically correct" assessment of linguistic ambiguity offered by deconstructive readings). Whether that offering of linguistic determinism constitutes "a triumph or a fall" de Man leaves up in the air (p. 20).

"A literary text simultaneously asserts and denies the authority of its own rhetorical mode," de Man argues.[8] Certainly that description applies to de Man's own texts, which make use of a rhetorical authority even as the readings offered deconstruct that authority. De Man continually suggests that the deconstructive rhetoric of mastery can only be rhetorical. For example, he explains Jacques Derrida's deconstruction of Rousseau in *Of Grammatology* by arguing that Derrida is not correcting Rousseau or pointing out his blind spots. Rather, if Derrida uses the language of correction (the rhetoric of rigor), it is because that particular rhetoric makes "a good story," not because Derrida's reading is true in any absolute sense.[9] Yet it is precisely the rhetoric of authority—indeed, of mastery—that has tantalized or vexed de Man's readership, despite his claims of non-mastery, despite "the lesson of deconstruction." Surely the "triumph or fall" of that discourse has everything to do with its masterful rhetoric of non-mastery and, more specifically, with the ways in which communities of readers have felt empowered or disempowered by that rhetoric.

For nontheorists—that is, just about everybody at the time that deconstruction was emerging as a novel approach to interpretation—the hermeneutic offering was decidedly a "fall," precisely because it appeared to assault the masteries of interpretation to which critics have (almost) always laid claim in their writings and pedagogy.

Moreover, deconstruction seemed to many to invite a mutiny of the non-masters within the educational system; antideconstructionists seemed particularly annoyed by student interest in the new theory.[10] Partly for this reason the New Criticism was deemed by many in the 1970's and 1980's to be arrogant, nihilistic, or amoral.[11] More recent attacks on the young de Man's anti-Semitism exult in this supposed verification that fascism is inherent in deconstructive thought.[12] As we shall see, the discourses of non-mastery have traditionally been experienced as threatening to those who feel disempowered by them; deconstruction was, and basically remains, no exception.

The outcry against deconstruction during the 1980's can be partially attributed to the "effect of mastery," the perceived absoluteness of this mode of interpretation, that seemed to undermine or undo all previously held masteries of western logocentric culture.[13] Yet the deconstructive philosopher Jacques Derrida, like de Man, insists that the project of mastery could not be more contrary to his writing, which, as Jonathan Culler says, "explores precisely the impossibility of such comprehensive mastery, the impossibility of constructing a coherent and adequate theoretical system."[14] Vincent Descombes describes Derrida's philosophical enterprise as a game with a "formidable Master" (Hegel and, more generally, logocentrism). "In what silent region was the insurgent able to hatch his plot against the Logos, while pretending to speak the language of the Master?" Descombes asks. Like a double agent, Derrida follows the rules of philosophical inquiry (e.g., by adhering to some standard of philosophical rigor), while at the same time entrapping that discourse by pointing out its insoluble (and therefore repressed) problems and contradictions. The outcome of this game waged by deconstruction from within and against logocentrism is necessarily a stalemate: "The game [Derrida] is playing against the Master-philosopher will last forever"; "the outcome of the game is undecidable."[15]

In this manner deconstructionists have claimed neither to master nor to be mastered by the intellectual tradition they critique, to which they are inextricably linked. Thus deconstructive "practice" differs from other critical practices in the measure of authority or truth it claims for itself. Because it undermines its own authority as a hermeneutic approach, deconstruction operates, Derrida says, "without any pretension to mastery." It operates, too, against the claims of mastery basic to philosophical, scientific, and hermeneutic discourses. In this way we might say that deconstructive non-mastery is also a mastery, because while it self-deconstructs, it also deconstructs the authority of all privileged discourses. Deconstruction is "not *neutral*," says Derrida; "it *intervenes*."[16] Such theoretical interventions, he suggests to those who consider deconstruction politically lukewarm, constitute powerful ideological attacks.

Indeterminacy as Determinism

However, despite the various defenses offered by Derrida and others, the critical establishment had largely rejected deconstruction by the late 1980's on the grounds of its amorality and/or irrelevance. Yet this characterization of deconstruction cannot be taken at face value. After all, amorality and irrelevance have been the strong points of many interpretive schools. Rather, the debate over deconstruction must be understood as a struggle between rival interest groups and as a mark of how different communities of readers felt empowered or disempowered by the deconstructive hermeneutic.

These recent discussions of mastery, agency, and the ideology of the subject are but the latest installments of traditional free will / voluntarism debates. Deconstruction, like several other forms of poststructuralist non-mastery, is often viewed as a determinism, a term generally designating the "determination of human choices or actions by antecedent causes," that is, by limitations on the will.[17] Deconstructive non-mastery embodies, at least for many nonpractitioners, a specifically linguistic determinism. According to J. Hillis Miller, "linguistic (i.e., deconstructive) explanations tend to imply or even openly to assert that society, psychology, and religion are 'all language,' generated by language in the first place and ultimately to be explained by features of language."[18]

Yet no determinism, no non-mastery, can gain ideological ascendancy unless those who use or contemplate it find it empowering; therein lies the paradox of successful determinisms, such as Martin Luther's or John Calvin's. This is to say that every apparent determinism must in some sense function or be experienced as a voluntarism—an ideology of human freedom and mastery—if it is to persuade and to survive. This argument might be understood as a corollary of Fredric Jameson's theory that "the effectively ideological is also, at the same time, necessarily Utopian." Jameson holds that any ideology persuades (indeed, is capable of persuading) because of the "substantial incentives" it offers, and that "we might say that such incentives . . . are necessarily Utopian in nature."[19] It will be argued below that such utopian incentives, however they are imagined within a given ideological system, offer some sense of freedom or liberation to those who embrace them. There is, then, within any non-mastery, any determinist ideology, some simulacrum of voluntarism, by which I mean the effect of mastery.

To assert that any ideology, whether overtly voluntarist or determinist, must in some sense be experienced as mastery by those who embrace it is scarcely to deny the reality of ideology's generally repressive effects. Rather, as Michel Foucault has argued, power begets its own "truth," and the repressive force of this necessarily contingent truth is felt less as a check than as a goad, as "right" and often as "a right." "We are forced to produce the truth that our society demands, of which it has need, in order to function: we *must* speak the truth; we are constrained or condemned to confess or to discover the truth."[20] In this way Foucault suggests that even the most absolute non-mastery generates a self-legitimating truth that those subjected to it must experience as "right." The effect of mastery, in Foucaultian terms, is our willing assent to ideology, an assent that is nevertheless compelled by "truth." Our assent is not only willing but willful, insofar as the "substantial incentive" of mastery, the fantasy of control, induces our submission.[21] We shall study in greater detail this mechanism of assent, the ransoming of the will, in the chapters that follow.

Let us consider this effect of mastery within deconstruction. How was it that a few (and later a great many) critics felt liberated by an apparent determinism, a certain ideology of the nonfreedom of the subject, that was largely alienating to others? For those who did (and perhaps still do) feel empowered by this new theory, deconstructive non-mastery offered plenty of inducements for inhabiting the space of cognitive suspension. There were, and are, those "technically correct rhetorical readings," of course, plus subsidiary masteries, such as the remarkable new vocabulary for describing all hermeneutic activity, a philosophical vocabulary not readily grasped by all. Furthermore, the radical suspension of belief demanded by deconstruction was invigorating to those willing to test the waters. Barbara Johnson, for example, has written of the power of deconstruction to generate intellectual surprise, which she seems to characterize as pleasure, if not knowledge.[22] The "rhetorical" mastery offered by deconstruction is not a voluntarism in the usual sense of an ideology of human will or control (such as the control of textual meaning); nevertheless, deconstructive mastery functions like a voluntarism by extending to its practitioners forms of psychological, as well as political, empowerment—certainly within the academy, and even to a degree outside of it.

Many critics have described this effect of mastery as the result of very particular power struggles within the academy. As John Ellis has argued, opponents of deconstruction, armed with commonsense arguments about language, reference, and intentionality, were frequently set up as straw men; deconstructionists "lured their opposition into taking the very position they need[ed] them to be in—the apparently solid and square, but actually naive and unthinking, ground of common sense that refuses to question habitual thinking." For Ellis, the problem is not that deconstruction is false, but rather that it has been done before—versions of it, at any rate—by a host of critics and philosophers for over a century. Ellis, then, also focuses on the rhetoric of mastery in deconstruction, which he calls "an illusion of intellectual tour de force . . . not backed up by any theory of substance."[23]

Thus to Ellis and many others, deconstruction boiled down to "a local political squabble between rivals for critical prestige and power"[24]—that is, a very concrete struggle for institutional mastery. Howard Felperin, writing in 1985, just past the zenith of the deconstructive movement and shortly after the death of Paul de Man, explained within a specifically institutional context the contradictory attitudes toward mastery that seemed to abound within that movement. On the one hand, deconstruction freely challenged institutional authority, while on the other, it remained "unwilling quite to relinquish any claim to institutional authority for its own practices." Intriguingly, Felperin locates the traditional—that is, the "masterful" and nonanarchic—side of deconstructive literary studies in a "distinctly puritan work-anxiety it continues to share with the older institution, whose forms it largely accepts despite its declared differences with the traditional rationale for those forms."[25] Felperin implies that any non-mastery experienced by deconstructionists was generated not so much by the vexing nature of linguistic determinism as by the demands of academic institutions grounded in a work ethic that was and remains antithetical to the implicit hedonism of deconstruction—especially the French variety.[26]

Katherine Hayles offers a different take on the deconstructive effect of mastery when, in response to "The Resistance to Theory," she asks, "Why does de Man want to push the local into the global?" Hayles then explores the notions of mastery that are undercut by de Man, only to be paradoxically reasserted by him:

"Mastery," in de Man's usage, connotes universalizing moves made by opponents to limit the scope and power of rhetorical theory. . . . When de Man creates a global theory of local knowledge, he simultaneously repudiates and practices mastery in this sense, for he resists totalization by totalizing. Mastery is intolerable because it is identified with totalitarianism; but it is also unavoidable, because the only way *always* to resist totalizing moves is through a theory more universally applicable than what is resisted. The ideology of local knowledge, pushed to the extreme, is thus inextricable from the totalitarian impulses it most opposes.

Struck by de Man's "unflinching honesty" in facing this paradox,[27] Hayles goes on to explore the ways in which other contemporary theories of local knowledge are, like deconstruction, self-subvertingly global. Hayles's reading would seem to suggest that the deconstructive rhetoric of mastery cannot be altogether distinguished from a conventional epistemology of mastery, except, perhaps, in its self-consciousness.

However we might define the deconstructive effect of mastery and the "substantial incentives" it offers, why, we must ask, has this compelling critical ideology gradually ceased to persuade? I will address this question later, but for now suffice it to say that deconstruction, viewed by many as the quintessential determinism of recent decades, did not survive—arguably, it was suppressed. Never-theless, virtually all post-poststructuralists claim to have learned "the lesson of deconstruction." We might understand that lesson as two-fold: how to decenter rival ideologies, and how to make one's own ideology more persuasive. Hence the remarkable resurgence during the last ten years of ethical criticism, under which rubric can be in-cluded political criticisms as well as a refurbished, "ethical" decon-struction.[28]

Masterful Non-Masteries

It was not only deconstruction that offered critics of several decades alternative methods of interpretation. Countless decenter-ing theories—hermeneutics of non-mastery—achieved critical mass from the mid-1960's to the mid-1980's; their abundance suggests that for a while, at least, critiques of subjectivity, agency, bourgeois individualism, and other metaphysical notions were experienced as empowering to those who subscribed to them. Let us consider three such critiques: those of Jacques Lacan, Louis Althusser, and Michel Foucault.

The works of French psychoanalytic theorist Jacques Lacan gave rise in the past several decades to a cult of non-mastery distinct from but not unrelated to other poststructuralist critiques of the subject. Lacan's study of the "mirror stage" in the development of the psy-che offers a clear example of post-Freudian non-mastery. At a given stage of development the *infans*, the infant child as yet without lan-guage, recognizes in the mirror a primordial I, an "Ideal-I," before that identity "is objectified in the dialectic of identification with the other, and before language restores to it, in the universal, its func-tion as subject."[29] But for Lacan this moment of identification marks the beginning not of stable subjecthood, but of a permanent psychic delusion, "the belief in a projected image."[30] The fragile imago in the mirror, he suggests, is but the first of a never-ending series of at-tempts to envision a unified ego with which to defend "oneself" (for want of a better word) against the perpetual underminings of such fantasies of selfhood that mark the symbolic order, the realm of lan-guage.

The theory of the mirror stage is but the beginning of Lacanian non-mastery. As Shoshana Felman has argued, Lacan understood non-mastery as characteristic not only of the subject, but also of theories of the subject—that is, of psychoanalytic thought itself. Felman points out that for Lacan, the process of psychoanalysis is the locus of a profound unknowing by both the analyst and the analysand: "There is no language in which interpretation can itself escape the effects of the unconscious; the interpreter is not more immune than the poet to unconscious delusions and errors." What "knowledge," then, does the analyst, the recipient of the patient's cathexis and large payments, bring to light? What the analyst does not produce is a definitive and conclusive account of an illness or problem, an account wrested from the unconscious of the analysand. "The unconscious," Felman writes, "is the radical castration of the mastery of consciousness, which turns out to be forever incomplete, illusory, and self-deceptive." Rather, what analyst and analysand discover through dialogue are questions and insights about how the necessarily unmastered unconscious of both participants works— namely, like a language.[31]

The overall effect of the psychic non-mastery proposed by Lacanian theory was a decentering of vestiges—psychoanalytic and otherwise—of the notion of the unified and self-determined subject. Such a decentering motive characterizes as well the work of marxist philosopher Louis Althusser. Like Marx, Althusser holds that subjectivity is a function of social class. But unlike Marx, he does not acknowledge the possibility of an end of ideology—a utopian future in which individuals have been purged of false consciousness.[32] In his well-known 1969 essay "Ideology and Ideological State Apparatuses," Althusser compares ideology to Freud's concept of the unconscious, stating that both are "trans-historical" structures of human society. Not only is there nothing outside of ideology, but there is no subjectivity (actual or potential) that is not constituted by ideology. "As St. Paul admirably put it," Althusser writes, "it is in the 'Logos,' meaning in ideology, that we 'live, move and have our being' " (p. 171).

Ideology molds and transforms "concrete individuals" into subjects, Althusser explains, through the process of "interpellation," or hailing. Just as a person in the street who turns and responds to "Hey, you!" presumes himself or herself to be the subject of the hailing, so does the individual respond to the call of a particular ideology. Moreover, the individual is interpellated in order to be made a subject—in both senses. That is, within a given ideology, the individual is constituted as both "a free subjectivity, a centre of initiatives, author of and responsible for its actions," and "a subjected being, who submits to a higher authority, and is therefore stripped of all freedom except that of freely accepting his submission" (p. 182). According to Althusser's determinist model of subjecthood, a person's only "freedom" is that of consenting to be dominated by whatever serves as "Absolute Subject," the center of an ideological system—such as God, the Führer, Mommy, the boss, or the theorist.

Althusser gives the example of Moses as an archetypal subject within Judeo-Christian religious ideology; having been called by his Name, having recognized that it "really" was he who was called by God, Moses "recognizes that he is a subject, a subject *of* God, a subject subjected to God, a *subject through the Subject and subjected to the Subject*. The proof: he obeys him, and makes his people obey God's Commandments" (p. 179). One becomes a subject, in other words, in the manner of Moses—that is, through a process of recognition and conversion. One hears the call, recognizes oneself as its subject, and thereby is constituted by it. Far from self-determining, Althusser's subject is completely a function of the ideological systems that he or she inhabits.

The works of Michel Foucault, like those of Lacan and Althusser, can be viewed as an extended critique of traditional notions of subjecthood. His studies of illness, madness, and sexuality,[33] for example, have further problematized the vision of the subject centered by and in health, sanity, and clearly circumscribed gender. And in the essay "What Is an Author?" Foucault puzzles over an assumption fundamental to western hermeneutic practice over many centuries, namely, the concept of authorial identity as it relates to hermeneutic practice.

In that essay Foucault points out the historical contingency of the idea of the author—the idea, that is, that the author is somehow relevant to an understanding of a text (pp. 143–53). Foucault argues that this idea of the author has actually been dead at least since Nietzsche's time. However, the fact of that death has yet to register with all critics, philosophers, and historians, to the extent that the "man-and-his-work" approach to textual interpretation is still widespread. Foucault explains:

> Modern literary criticism . . . still defines the author in the same way: the author provides the basis for explaining not only the presence of certain events in a work, but also their transformations, distortions, and diverse modifications (through his biography, the determination of his individual perspective, the analysis of his social position, and the revelation of his basic design). The author is also the principle of a certain unity of writing—all difference having to be resolved, at least in part, by the principles of evolution, maturation, or influence. (p. 151)

Critiquing the bourgeois individualism implicit in this approach, and also announcing that such notions of the subject are obsolete, Foucault proposes a different approach to what he calls "the author-function." Instead of wondering, "How can a free subject penetrate the substance of things and give it meaning?" the critic will ask, "How, under what conditions and in what forms can something like a subject appear in the order of discourse? What place can it occupy in each type of discourse, what functions can it assume, and by obeying what rules?" (p. 158). Foucault's approach denies the subject its long-held authority, its status as "originator."

Lacan's concept of the mirror stage, Althusser's theory of interpellation, and Foucault's critique of the author all present versions of the decentering move standard to much late-twentieth-century French and American criticism—standard until recently, that is. What is decentered in each case is some notion of the subject, as well as related theories of individual freedom, competence, will, or power—that is, of mastery. These arguments put forward one or more varieties of determinism, identifying the subject's authority as limited by external forces such as language, the structure of the psyche, ideology, or historical change. What links these critiques is the authors' insistence on the discursivity of the subject—that is, the subject's inscription within the texts of western culture as they are variously conceived of and emphasized.

But though they decenter the subject, these three critical approaches seem to lay claim to certain masteries that privilege the critics' authority, even as they undercut that authority and "reinscribe" it within the framing determinism. Thus, for example, Lacan makes proclamations about the true insight of Freud or the true illness of Dora;[34] Althusser speaks transhistorically and "scientifically" about how subjects are constituted in and by ideology; and Foucault undertakes his historical critiques with a distinct positivism. Derrida and other deconstructionists have taken these theorists to task for their reliance on some version of the metaphysics of presence—that is, for their claims to mastery above and beyond the merely rhetorical.[35] But such debates have been succeeded to some extent by the critical backlash against non-mastery and against too-determined theories of the subject. As Cathy Caruth has noted, this backlash betrays the fear that poststructuralist theory, and deconstruction in particular, automatically results in "political and ethical paralysis."[36]

Feminism and Mastery

From the late 1960's through the early 1980's, the poststructuralist ideologies of non-mastery were at their peak of popularity. As I have suggested, this popularity was due to the paradoxical fact that decentering determinisms were experienced as empowering— certainly for many in France and then in the United States, where these critical theories found a stronghold. But by the late 1980's, theoretical non-masteries—deconstructive and other poststructuralist critiques of the subject—were regarded with less enthusiasm by many who had once embraced them. Ethical criticism has largely eclipsed deconstruction. Moreover, we have seen the provisional (and not-so-provisional) resurrection of the subject, a subject that has learned the "lesson of deconstruction"—the lesson that there is really no such thing as a subject, but that there are serious political problems with pressing that argument. It is misleading to speak of the return of the subject, though, both because few political critiques of deconstruction long for Old Mastery and because, as Foucault pointed out, the ideology of the subject as traditionally understood has never really disappeared. Indeed mastery, in terms of subjecthood, was never completely out of vogue, but the concept of non-mastery has fallen out of fashion with the critical avant-garde for many reasons—the most important of which is that it is no longer experienced by many groups of readers as empowering. Increasingly, feminist, marxist, and other political critics have been uncertain about the value of deconstructing the subject. This shift in sensibility is perhaps most marked among those critics—such as students of Lacan—who were particularly fluent in the discourses of non-mastery. In an intriguing mid-1970's exchange in *The Newly Born Woman*, Catherine Clément and Hélène Cixous debated the fiction of mastery from within the framework of Lacanian theory. "What is the discourse of mastery?" Cixous asked, referring to the decenterings of Kafka and Lacan:

There is but one. It is what calls itself "the law" but is presented as "the open door" in precisely such a way that you never go to the other side of the door, that you never go to see "what is mastery?" So you never will know that there is no law and no mastery. That there is no master. The paradox of mastery is that it is made up of a sort of complex ideological secretion produced by an infinite quantity of doorkeepers. (p. 138)

But even though mastery has been deconstructed, is it clear that anyone can be rid of it? Furthermore, is it clear that women want to be rid of it? For Cixous the answer to the second question is "yes"; mastery, even as a fiction, entails repression, because the discourses of mastery are necessarily mystified (p. 139). Clément, however, disagrees; mastery is not to be entirely deconstructed or rejected:

It has to be said straight out: for me mastery is fundamental and necessary. I don't particularly think one can transmit certain knowledges—*the* knowledges—except through mastery. That involves everything having to do with democratic transmission. Paradoxically, information contained in a system of knowledge cannot be transmitted outside of mastery. It is dependent on the "law" of the Symbolic, like the doorkeeper, like the honest man. Subjectivity can be taken in, deluded, by it, of course, but it can also find there an explicit coherence, a certain number of connections shared by all, so that when the statement is transmitted, the receiver has access to it either immediately or through mediation. (p. 138)

Clément's statement is puzzling, because it seems to move in two directions. On the one hand it acknowledges, à la Derrida, that deconstruction is never absolute, that one necessarily remains inscribed within logocentric discourse (mastery has many names). On the other hand, Clément embraces for herself and for other women some quite traditional ideas of mastery. "Subjectivity can be taken in," she writes, suggesting that it can also *not* be taken in—in other words, that it is possible to be a master without embracing the usual fantasies of mastery. This last view of mastery seems both voluntarist and conservative, an outright rejection of "the lesson."

Cixous rejects this voluntarism but nevertheless invents one of her own. Like de Man, she invokes mastery only as a strategy:[37] "I use rhetorical discourse, the discourse of mastery, orally, for example, with my students, and obviously I do it on purpose; it is a refusal on my part to leave organized discourse entirely in men's power. I never fell for that sort of bait" (p. 136). To have authority as a feminist, Cixous plays the role of the master tentatively, rhetorically. "I demand," she writes, "that love struggle within the master against the will for power" (p. 140). Even Cixous leaves partly intact a very traditional notion of the thinking and willing subject—namely, that of the subject who is, at least in part, capable of autonomy and of authority. This subject employs rhetoric, the Law of the Father, the Symbolic order, or logocentrism for political gain.

Reconstructing the Subject: The Neo-Erasmian Moment

Since Clément and Cixous debated the uses and abuses of mastery, feminists, neo-marxists, and theorists of race and ethnicity have further questioned the value of deconstructing the subject. Ernesto Laclau and Chantal Mouffe contend that the notion of the decentered and dispersed subject falls prey to the same charge of essentialism that was levied against the old subject.[38] Moreover, the decentered subject of poststructuralist debate causes not only conceptual problems but also political ones for the radical critic.

In *Discerning the Subject*, Paul Smith reexamines the critiques of subjecthood advanced by recent theory. In the chapter entitled "Feminism," Smith questions the success of some poststructuralist theories of the subject, taking Toril Moi to task for her use of "the blandest clichés of poststructuralism." In Smith's view, the political ends of feminism, together with the specificity of feminist discourse, have been undermined by the deconstructive vision of indeterminacy that characterizes the thought of many French feminists and their advocates, like Moi (pp. 134–38). At the same time, Smith rejects certain aspects of the more pragmatic Anglo-American feminism. In particular, he criticizes some feminists for their naive reliance on traditional notions of the subject. Elaine Showalter, he argues, seemingly relies on "depressingly familiar" assumptions about subjecthood, which depend on "a set of demonstrably humanist values and ideologies." The basic problem with this kind of feminist theory, Smith argues, is that it falls back on many of the same essentialist notions of female or human identity that have plagued patriarchal thought (p. 136). While Smith questions the value of some poststructuralist feminism because it strikes him as politically ineffective, he also fears the reactionary (pre-poststructuralist) visions of the self in much Anglo-American feminism.

Rejecting both traditional and poststructuralist theories of the subject and of will, Smith suggests a third course: the adoption of a provisional identity or essence, a subject half under erasure. In proposing this approach, Smith theorizes Gayatri Spivak's idea that feminists and other marginalized groups must "take the risk of essence,"[39] which entails constructing a subject—an agent—somewhere between the traditional humanist formulations of the individual and the deconstructive dispersions of identity. One may assume a concept of subject-as-agent without believing either in the bourgeois, patriarchal concept of a centered, fully self-conscious, autonomous individual or in the determined subject of deconstruction. "A person," Smith writes, "is not simply the *actor* who follows ideological scripts, but is also an *agent* who reads them in order to insert him/herself into them—or not." This concept of agent emerges from, and is problematized by, its doubleness, for it contains within itself a dialectic between antithetical notions of subjectivity (p. 150). It is this version of the subject, Smith contends, that is most capable of resistance. For Smith, the human agent "is the place from which resistance to the ideological is produced or played out" (pp. xxxiv–xxxv). Smith's corrective is actually a strategy for accomplishing the political ends of feminism and other radical theories; he recommends that revisionary theorists assume a version of the subject position, but self-consciously, critically, in order to become more effective agents of political change.

Smith is not alone in rejecting the determined subject of post-structuralism in favor of a less dispersed or subjected "agent." Indeed, the backlash against deconstruction has been directed at the apparent ethical dilemmas posed by notions of non-mastery, for in the eyes of many politically oriented critics, a determined subject is not a responsible subject; that is, it is neither responsible for its actions nor an epistemologically responsible construction of subjecthood. Discontent with the deconstructed subject has been widespread, and reconstructions are the order of the day. Such reconstructions have been put forward by Smith, by Laclau and Mouffe, by Diana Fuss, by philosophers Manfred Frank and Fred Dallmayr, and by countless other participants in what has become an uprising against the overly determined subject.[40]

In a recent review article, John H. Smith notes that according to many critics, "the attack on the subject undermines . . . the possibility of responsible, and liberating, praxis which requires a signifying agent willing to stand by his (or her) values." Instead of either affirming or rejecting the idea of the individual, some critics and philosophers now follow versions of the third course: "a 'reconstruction' of the individual . . . that avoids the nostalgia for an undeconstructed self."[41] Likewise, in *Reconstructing Individualism*, the proceedings of a 1984 Stanford conference, the editors insist that "reconstruction does not imply a return to a lost state but rather an alternative conceptualization of the experience of subjectivity, enriched by the chastening experiences of the last century."[42]

Yet despite the many significant differences between the refurbished subject of recent theory and the supposed humanist subject of yore, current theory has ransomed from deconstructive bondage a significant element of the traditional concept of the individual— namely, a version of the will. As John Smith has noted, "in discussions among literary theorists and critics concerning issues like the significance of authorial intention, the supra-subjective force of literary traditions, the self-referentiality of poetic discourse, and the elusive uniqueness of style, nothing less is at stake than notions of 'freedom'—understood as freedom of or from the individually ut-tering (writing) self—and 'humanism'—understood as the ideology of the creative individual."[43] Freedom, as Smith correctly suggests, is the goal of theory, although critics differ on the question of what holds us most in bondage. Despite their denial of any truck with hu-manism, theology, or metaphysics, countless critics today fear and defend against the ethical consequences of a too-determined theory of subjecthood. For that reason we might describe this particular moment in the theoretical debate as neo-Erasmian, after the six-teenth-century humanist who defended a limited notion of human agency, or will, in the hope of navigating between two antithetical positions on subjectivity: the voluntarist theology of human auton-omy (long known as the Pelagian heresy) and the determinist (pre-destinarian) theology asserted by Luther and by radical Protes-tantism.[44]

On the one hand, Erasmus admitted that Luther's determinist theology made sense, even though it challenged several cherished no-tions of human free will. On the other, he feared that this new de-terminism, if publicized and taken to its logical conclusion, would generate social anarchy. Erasmus held that doing away with some notion of human agency was not, finally, practical. Thus he sought to reconstruct the subject as a nonunified, nonautonomous entity subject to divine foreknowledge and forewilling, but still in some sense capable of free choice. In a famous parable about a father and son, Erasmus attempted to recuperate the subject according to, we might say, a third course:

A father raises his child, which is yet unable to walk, which has fallen and which exerts himself, and shows him an apple, placed in front of him. The boy likes to go and get it, but due to his weak bones would soon have fallen again, if the father had not supported him by his hand and guided his steps. Thus the child comes, led by the father, to the apple which the father places willingly into his hand, like a reward for his walking.

. . . Let us assume it is the same with God. What does the child do? As the boy is being helped up, he makes an effort and tries to accommodate his weak steps to the father's guidance. The father could have pulled him against his will. A childish whim could have refused the apple. The father could have given the apple without his running, but he would rather give it in this manner, because it is better for the boy. I readily admit that our striving contributes less to the gaining of eternal life, than the boy's running at the hand of his father.[45]

Erasmus's imagined resolution of freedom and necessity, though far removed in language and sentiment from contemporary theory, nevertheless shares certain features of post-poststructuralism—specifically the idea that the reconstructed subject is capable of "resistance"; indeed, that it is continually reconstructed precisely in order to resist. Whether that subject is capable of resisting Christian notions of sin (as in Erasmian thought) or the modern sins of patriarchy, racism, and capitalism (as in much contemporary criticism), it maintains, albeit in a limited and generally self-questioning mode, some autonomy or self-determination. As we shall see in the chapters that follow, the early modern dialectic on will, mastery, and the status of the subject resembles contemporary debates in many intriguing ways, suggesting that in some senses recent theory has reinvented the wheel.

As suggested above, no ideology persuades effectively unless it contains a utopian appeal—an appeal invariably directed toward freedom or mastery, as those concepts have been variously understood. In different ways, poststructuralism and the backlash against its determinisms offer their subscribers some version of mastery, despite their mutual rejection of Old Mastery. Though the theoretical discourses of non-mastery often present themselves as correctives of past illusions, the differences between the rhetoric of mastery and that of non-mastery are relative at best.

The Early Modern Unconscious

The myth of the unified self as the chief premodern view of identity deserves renewed attention, if only to clarify the value and persistence of the stereotype of Old Mastery: full self-possession, self-consciousness, self-control. If many recent theories of the subject—those of deconstruction, those of psychoanalytic theory, post-marxisms, and post-feminisms, to name a few—hinge on their dialectical opposition to a shared reading of early modern history and the views of identity and authority that they extract from it, then it is necessary to test the assumptions of that shared reading.

Old Mastery, as a Renaissance idea and as an idea of the Renaissance, functions oppositionally within poststructuralism as the category of thought to be critiqued and destabilized. More recently theorists have treated Old Mastery—the theory of the autonomous, unified subject generally thought to have originated in the Renaissance—as the first term in the dialectical evolution of the conceptualizing of the subject; the third term of this dialectic, the reconstructed subject, synthesizes elements of Old Mastery and of its deconstructive antithesis.[46] In both cases, poststructuralism and the backlash against it, Old Mastery is a suspect category to be deconstructed.

Why, we might ask, is it necessary continually to redefine agency, both in terms of perceived determinisms that threaten to undercut the possibility of individual choice and responsibility and in terms of Pelagianism, which could be very loosely described as the fantasy of autonomous, unified subjecthood, and which is continually reinvented and invoked as heresy (though not all pelagianisms are interchangeable)? This is a complicated question that we will explore further after investigating several early modern conceptions of freedom, necessity, and subjecthood. For now, let us turn again to Paul Smith's theory of the reconstructed subject-as-agent, a theory that I take to be paradigmatic of trends in recent ethical criticism, and focus on the categories of early modern thought discernible within his argument. The dialectic of that argument involves not only antithetical trends in contemporary theory, but implicitly another antithesis, that of the present and the past. It is striking, for example, that whenever he wishes to discredit a contemporary method or school, Smith alludes to its archaic and reactionary content. For example, Elaine Showalter's downfall is her "humanism," whereas Julia Kristeva's is her "bourgeois individualism."[47] Ironically, in his analysis these representatives of antithetical theories of mastery and subjecthood turn out to embody versions of the same thing—that is, the early modern subject position as it is usually understood.

Smith's argument pertains mainly to twentieth-century theory, yet his vision of what is to be rejected clearly derives from commonplaces about the early modern period and its presumably outmoded notions of will. Not coincidentally, the words "humanism," "bourgeois," and "individualism" connote not only negative trends in both poststructuralism and its counterpart (prestructuralism), but also the standard attributes of the Renaissance. Smith suggests that at present only one theoretical strategy avoids the ideological (that is, early modern) pitfalls of Old Mastery—namely, the feminist "risk of essence."

One need not reject Smith's practical theory of will to observe that the structure of his argument depends on an opposition between what is modern and what is early modern. In unacknowledged, perhaps unconscious, ways, Smith's argument replicates precursor debates on subjectivity and will in the early modern age, both thematically and rhetorically. The most prominent similarity between Smith's work and the early modern discussions of will treated in the following chapters is their mutual acknowledgment of the bondage of the subject to various determinisms (such as ideology or divine Providence), together with their shared desire for a subject that is, despite its limitations, willful (e.g., capable of political resistance or ethical choice).

The schematic and usually (as in Smith's case) tacit rejection of early modern theories of will characterizes much contemporary theory. This rejection can be understood as a refusal to acknowledge how today's theory rehearses in new contexts much older debates on identity, freedom, and their unraveling. It also disguises the desire and pursuit of mastery within current theory through a displacement: it assumes that all mastery is necessarily Old Mastery. The early modern, as it is stereotypically and ahistorically conceived, functions in many ways as the unconscious of contemporary theory. As the premier concept from which theory has sought to distance itself—that is, which it has sought to repress—Old Mastery resurfaces as the desire for hermeneutic authority and as anxiety over its impossibility. By reading contemporary theory through related early modern controversies on will and power, we can understand more clearly the configurations of the late-twentieth-century controversy over will and determinism, over Old Masters and new subjects.

CHAPTER 2

Humanism

The Fortunes of Francis Petrarch

⟨∾⟩

The Origins of Humanism

Humanism, more than any other Renaissance discourse, has been associated with the idea of mastery: mastery of the cultural inheritance of Greek and Roman antiquity; mastery of a syncretic blend of history, poetry, and moral philosophy; mastery of the art of rhetoric.[1] In its secondary senses humanism also celebrates other kinds of mastery: the achievements of the individual, of the self humanized by a certain pedagogy and set of values, and the achievements—the masterworks—of the culture.[2] Partly for that reason, the term "humanism" is often encoded within poststructuralist writing as "Old Mastery," the theoretically premodern belief in a unified, fully conscious, and freely willing self. The convention of the great divide between modern and early modern thought on which much contemporary theory relies can be quickly conjured up by the often derogatory terms "humanism" and "humanist." Of course, these terms now have multiple connotations, some neither early modern nor, strictly speaking, historical. But given the generally negative valuation of humanism within poststructuralist theory, and given the long association of humanism with the ideology of individualism, it is worth returning *ad fontes*, to the origins of humanist discourse, to reappraise that rhetoric of mastery as it was originally disseminated. In so doing, we might better understand the current dialectic of mastery in relation to its early modern counterpart.

"Renaissance man has been described as individualist," historian R. R. Bolgar writes, "and the historians of the period have noted the spread of capitalist relations in the economic field and the parallel spread of rationality in administration, the general acceptance of materialist values and a greater emphasis on social mobility, conspicuous expenditure and the cult of personal glory."[3] Bolgar suggests that in order to understand this early modern shift in consciousness, marked by a new individualism, one must look to the fourteenth-century poet and "first modern man,"[4] Francis Petrarch. On the matter of Petrarch's modernity, Bolgar expresses the consensus of many generations of historians and critics—a consensus influenced, no doubt, by Petrarch's own suggestion that he was a lone visionary standing at the threshold of a new, improved era, as he wrote in his epic poem, the *Africa*:

> At tibi fortassis, si—quod mens sperat et optat—
> Es post me victura diu, meliora supersunt
> Secula: non omnes veniet Letheus in annos
> Iste sopor! Poterunt discussis forte tenebris
> Ad purum priscumque iubar remeare nepotes.

> But if you, as is my wish
> and ardent hope, shall live on after me,
> a more propitious age will come again:
> this Lethean stupor surely can't endure
> forever. Our posterity, perchance,
> when the dark clouds are lifted, may enjoy
> once more the radiance the ancients knew.[5]

If Petrarch was indeed the prophet of modernity, the "more propitious age" foretold in the *Africa*,[6] he was also the high priest of the early modern cult of fame, combining individualism and humanism in his pursuit of international renown as a poet and scholar.[7] Petrarch's reputation in both of these areas was founded, above all, on his desire to recover and revitalize the inheritance of Greek and Roman antiquity, his modernity being a function of a certain backward gaze, together with the novel forms of mastery that such a gaze presupposed.

Petrarch wrote profusely of his reverence for the poets, orators, and moralists of pagan and Christian antiquity, the classical precursors whom he sought to emulate in his writings and in his daily life. Collectively his works reflect an obsession with mastery, the desire to understand, to imitate, and to surpass his literary and philosophical models—especially Cicero, Virgil, and Augustine. It was upon this foundation of his familiarity with what he considered the all-but-lost heritage of remote antiquity, and of his attempted reappropriation of that heritage, that Petrarch sought to establish his fame. Critics and historians ever since have debated the nature and degree of Petrarch's mastery, the success or failure of his various imitative projects: his *Canzoniere* and other lyric works; the *Africa*, his unfinished epic; his disquisitions on political, philosophical, and religious topics; and his intriguing letters, which he conveniently collected and organized for posterity. But although their assessments of those projects vary, Petrarch's humanist heirs nevertheless continue to accord him standing as "first modern man"—which is itself a paradigmatic kind of mastery, as we shall see.

Petrarch, then, has long served as a figurehead for the humanist movement he is said to have inaugurated, and he has been understood as the original repository of that strange beast known as modern consciousness. In his writings scholars have detected elements of his fundamentally different, nonmedieval perception of the world, of subject-object relations,[8] of self-as-individual. According to such arguments, Petrarch's reputation as father and founder is secure because his perceptions, his state of mind, and his insights are verifiably unlike those of the generations before him—that is, in some essential way original.

The problem with many such evaluations of Petrarch, however, is that they fail to acknowledge or even to recognize the disciplinary stakes involved in the "discovery" of origins. Renaissance scholars have shown a "virtually irresistible" tendency, as David Wallace has noted, not only to claim Petrarch as the source of humanism, but also "to interpret the origin of humanism by reference to its ends." He contends that by interpreting Petrarch as a mirror, however tarnished, of the modern, critics and historians in certain ways neglect the context of Petrarch's writing—namely, the particular social, economic, and political circumstances of his work. Wallace argues for a different approach more attentive to the "concrete historical moment." Such a historical (or new historical) rereading does not entail the pursuit of authorial intention or any other form of transcendent meaning,[9] but it does entail a study of the temporal contingencies of Petrarch's writing, as well as those of one's own critical perspective.[10]

One sort of contingent reading demands that the critic acknowledge the ways in which historical appropriations—for example, of Petrarch as father of the Renaissance and of modernity—are never disinterested. Thus it might be argued that Petrarch's fame abides precisely because for centuries, humanists have retroactively accorded him the enduring status of prophet and founder of that "more propitious age" we call modernity. Barbara Smith has analyzed the "dynamics of endurance" of foundational texts by arguing that "classics" survive because they perform some desired function for those who appreciate, appropriate, and perpetuate them. The classic that endures must be repeatedly found to possess features "of value"—features that typically call for and legitimate "the characteristic resources of the culturally dominant members of a community," such as their "specific training" and "competence in a large number of cultural codes."[11] The masteries of the author, in other words, confirm the masteries of the readers—in this case, the readers of Petrarch and of Renaissance texts in general.

Seen from this perspective, Petrarch's enduring reputation as the "first modern man" and "first humanist," together with his high standing among scholars of the early modern, suggests that in a complicated fashion Petrarchan texts reproduce and legitimate the various competences not only of those who devote their lives' work to Petrarch and to the Renaissance, but more broadly, perhaps, of members of the academy, the institutional locus of humanist mastery during the many centuries since Petrarch simultaneously lamented the loss of classical learning and announced his recovery, at least in part, of that tradition. Petrarch scholarship is itself about mastery, and not simply because it takes as its subject a man obsessed with the past and his own grasp of it. Indeed, this six-hundred-year-old tradition of scholarship in myriad ways describes, as well as reproduces, the questions of mastery raised by Petrarch—namely, those of the possibility of differentiating the present from the past, and of distinguishing oneself from that past, as well. The "Petrarch story" functions as an allegory of academic mastery, particularly of how one attempts to read and appropriate the past, or one's precursors. That story, still serviceable, is thoroughly bound up with other foundational narratives of the academy and with academic practices of the last several centuries, with masteries new and old. The narratives of mastery, successful or not, that critics inevitably uncover in Petrarch's work not coincidentally mirror certain narratives of the university, of the arts of humane letters, and of the disciplines of criticism and history.

Moreover, the "Petrarch story" is predicated on the possibility of conducting one's humanist practices in a space removed from the workaday world, from the crassly materialist preoccupations of other humans. Indeed, one of the central masteries attempted by Petrarchan humanism is the transcendence of the economy against which that humanism operates differentially. It is precisely the idea of humanistic transcendence that to this day shapes the principles of liberal arts curricula, of pedagogic practice, of university structures. This fundamental mythology of the humanities—that its discourses transcend the banalities of the everyday world by offering an uncontaminated vision of human culture and perfection—obscures the social relations of mastery.

"The most elusive factor in any education is the ideology on which it depends," Anthony Grafton and Lisa Jardine have remarked in their study of the evolution of the humanities as a university program during the fifteenth and sixteenth centuries.[12] Generally speaking, the humanist tradition has been thought to offer "such vistas of intellectual and spiritual freedom as to make it irresistible,"[13] a formulation that bears out the notion that utopian incentives are intrinsic to every ideology, as discussed in Chapter 1. Grafton and Jardine historicize the liberating and egalitarian ideals of the humanities in order to show how those ideals have always been at odds with the reality of humanist education, which is a process of cultural legitimation and indoctrination of social elites.[14] The ideologies of humanism and the humanities, in other words, represent mastery as disinterested (as in Kantian judgments of taste), as egalitarian (available to all), and as somehow outside the market-place.

Some Questions of Method

Thus far this chapter has been complicated by two very differ-ent views of Petrarch in relation to humanism. According to the first, which suggests a traditional, "old historicist" perspective, Petrarch is the first modern man, the originary humanist and old master. De-fenses of this view tend to rely on positivist criteria, such as proofs of Petrarch's originality based on various forms of textual and bio-graphical evidence. The second range of views encompasses new his-toricism, neo-marxism, and neopragmatism—that is, forms of post-structuralism. In contrast to most traditional interpretations, post-structuralist readings of Petrarch tend to critique both the idea of origins and the mastery customarily attributed to him, as well as the masteries assumed by his unself-conscious reader. According to one such argument sketched above, for example, "Petrarch" functions not as an authentic creative intellect, but as an ideological com-modity ("first modern man") used to legitimate and perpetuate cer-tain privileges of the readers who appropriate and disseminate his texts as cultural artifacts. These two interpretations of Petrarch, then, would seem in many ways to be mutually exclusive, the second prob-lematizing or even repudiating the first.

Perhaps the reader is wondering which of these methods will ob-tain here. This book begins with the traditional assumption that there was at one time a Renaissance, which can now with impunity be referred to as the early modern age. Moreover, this chapter, the first of the early modern chapters of this study, begins with Petrarch and a return *ad fontes*, to the sources of humanism. Yet the chapter also remains poised at the brink of a decentering—of Petrarch as first modern man, and of the assumptions of contemporary humanist practice. For that reason the reader might anticipate further post-structuralist turns in the presentation. What does it mean to begin with Petrarch (even though this is actually Chapter 2)? Possibly this setup is a rhetorical ploy, a convenient way to begin a chapter, like "Once upon a time."

Or perhaps both methods can obtain at the same time. As I argued in Chapter 1, the differences between pre- and poststructuralist modes of interpretation are not all that they seem to be. An unreconstructed deconstructionist would argue, for example, that both sets of approaches to Petrarch rely on positivist forms of evidence, although they reach very different conclusions with it.[15] But besides that, the opposition between old and new historicism, between "traditional" scholarship and the new criticism, between "unself-conscious" and self-conscious theoretical perspectives, replicates the opposition between poststructuralism and humanism. To choose a more contemporary interpretive mode informed by some combination of poststructuralist theories is to assent to a form of mastery over the past—to a transcendence, in particular, of humanism. The most determined poststructuralist, in CIA style, would neither confirm nor deny participation in this *aufhebung*, but the deconstructive rhetoric of mastery remains the functional equivalent of an epistemology of mastery. Moreover, given that transcendence and mastery are thought to be the defining features of humanism (either the main virtues or "the Problem," depending on one's point of view), it is important to reflect on this mirroring of humanism by poststructuralism. The trope of the mirror could evoke the standard specular metaphors of old historicism or the generic "mis-en-abîme"— or possibly both.

To return to the question of origins, there are several reasons to begin with Petrarch, reasons that shed light on the critical methods operating in the impending argument. First of all, Petrarch is a functional choice for an opening, and possibly for an origin, because he left his future audience a paper trail of hundreds of letters, treatises, poems, and meditations—in other words, because he's there.

There is a further justification, however, for approaching early modern and poststructuralist mastery through the works of the "first humanist": the fact that Petrarch wrote profusely on the subject of will. One work in particular, known as *De secreto conflictu curarum mearum*, or simply as the *Secretum*, explores in detail questions of freedom and determinism in relation to humanist practice. Representing itself as autobiography,[16] the *Secretum* is structured as a dialogue between Francis, the humanist poet, and Augustine, the fourth-century bishop of Hippo and preeminent Christian theorist of the will, who has returned to earth for the express purpose of advising his protégé.[17] The premise of the dialogue is that the soul-sick Francis attempts to will a moral change of heart, a conversion, in order to improve his spiritual life and relieve his depression. With Lady Truth standing in silent attendance, the two discuss the poet's desire for moral mastery (the piety and virtue associated with late medieval Christianity) in the context of humanist mastery (the command of the cultural heritage of classical antiquity, as well as literary and social success). In their discussions of freedom and fate, Augustine and Francis weigh the possibility of achieving both types of mastery through conscious acts of will. It is this complex interrelation of Francis's assertions of humanist ambition, desire for moral probity, and puzzlement about the status of the will that makes the *Secretum* a particularly rich text for an investigation of the problematic of mastery in the early modern age.

A third justification for beginning with Petrarch is that it is possible to use his debate on will in the *Secretum* and other writings not so much as a resolution to the mystery of method traced above, but as a paradigm of the theoretical problem contemplated by this book. Petrarch's debate on the will can be read as an allegory of the continuing crisis in theory—a "crisis" in the sense of its Greek etymology, a "deciding" or "determining," but also a "trial," a "dispute," and a "quarrel."[18] The quarrel in theory concerns its subject—that is, its proper object of study. The issue is inseparable from questions of the person/agent/individual (there is no neutral term) who acts upon the world or is acted upon. Petrarch's debate on will in the *Secretum* is in effect a debate about theory.

It is also a debate about a crisis in the more modern sense of the term (a turning point, a time of distress or extremity). The subject of that crisis would seem to be Petrarch himself, or so most critics have assumed, because "Petrarch" announces at the outset that his dialogue is autobiographical. But if the *Secretum* explains something about the historical Petrarch, the nature of his crisis, and perhaps the crisis of late medieval Europe, there is no consensus as to its meaning—or rather, there are only multiple determinations, that succession of critical "crises" known as historical or referential readings.

The same questions remain, of course, after many such readings:

Did Petrarch, the original, official, and authentic Petrarch, have a crisis, as the *Secretum* suggests? When? Why? What was it like? Petrarch challenges his readers to make such historical determinations, and critics have always complied. Most recently, Francisco Rico and Hans Baron have argued for a redating of the *Secretum,* offering new evidence that the dialogue was first composed in 1347 and then revised periodically until 1353.[19] As we shall see, the dating of this work has a great deal of bearing on its interpretation and on the configuration that the reader gives to its crises. If Petrarch did, in fact, begin the *Secretum* in 1347, as Rico and Baron have argued through careful philological analysis, then it is useful to explore the rather abstract debates on will and mastery within the dialogue in relation to the events of that remarkable year. I will venture some historical determinations of my own by reading Petrarch's *Secretum*—especially book 2—in the context of certain other writings of 1347 and by connecting the theological debates on will and mastery in that dialogue to specific political events of that year. I will also theorize what such determinations—that is, historical readings—suggest about the freedom and bondage of the critical will to read.

Misery, Memory, and Will in the *Secretum*

Engaged in his own process of historical reading, the character Francis sets out to determine in the *Secretum* his relation to the past—his own past, first of all, which he hopes to transcend through the process of spiritual transformation, and secondly a collective past, that of Greek and Roman antiquity, which he strives to appropriate as a humanist philosopher and poet. His relation to the past hinges on questions of will: specifically, the will to make the spiritual changes that Augustine recommends, thereby rejecting and transcending his former self. These changes would require that in preparation for the next world Francis abandon his attachments to this world, attachments most manifest in his desire for earthly fame. Thus for Augustine, humanist mastery is antithetical to the program of spiritual mastery he puts forward, and Francis remains free to choose either course. However, it is precisely this notion of freedom that Francis continues to resist.

During the three-day encounter, the two discuss the psychology of will in relation to memory and reason (day 1); the seven deadly sins as contemplated or committed by Francis (day 2); and two overarching sins, lust for the angelic Laura and for poetic fame, that continue to dog Francis (day 3). On the first day, Augustine attempts to cure Francis's unhappiness by exhorting him, "Have you forgotten that you will die?" Nothing better can be found to calm the soul's tempests, says Augustine, than the memory of one's own misery and continual meditation on death. Francis assures him, here and in general, that he has not forgotten his mortality, but that although his meditations on mortality are frequent, they in no way relieve his anxiety (S, p. 41).[20]

In contrast, Augustine holds that Francis wills his own misery and thus is largely responsible for it. Conversely, he can achieve happiness simply by desiring it and engaging in a three-part meditative exercise:

> We have agreed that if a man is very clear in his mind that he is unhappy, he would desire to be happy; and that once he has conceived a desire for happiness, he will pursue his goal energetically. The third point is this: if a man expends every effort to become happy, it is in his power to do so. But this third point holds true if the second holds true, and the second in turn depends on the first. (S, p. 42)

According to Augustine, the person who performs this exercise cannot avoid confronting his own misery and will eventually will his own happiness.

Francis questions the value of this advice, claiming that if his will remains unconverted, then certainly it is through no fault of his own. He insists that he cannot change, though Augustine argues that he simply does not will the change. To support his views, Augustine describes his own freely willed conversion experience:

> I pulled my hair, I struck my forehead, I wrung my hands; I doubled up and beat my hands together; I filled the heavens with my bitter sighs and watered the earth with floods of tears. And yet, through all this, I stayed the same man I was until at last a deep meditation brought home to me the full extent of my unhappiness. And so, after I committed my will fully, I was instantly able to act [Itaque postquam plene volui, ilicet et potui] and with amazing and blessed swiftness I was a changed man. I am sure you know all this from your reading of my *Confessions*. (S, p. 48; OL, p. 66)

As many have noted, this voluntarist account of personal change does not square with *Confessions* 8, where the historical Augustine describes his conversion under the fig tree.[21] Petrarch's Augustine does not mention the mysterious voice in the garden telling him to "take up and read," nor does he suggest the role of grace or divine intervention in his conversion. In contrast to the subtext in book 8 of the *Confessions*, this Augustine stresses his own will to change—a point crucial to his persuasion of Francis.

The entire *Secretum* hinges on this battle of wills—or rather, of theories of the will. Augustine continues to insist on a kind of voluntarism (though by no means an absolute one), arguing that man in general and Francis in particular can freely will spiritual or psychic change. Francis, in contrast, insists that matters of will are not under human control. By the end of the third day, Francis remains unconvinced of his confessor's theory of will, and Augustine reluctantly acknowledges that their argument over the nature of will remains unresolved: "You are labeling the will as lacking in power [Voluntatem impotentiam vocas]." Augustine prays, nevertheless, that God will somehow lead Francis "to salvation" (*S*, p. 144; *OL*, p. 258).

The *Secretum*, especially its open-ended conclusion, has evoked very different responses, but critics have tended to read it as a quasi-allegorical treatment of the tensions between a purely spiritual life (exemplified by the historical Augustine, for example, or by Petrarch's ascetic brother Gherardo, a Carthusian monk) and the more worldly spirituality of the late medieval humanist. In various ways these readings reinforce the theory that Petrarch was a transitional figure between the medieval and modern eras. Klaus Heitmann, Charles Trinkaus, William Bouwsma, David Marsh, Jaroslav Pelikan, and Albert Rabil emphasize, though in different ways, the disjunctions in the *Secretum* between medieval Christianity and Renaissance humanism.[22] Francesco Tateo, while cautioning against critical generalizations about medieval/Renaissance dichotomies in the *Secretum*, reads the dialogue as an adaptation of Stoicism and Augustinian thought to Petrarch's own epoch and sees the character Francis as a nonautobiographical foil for the updated and synthetic theology offered by Augustine.[23]

The dichotomy between past and present in the *Secretum* has been represented not only in larger, ideological terms (what might be called "paradigm shifts" in the history of ideas), but also in the biographical terms of a conversion narrative. Luigi Tonelli, Carlo Calcaterra, and many others have read the *Secretum* as a reflection of a religious crisis supposedly experienced by the historical Petrarch in the early to mid-1340's.[24] Though he argues for a later dating of the *Secretum* (1347-53) and hence against the conversion theory, Francisco Rico also reads biographically; he interprets Augustine as the image of Petrarch as he would like to be, and Francis as his former self, the self to be transcended.[25] Hans Baron defends the idea that the dialogue dates from 1347 and after but rejects Rico's interpretation of the two speakers. Rather, Baron argues that the *Secretum* presents the conflict between Petrarch's worldly humanist goals and his Christianity.[26]

A third category of interpretations of the *Secretum* stresses Petrarch's historical difference in hermeneutic terms. For Thomas Greene, Petrarch is the innovator of a humanist hermeneutic tradition vastly different from the medieval, allegorical mode of reading. Greene interprets the *Secretum* as an account of Petrarch's humanist agon with Augustine and other classical precursors.[27] And Victoria Kahn has argued that the *Secretum* expresses a partial resistance to classical and medieval modes of reading and embodies a new, essentially modern mode of interpretation. Francis, the Petrarchan persona, is characterized "not as the ideally passive reader but rather as the willful (mis)reader who fails to imitate his master."[28]

We might think of this sampling of interpretations as allegorical, to the extent that they detect in the content or structure of the *Secretum* a narrative about differences—invariably, the differences between the medieval and the modern—by drawing a distinction between what existed before Petrarch (a theology, a philosophy, a literary tradition, an economy between writer and reader) and the kind of separation from that past, however construed, that Petrarch engineers in the *Secretum* and, perhaps, in his personal life. That allegory of mastery, generally understood as a transcending of the past (that is, as an embodiment of some notion of progress), typifies not only the range of meanings attributed to the *Secretum*, but also the structure of the readings themselves. Regardless of their theoretical orientations, such readings make a claim of novelty; they attempt to secure their own distance from the past (from recent rather than ancient critical tradition, however), just as they locate such distance in Petrarch's text. One aspect of humanist practice since Petrarch's time, and certainly in the late twentieth century, is the will to read the past through its artifacts and to find mirrored in those artifacts one's own gestures of mastery.

What does the humanist critic's claim to historical difference—that is, to originality—imply? Above all, it implies a sort of hermeneutic or poetic voluntarism, the power to reread, to appropriate, even to create a literary tradition. Interestingly, this will to power bears some resemblance to the method of deliberate conversion outlined by Petrarch's Augustine. Yet the *Secretum* also exposes the humanist's nonfreedom—generally, though not exclusively, through the objections of the character Francis. Book 2 of the dialogue opposes the humanist's poetic voluntarism (the will to originality, creativity, difference) to the bondage of the humanist's will to "fortuna."[29] Let us examine this relation of humanist hermeneutics to fate, or, in the critical terms of this reading of the *Secretum*, the will to read and to write in relation to the determinisms, real and perceived, of the late medieval social order. Not surprisingly, this conflict has some bearing on contemporary humanism and poststructuralism.

The Earthly Paradise and the Humanist Ethic

On the second day of the dialogue, Augustine adopts the interrogative techniques of the medieval confessional in order to determine the precise nature of Francis's crisis.[30] While studying the humanist's degree of involvement in each of the seven deadly sins, the dialogists discuss at length two of those sins, *avaritia*, or greed, and *accidia*, the late medieval version of sloth. Interestingly, these discussions foreground an economic dimension of the free will / determinism problem: namely, the possibility of the humanist's escape from what he experiences as economic and political servitude.

The section of book 2 devoted to avaritia and the related vice of *ambitio* opens obscurely; Augustine alludes to the greed and ambition of his charge without giving particulars. He asks, quoting Horace, why Francis counterproductively nourishes such long hopes (of wealth, presumably) when life is so short ("Quid necesse erat in tam brevibus vite spatiis tam longas spes ordire? 'Vite summa brevis spem nos vetat inchoare longam' ") and adds, "You will say, I suppose, that you do it out of love for your friends" (*S*, p. 72; *OL*, p. 114; quoting Horace, *Carmina* 1.4.15).

Annoyed by this charge of greed, Francis insists on the modesty of his own pecuniary desires:

I am not so selfish and inhuman as to be unconcerned about my friends, especially those whose virtue and merit have drawn me to them. For it is they whom I esteem, revere, love, and take pity on. On the other hand, I am not so generous that I would ruin myself for my friends. No, hardly that. What I want is enough to live on. And since you shoot darts at me from Horace, I shall shield myself with something taken from the same poet. What I want is "a supply of books and stores for one year so I do not have to worry from one hour to the next" ["sit bona librorum et provise frugis in annum / copia, ne fluitem dubie spe pendulus hore"]. (*S*, p. 72; *OL*, p. 116; quoting Horace, *Epistulae* 1.18.109–10)

Leaving aside for a moment the question of reference (whether Petrarch is alluding to specific friends and events in his life), let us consider the force of the Horatian allusions in these passages. Both Augustine and Francis invoke the Roman poet, who, under the official patronage of Maecenas, aide to the emperor Augustus, wrote eloquently of love, fine wine, good country and bad city living. The worldly yet reclusive image of the poet cultivated by the historical Horace and immortalized in his poems and letters becomes in the *Secretum* the ideal to which Francis aspires.[31] Thus the greatest ambition of the latter is simply to be left alone, because human entanglements interfere with his studies, and to be left alone simply. Intriguingly, Francis ignores the question of patronage when he expresses his modest wish to be on the receiving end of books, provisions, and time.

Next Augustine exhorts Francis to remember his former, nonmonetary wealth:

Do you recall with what delight you once wandered far into the country and listened to the murmur of the swirling streams as you lay on a bed of grass? At another time, you would sit on a mountain top and with unobstructed view you would gaze at the fields stretched out below. At other times, you would sleep peacefully in a patch of shade in a sunny valley and revel in the silence. Never at a loss for something to do, you were always deep in meditation and, with the Muses for companions, you were never alone. And as you returned at sunset to your little house, like the old man in Vergil who "To his way of thinking matched the wealth of kings and returning late / Set his table with food from the garden" ["regum equabat opes animo, seraque revertens / nocte domum, dapibus mensas onerabat inemptis"], do you not think that of all men you were by far the richest and most fortunate? (S, pp. 73–74; OL, p. 118)[32]

In this vivid evocation of prelapsarian freedom (before Francis's fall into greed and ambition), Augustine reminds his charge that once he was rich—"as rich as kings"—in his rural habitat. Such pastoral riches, he suggests, are self-generating. Those who dedicate themselves to the Muses can listen to water music all day and still find simple but tasty food on their tables at night. Moreover, their private paradise depends on no contact with the rest of humanity; it is self-sustaining, completely free of all the economic, emotional, and other daily transactions that distract regular (and presumably more venal) people. Augustine insists not only that the humanist should try to live according to this class-crossing pastoral ethic, but also that it is possible to do so—Francis being a case in point at an earlier, less ambitious stage of his life.

Pastoral proscribes many vices, Renato Poggioli argues, especially those "related to the misuse, or merely to the possession, of worldly goods." That is not to say that the pastoral world lacks an economy of its own, but "money, credit, and debt have no place in an economy of this kind. By a strange and yet natural miracle, the system seems to avoid any disproportion between production and consumption, despite its lack of planning and foresight."[33] It is precisely this ethos that Petrarch incorporates into his humanist's version of the pastoral paradise, where the scholar enjoys his freedom from the economic and social demands of the "outside" world.

Petrarch's use of Virgil in framing the humanist's pastoral retreat is significant, because, as Annabel Patterson has noted, Petrarch interpreted Virgilian pastoral as an allegory of the poet and his culture, specifically as "a self-conscious admission of the problems faced by all writer-intellectuals, who must weigh their need for survival

and recognition against the demands of personal freedom and inte-
riority."[34] Furthermore, within the *Secretum*, elements of pastoral
function as allegories of the poet/humanist's social and economic
predicaments (such as the "servitude" of patronage)—allegories that
on the one hand deny his compromised relationships with the powerful and on the other legitimize them. Indeed, the "first humanist"
had many such compromises to defend. The peripatetic Petrarch
sought out the patronage of nobles and tyrants throughout Italy and
France, including the Milanese Visconti during the years 1353–61.
Petrarch's ties with that autocratic and ruthless clan appalled friends
and admirers all over Europe.[35] The defense provided by the pastoral
myth at the center of the *Secretum* suggests that it is possible for the
humanist to transcend the political economy of his age and to remain untouched by the crass realities of monetary need. Clearly at
variance with the economic realities of Petrarch's life, which was sustained not by his agrarian skills but by the patronage system, this
version of pastoral nevertheless constitutes a powerful and still serviceable myth. Petrarchan pastoral can be said both to deny and to
legitimate the humanist's relation to power, principally by obfuscat-
ing that relation. This is not to suggest that Petrarchan pastoral can
only serve this ideological function. It is conceivable, for example,
that Petrarch had a distinct appreciation for country living, or that
the desire for a "golden world" might have some other meaning—
for example, as "a symbol for man's inner need and desire for peace
and harmony," as A. B. Giamatti wrote of the idea of the earthly
paradise.[36] Nevertheless, the political uses of Petrarchan pastoral
should not be discounted.

But if the *Secretum* presents the myth or, more accurately, the
ideology of humanist freedom, in the form of a pastoral escape from
economic servitude, at the same time it critiques that myth through
certain accounts of economic necessity. For example, Francis implies
that he has abandoned his pastoral paradise and moved into the public sphere out of legitimate financial need: "Well, if I look ahead to
the poverty of old age and provide for when I can no longer work,
what is so reprehensible about that?" (*S*, pp. 74–75). It is both sen-
sible and normal, he argues, to prepare oneself for the economic
needs of the future and for the potential downturns of fortune. Fran-

cis points out that the humanist is never as free from need as Augustine's pastoral myth would suggest. He indicates, too, that economic voluntarism (the myth of pastoral self-sufficiency) fails because one cannot will financial security.

In his counterarguments against economic necessity—the survival needs framed by Francis in quasi-determinist terms—Augustine analyzes human need and how best to respond to it. "I think moderation should be sought in every situation [Mediocritatem sane in omni statu expetendam censeo]," he rejoins (S, p. 75; OL, p. 122). Poverty is not a condition to be actively pursued, but neither is wealth. Augustine then responds to Francis's claim of financial need with a more general theory of necessity: that to be human is to want, and that man's condition of need is ineluctable. "Just look at him— born naked and unformed amid wailing and tears, comforted by a little milk, trembling and crawling, restless, beset by all kinds of diseases, subject to all kinds of passions, lacking in wisdom, fluctuating between sadness and joy, unable to master his will, unable to control his appetite" (S, p. 77). In this account of necessity, which combines elements of Ciceronian Stoicism and of the historical Augustine's theories of frustrated desire, Petrarch's Augustine acknowledges that men and women are always subject to the plays of "fortuna." Like Francis, he acknowledges a form of determinism or destiny operating in everyone's life: namely, the inability of human will to eradicate need completely. But for Augustine, the site of resistance to will is not so much an external force, malevolent "fortuna," as an internal one basic to human nature.

Regardless of social position, Augustine continues, no person's power over want, or over others, can ever be absolute: "Certainly the kings and lords of the earth whom you think so rich need countless things. And the generals of armies are subservient to those they seem to control; surrounded by their armed legions, they ought to fear the soldiers who cause their leaders to be feared" (ibid.). Here Augustine reduces Francis's statement of his particular monetary needs to a general statement about human desire, independent of class position. Nested within this account of the vulnerabilities of man, and especially of the powerful, are several ideas about need. One is that desire is virtually insatiable (as proven by the fact that few, if any, can control their appetites and passions). A second is that kings and generals are not really in control of their lives, because they still experience need. A third is that all humans are, relatively speaking, stuck in the same predicament of wanting. Because this condition of want is an aspect of one's humanity and therefore cannot be changed, one's best alternative is to make a virtue of necessity:

Then stop hoping for the impossible and content yourself with your human lot; learn how to live in need and how to have more than you need, to command and to obey. Do not by living your life according to your own ideas try to cast off the yoke of Fortune to which kings submit. You will know you are free of the yoke at last, when you have renounced all your human passions and have yielded completely to the rule of virtue. From that time on, you will be free, subject to no man, and finally a king, truly powerful and completely happy. (*S*, pp. 77–78)

Clearly Augustine's voluntarism is not absolute, particularly in this Stoic frame. Yet one of the basic assumptions of Stoicism is that even if humans cannot control "fortuna," it is still possible for the individual to experience a kind of inner freedom through a virtuous detachment from human desire and from the fluctuations of fortune.[37] The ideal of pastoral freedom is partially offset by the fact, acknowledged by Augustine, that no one is ever completely free. Yet evidently humanists and priests come closest to achieving freedom; they do so by avoiding the lure of gold and the hooks of avarice (*S*, p. 75). Augustine argues that by transcending desire, especially the desire for money, Francis can ransom his will from the "necessities" of the marketplace.

Barbara Smith has analyzed the conventional distinction, made by Petrarch's Augustine, among others, between the realm of the marketplace and that of spirituality, wisdom, taste, and other qualities thought to transcend "mere" economic value. Often that distinction is represented as "the priest/humanist's struggle to chase the money changers from the temple, to preserve the sacred objects from the merchant, and to name and isolate their value as absolutely different from and transcendent of exchange value and use value." Smith argues that the effect of such distinctions between what is base (figured principally by the monetary or economic) and what rises above it is to obscure that "broader and more continuous struggle between those with something to *lose* from a reclassification and circulation of goods and those with something to *gain* from them."[38] Thus the claim to have escaped the realm of mammon is simultaneously a claim of mastery against any contenders, who by definition embody the values of the marketplace. The rhetoric of economic transcendence bolsters the authority of anyone—such as professional humanists and other keepers of the flame—claiming the powers of aesthetic, intellectual, or moral discrimination against rival interest groups. In the case of Petrarch, such rivals would include all non-humanists, especially those who, in a "base" sense, are more free than Francis—his patrons, actual and potential: popes, cardinals, barons, and assorted despots who happen to have significantly more money and power than he does.

Smith argues that the rhetoric of transcendence masks a strategy for controlling whatever turf, intellectual or otherwise, one hopes to claim. It might also be argued that such rhetoric masks the impossibility of transcendence—of a ransoming of the will from economic "necessity." Thus Augustine's language of freedom, moral choice, and self-control represents a denial of the realities of the marketplace—in particular, the relative nonfreedom of the humanist. For that reason we might say that the myth of pastoral bliss fondly recalled by the two speakers in the *Secretum* expresses a fantasy of escaping the "predestinarian" bondage of the humanist to the class he generally serves and on which he depends for his livelihood.

Accidia, the Bondage of the Wallet, and the Dating of the *Secretum*

It is indeed economic bondage to others that drives Francis to despair, as he later confesses during an investigation of accidia. Toward the end of the second day Augustine introduces accidia as a "[deadly] disease of the mind [funesta . . . pestis animi]," a spiritual torpor that borders on despair (*S*, p. 84; *OL*, p. 140).[39] When Francis tries to identify the source of that despair, he immediately points to the brutal turns of fortune he has had to endure:

I am like someone surrounded by countless enemies. There is no possibility of escape, no hope of mercy, and no solace. Everything threatens death. The enemy has raised his batteries and has tunneled beneath the wall; already the towers begin to fall, the ladders lean on the ramparts, the grappling hooks are fastened to the walls and fires rage out of control. And as a man looks upon the flashing swords and the fierce face of the enemy, thinking destruction is at hand, is it any wonder that he would be utterly overwhelmed by fear and sorrow? Even if destruction were avoided, the very loss of freedom is devastating for courageous men. (*S*, p. 85)

Once again Francis explains his predicament in terms of a loss of freedom, without explaining the circumstances of his downfall or whether anything in particular has provoked this paranoid image of besiegement. He does assert, however, that fortune has singled him out for special punishment: "I am taking it badly that out of all my contemporaries whom I know, no one has developed more moderate goals than I and no one has encountered more difficulties than I. Truth, who is our witness and who sees all, will tell you that I have never desired the highest ranks" (*S*, p. 88). Echoing themes of the earlier debate on avarice and ambition, and alluding once again to the Horatian "golden mean [aurea mediocritas],"[40] Francis insists that it has always been the "middle road [mediocritam]," rather than the "highest rank [summum locum]," that he has sought, yet that unassuming position has consistently been denied him (*S*, p. 89; *OL*, p. 150).

When Augustine suggests that in reality Francis's position has always been far better than middling, the latter confesses that his real complaint is that "up to now, I have lived dependent on others" (*S*, p. 90). Augustine confirms that the real complaint here has to do with dependence rather than want: "As to your complaint that you do not live a life of your own, what that means is that you are not living in poverty, but dependent on somebody else [Quod vero non tibi te vixisse conquereris, non inopie sed servitutis est]" (*S*, p. 90; *OL*, pp. 152, 154).

Throughout this section on accidia and the earlier section on avaritia, the themes of frustrated ambition, unstable fortune, problems of patronage, and the humanist's lost paradise recur. There remain, of course, certain puzzling questions of the dialogue's referentiality: is the *Secretum* autobiographical, and, if so, do its characters refer to incidents in the life of the historical Petrarch? Moreover, what does it entail, in the wake of poststructuralism, to read literally, making assumptions about the greed, ambition, and depression of this fourteenth-century humanist? As described above, twentieth-century critics of the *Secretum* tend to read the dialogue somewhat generally, as well as allegorically, exploring the differences between the medieval and modern, or proto-modern, views seemingly expressed by the two characters.[41] That is not to say that readers exclude questions of historical or biographical reference, although Francis discusses his vices and shortcomings in a remarkably abstract way, and although the "history" that emerges in the dialogue is drawn, for the most part, from the plots of other books—the *Confessions*, the *Aeneid*, Horace's odes, and a host of other classical sources.

It is partly on historical and biographical considerations that Rico and Baron have based their arguments that the *Secretum* was first written in 1347 and revised in 1349 and 1353, although the dialogue seems to be set in 1342 or 1343.[42] Rico points out that in book 3 Augustine says Francis has been caught in a web of amorous deception for sixteen years.[43] Petrarch describes his own first meeting with Laura as taking place on April 6, 1327 (*Canzoniere* 211.12–13), which would seem to place the action of the *Secretum* between April 1342 and April 1343.[44] But Rico argues that the time of the action of the *Secretum* has been confused with the time of its writing, and that there are strong reasons for assigning the original composition of the dialogue to 1347.[45] Summarizing the arguments that the *Secretum* was first drafted in 1347, Baron points out that there is no evidence of Petrarch's having had a religious crisis in 1342–43, but that the *Secretum* does show some similarities to the *De otio religioso* of 1347, especially in its reliance on the *De vera religione* of Augustine.[46] Moreover, Francis's decision to finish his *Africa* and *De viris*, voiced at the close of the *Secretum*, does not seem to square with Petrarch's literary production during the years following 1343. Most significantly, Petrarch is known to have invented dates for his correspondence and possibly for other documents; thus there is no reason to assume that the temporal settings of Petrarch's works necessarily coincide with their dates of composition.[47]

It is difficult, of course, to date many of Petrarch's works with certainty, as Rico and Baron admit, because of Petrarch's habit of rewriting his texts over the course of years or even decades. As David Wallace has noted, "Petrarch's epistles, though full of historical detail, tend to escape or erase the specific moment of their historical origin. The same may be said of Petrarch's other works, which, through a series of minute revisions extending over decades, conceal the chronology of their making."[48] Arguably the overall lack of historical specificity in works such as the *Secretum* might be taken as a conscious strategy on the part of Petrarch to erase the traces of his political entanglements, the compromised reality of his career, and to erect in their place a more flattering image of the poet, largely removed from a historical context. Like the humanist's pastoral paradise, free from the contamination of the political and economic marketplace, the confessions of Francis in the *Secretum* seem to transcend the particular realities of daily life (Petrarch's or anyone else's, for that matter) and to become part of a transhistorical dialogue between the great minds of antiquity and, of course, Petrarch. The fact that Francis falls, either by choice or by necessity, from the earthly paradise of humanist detachment into the cesspool of urban life[49] cannot automatically be fixed as a historical event, because the *Secretum* itself partly allegorizes that fall (as caused by the turns of Lady Fortuna, the hooks of greed, and other factors).

If the *Secretum* remains, then, a convenient text for allegorizing because of its effacement, deliberate or not, of historical detail, it is nevertheless possible to conjecture, as Rico and Baron do, that the dialogue dates from a period of Petrarch's life later than the apparent time of the action, 1342–43—specifically from 1347 and after— and to corroborate that thesis with historical and philological evidence. Surprisingly, however, Rico and Baron do not discuss in any detail what was probably the most remarkable event of 1347: the rise and fall of Cola di Rienzo, the revolutionary innkeeper's son who led a populist uprising in Rome in the hope of restoring that city to its former glory. They also do not focus on the fact that 1347 ended with the arrival in Sicily of the Black Death, surely the greatest calamity of that century.

For Petrarch as well, 1347 held many changes and reversals. Sometime in its first months he traveled to the Carthusian monastery of Montrieux to visit his brother Gherardo, whom he had not seen since the latter's arrival there in 1343. Inspired by his visit with the austere monks, Petrarch wrote the *De otio religioso* during Lent, which fell during February and March of that year.[50] Rico and Baron believe that Petrarch began the *Secretum* sometime after the *De otio*, while he was still living in Provence, most likely as a further response to his chastening visit with his brother. Because these critics contend that Petrarch finished the first draft of the *Secretum* in the early months of 1347, they do not consider in any detail the dialogue's possible relation to the main event of the summer and fall of that year: Cola di Rienzo's coup in Rome and his subsequent seven months in power. But given that Petrarch's deepest poetic and political aspirations were for a time bound up with those of Cola, it is entirely possible that this intriguing episode in Rome's history had some bearing on the elements of book 2 discussed above—Francis's revelations of his vaulting ambition and greed, his patronage problems, and the calamitous blow dealt him by cruel "fortuna"—and thus that Petrarch wrote several parts of the *Secretum* toward the end of 1347, as I shall argue below.

Petrarch's basic instinct was to transfer political issues from the realm of practical contingencies to that of philosophy, as Rodolfo de Mattei has argued.[51] Quite frequently critics accept at face value Petrarch's tendency—or rather, his strategy—to depoliticize any discussion. For example, readings of the *Secretum* that emphasize its theological and philosophical debates, or its copious allusions to classical authors, at the expense of the historical or political references perhaps deliberately obscured by the author participate in the obfuscation of class conflict, as well as of the humanist's particular role in those struggles. Such obfuscation is, I would argue, characteristically Petrarchan.

It is possible and indeed useful to read the *Secretum* less as a general, quasi-allegorical debate on the humanist's quest for greater spiritual perfection or as a representation of his philosophical or poetic struggle with his classical precursors, and more as a cost/benefit analysis of his compromised career. Such a reading gives the apparent allusions to specific events a significance quite different from that often ascribed to the dialogue. The reading shares, it should be noted, the "allegorical" pattern of those interpretations alluded to above, although the medieval/modern distinction it makes concerns the coming into being in late medieval society of the humanist scholar as a special agent and employee of the early modern state.

New Masters: Cola di Rienzo and the Rebirth of Rome

It is difficult to convey to the contemporary reader the truly extraordinary nature of populist leader Cola di Rienzo's political project. On Sunday, May 20, 1347, Cola successfully executed a political coup in the city of Rome.[52] In the absence of the papal court, which had removed to Avignon decades earlier, Rome had long been subject to the control of its ruling families, especially the Colonna and Orsini clans, who perpetually waged war on each other and on the inhabitants of the ancient city.[53] Cola's carefully planned takeover coincided with the temporary absence of the nobles and the army from Rome.[54] On May 20, Cola gathered his small militia and addressed a large crowd from the Capitoline Hill, promising to liberate the people from their oppression by the Roman nobility and to institute a new social order. An aide read out a new constitution that conferred the government of the city upon the people. The people, in turn, accepted their new constitution and Cola as their leader. A few days after the coup Cola convened a parliament, during which he took the title of tribune, as did Raimondo, bishop of Orvieto and vicar of Pope Clement VI; the vicar was soon to discover, however, that his authority existed in name only. Surprised, disorganized, and frightened by the popular revolt, the nobles soon swore their allegiance to the new tribunes.[55]

Cola's initial goals were not merely to eliminate the belligerent influence of the Roman aristocracy, but to re-create the republican values of ancient Rome and to reunify Italy.[56] The events of his brief months in power—especially his rapid transformation from populist hero to grandiose tyrant—reveal his passionate desire to restage the glory days of past empire. Whether Cola di Rienzo was a genuine man of the people, a proto-marxist, a mystic, a visionary idealist, a medieval Mussolini, a "fantastic madman,"[57] or something altogether different has yet to be decided.

In the early months of his rule, Cola instituted progressive social reforms on behalf of the common people of Rome and very much at the expense of the nobility.[58] He managed for a time to maintain the support of the papacy, which had long resented the turf war among the first families of Rome. Papal support soon faded, however, when news of Cola's increasingly extravagant activities reached Avignon.

On July 31, Cola, wearing a white silk robe and bearing a scepter, moved through the streets of Rome to the Lateran Palace. There he took a bath of purification in the baptistry's porphyry tub, once used by none other than the emperor Constantine, who was supposedly cured of leprosy in it by Pope Sylvester. Cola passed that night in a vigil, then had himself knighted the next day in a lavish ceremony, this time wearing scarlet and fur. Also that day he proclaimed, to the surprise of the pope's vicar, that Rome was the "caput orbis," that all Italians were citizens of Rome, and that only the people of Rome had the right to elect an emperor. All those interested in protesting that claim were invited to Rome to make their cases.[59] The pope's vicar did, in fact, protest; however, his notary, reading a counterproclamation, was drowned out by loud trumpets, drums, and cymbals.[60] Later that day Cola threw a massive party, with free food and wine for everyone in Rome who wished to participate. Perhaps the most extravagant symbol of Cola's largesse was the famed equestrian statue of Marcus Aurelius, rigged out for the day's festivities so that it squirted red wine from the horse's right nostril and water from the left.

During the first weeks of August Cola staged other lavish ceremonies and tournaments on behalf of some two hundred visiting dignitaries, and on the fifteenth of the month he had himself crowned as tribune.[61] One day later he dismissed the pope's vicar from office. Predictably, Cola's "imperium" began to unravel after these proceedings, as the Avignon establishment began to recognize the extent to which its interests in Rome were threatened. Cola further shocked and angered Avignon by allying himself to the invading Louis of Hungary against Naples, then under the protection of the pope.[62]

In Rome itself, matters went from bad to worse. Suspecting a conspiracy on the part of the nobles, Cola invited the Colonna, the Orsini, and other aristocrats to a banquet on the fourteenth of September. He then arrested them, threw them in jail, and condemned them to death, only to release them the next day with honorific titles and gifts. This chameleonlike behavior wore thin not only with the Roman nobility, but also with the general population, many of whom had already decided that Cola was insane. By the nineteenth of the month Cola had announced that the Roman people would soon be allowed to choose their next emperor; not surprisingly, Cola was the main contender.

Many events contributed to the rapid downfall of Cola di Rienzo, but one that was of great significance to Petrarch concerned the Colonna family, members of which had long been the humanist's patrons and admirers. On November 20, the nobles unsuccessfully attacked Rome, and four members of the Colonna clan were killed. On November 23, Cola brought his son Lorenzo to the bloody pool at the northern end of the city where the Colonna had died, and using those waters dubbed him a "knight of victory"—a ritual that did not impress many Romans with its tastefulness. Indeed, by this point the populace had decided that Cola was just another tyrant.[63]

By December, Cola's rule had run its short course. The tribune had lost much of the support of the Roman people, partly for the reasons mentioned above, partly because a grain embargo imposed by the nobles and the cardinal legate was causing shortages in the city, and partly because Cola had himself imposed an unpopular salt tax.[64] On December 15 Cola suddenly abdicated after a riot occurred in the Colonna-controlled neighborhoods of the city. Sobbing and escorted through town by a small group of supporters, also sobbing, Cola withdrew to Rome's Castel Sant'Angelo and soon fled to Naples. His odd story continued for several more years, but his dream of empire had collapsed only seven months after it had begun, and just months before the Black Death would drastically rearrange the political hierarchies of Italy and of Europe. Cola gave himself many titles—"Nicolaus, white-garbed Knight of the Holy Spirit, the severe and clement, liberator of the city, zealot of Italy, lover of the world, and august Tribune [Candidatus spiritus sancti miles Nicolaus, severus et clemens, liberator Urbis, zelator Italie, Amator orbis et Tribunus Augustus]"—but the ironic epithet that he gave himself in exile, "the dreamer-tribune [tribunus sompniator]," describes his enterprise best.

Humanist Bondage and the Will to Leisure

Petrarch's involvement in the attempted *restauratio Romae* was substantial, and his correspondence and poetry composed during Cola's months in power reveal much about the hortatory uses of humanist discourse. Beyond that, however, Petrarch's writings of mid- to late 1347 explain a great deal about humanist mastery in the context of late medieval politics—for example, the ways in which hermeneutic as well as economic freedom, mythologized in the *Secretum* as the humanist's pastoral retreat, were bound (linked, that is, but also "in bondage") to concrete political institutions and class conflicts.

Petrarch's ties to Cola di Rienzo date from 1343. Toward the end of the preceding year a delegation of Romans headed by Stefano Colonna had visited Avignon seeking to persuade the recently installed Clement VI to return to Rome, to accept the position of senator, and to make 1350 a jubilee year.[65] But while these men lobbied in Avignon, the baronial government that had sent them was overthrown and replaced by a council headed by various members of Roman guilds.[66] Early in 1343 Cola di Rienzo was dispatched by the new council to represent the new government of Rome and to garner the pope's support for this more democratic ruling body.

In Avignon, Cola demonstrated his extraordinary oratorical gifts by making passionate speeches in favor of the new government and against the plundering, murdering, and other antisocial behavior of the baronial houses of Rome. The pope is said to have listened sympathetically to Cola's speeches but then to have turned against him because of the interventions of Cardinal Giovanni Colonna, who was predictably angered by Cola's denunciations of his family.[67] Yet that same cardinal later restored Cola to favor at the papal court; this reversal may have been wrought by none other than Petrarch, protégé of the cardinal and friend to the Roman Colonna family for some seventeen years.[68]

Petrarch and Cola most likely met one or more times during the latter's visit and shared their visions of a Rome restored to its former greatness.[69] "Of all men then living," Ernst Hatch Wilkins writes, "Cola and Petrarch were doubtless the two who most passionately and intelligently desired the rescue of Rome from its shameful plight."[70] Gregorovius identifies Cola "as the political incarnation of [Petrarch's] own thought, as a hero who had sprung from his own brain";[71] probably no one captivated the humanist's enthusiasm and fueled his deep hopes for the return of Roman glory as much as Cola di Rienzo did. In 1347, when Avignon received word of Cola's May takeover, Petrarch revealed in his letters and through his interventions with the papal court the degree to which he shared Cola's ambition to reestablish Rome's former greatness. He also revealed much—too much, no doubt—about the nature of his loyalties to his patron Cardinal Colonna and to the Colonna family.

"Liberty stands in your midst [Libertas in medio vestrum est]," Petrarch writes to Cola and to the people of Rome in a long hortatory letter dating from late June of 1347:

Enjoy this great blessing, the realization of your dreams of many years. Rejoice in it, but do so with moderation, with discretion, and with calm. Give thanks to God, the dispenser of such gifts, who has not yet forgotten his most holy city and could no longer behold her, in whom he had placed the empire of the world, enchained in slavery. Therefore, brave people and descendants of brave people, if sane thinking has reasserted itself together with liberty, let each one of you prefer death itself to the loss of liberty. Without liberty life is mockery. Keep your past servitude constantly before your eyes [Praeteritam servitutem ante oculos assidue revocate].[72]

In this remarkable letter Petrarch congratulates Cola and the Romans for taking back their freedom, in the great tradition of their republican ancestors. For a brief moment in his career, Petrarch seems to identify with the classes below his own (in fact, once his own), urging the masses to rejoice in the liberty that they have long deserved but have neglected to seize.[73] He urges the Romans never to forget their former servitude and to kill or expel all those who hate liberty and who cruelly stand in the way of the people's freedom.

And who are those predatory "ravishers of your honor, the plunderers of your fortunes, the destroyers of your liberty"?[74] None other than the baronial families of Rome—most prominently the Colonna, Petrarch's patrons of nearly two decades. Petrarch had direct knowledge of the destructive effects of the perennial warfare among Rome's ruling families, having spent time in Rome in 1337 as a guest of the Colonna.[75] Despite his long-standing ties to the Colonna, on whose money and courtly intercessions he had relied since early in his career, the humanist decries the pretensions to power of the first families of the city, whose ancestry, he points out, is not even Roman. Their claims to power are based on "superabundant wealth" gained by theft and plunder, and on false declarations of their genuine "romanitas."[76]

In this hortatory letter, Petrarch urges Cola and the Roman people to take strong action against these ravening wolves, who are circling the city and waiting to pounce: "They now thirst equally for the blood of both the flock and the shepherd. They consider your liberty and the glory of your deliverer their dishonor and disgrace. Have faith in yourselves. Rise against your enemies. They will only be a contemptible handful if you stand united."[77] Here, as in book 2 of the *Secretum*, Petrarch links a call to freedom with a vision of pastoral self-sufficiency. Actually, this passage suggests two pastoral scenarios, one predatory and menacing, the other irenic. The image of predatory pastoral is actually a fair description of Rome during the Avignon papacies; historians have described the city as depopulated by baronial warfare, disease, and poverty. Overgrown and overrun with sheep and cattle, medieval Rome might be accurately described as a ruined and threatening pastoral landscape.[78]

Petrarch's letter associates Cola di Rienzo with the positive vision of pastoral. Through an act of will, Cola, the good shepherd, and the Roman people, good sheep, can determine the type of pastoral that will prevail in their hometown. To realize the better option, Petrarch says, they must drive out the predatory wolves. Thus the humanist incites the Romans to kill the Colonna, the Orsini, and everyone else who hates the people's liberty and plots against their state. With this kind of brute animal, he says, "all sternness is benevolence, all pity is inhuman."[79]

The class sensibilities of Petrarch's hortatory letter are surprising, not only because the author recommends the use of violence against his aristocratic patron family, but also because he seems in some way to identify with the class of men and women he typically deems the crass and vulgar horde. Arguably, the masses become acceptable to Petrarch when he can imagine them as good sheep, clean and cooperative denizens of the new, imperial Arcadia. The sign of their good behavior, as Petrarch conceives of it, is that they will not desire power or influence, but rather will make a game of being submissive:

> Take this friendly rivalry upon yourselves: not who is to be the more powerful, but who is to be the better and more patient citizen, who is to reveal the deeper love of country, the greater humility toward his neighbors and the more implacable hatred for the tyrants. Enter this contest with your tribune: as to whether he will show greater foresight in the honest administration of government than you readiness in obeying.[80]

Needless to say, no record exists of anyone in Rome having played this game.

Wilkins explains Petrarch's shift in class allegiance—if not wholly toward the Roman people, then certainly away from the Colonna—in terms of the humanist's great commitment to the values of ancient Rome, which he believed Cola di Rienzo would reinstate. Wilkins asserts that "despite his close associations with members of the Colonna family, Petrarch was bound by his ideals for Rome and by what he himself had seen in Roman territory to support Cola's attitude toward the great noble families that had been wrecking the city." Wilkins also claims that Petrarch offered his scholarly assistance to Cola's project "with no thought of personal aggrandizement."[81]

It is far from clear, however, that Petrarch's sole motive for inciting class warfare against his patrons was his idealistic and patriotic hope for the restoration of Rome. Arguably it was Petrarch's own experience of servitude to the Colonna family that in part fueled the rhetoric of rebellion in the letter quoted above. As we have seen, Francis touches on precisely this issue in the *Secretum*, expressing rage at the humanist's dependence on the wealth and power of others, together with a desperate desire to transcend that economy and to retreat to his pastoral paradise. Those meditations on the frustrated ambition and economic "servitudo" of the humanist dependent on aristocratic patronage suggest the depth of Petrarch's own resentment on that subject, as do many of his other writings.

Moreover, it is far from clear that Petrarch had nothing to gain personally from his vindications of Roman "libertas." In his hortatory letter, after suggesting the killing or expulsion of all adversaries, the poet offers his own services to the new republic; if the people do not disappoint him by failing to persevere, he will carry out his duty as a citizen of Rome (having been granted that status during his laureation in 1341) by writing lofty verses in praise of that great city: "Crowned with Apollo's wreath, I shall ascend lofty and inspiring Helicon. There, at the brim of the Castalian font, I shall recall the muses from their exile and sing resounding words in abiding memory of your glory, words that will ring throughout the ages."[82] At the very least, Petrarch hopes to further his career as poet laureate by offering his literary skills to the new government; the restoration of Rome after centuries of ruin offers intriguing themes for poetic exploitation. And, once again, he expresses his own will to leisure in pastoral terms.

There is also some evidence, however, that Petrarch hoped for more than poetic fame from Cola and the Romans. Roberto Weiss has brought to light a letter written by Barbato da Sulmona, humanist and close friend of Petrarch's, which suggests that Rome be managed by a "duumvirate" consisting of Cola and Petrarch. Weiss does not believe that Cola would have supported this division of labor, but he does suggest that Barbato was aware of Petrarch's desire to return to Italy during the fall of 1347 to advise Cola, and that Barbato believed in Petrarch's humanist qualifications as a potential leader of Rome.[83]

Petrarch was, in fact, invited to Rome by Cola, as a letter from the latter, dated July 28, 1347, reveals. In that missive the tribune thanks Petrarch for his many letters (very few of which survive, despite Petrarch's custom of saving for posterity almost every scrap that he wrote).[84] Cola assures the poet that liberty is alive and well in Rome, and that he and his people would be delighted if Petrarch were to join them, thereby adorning the city with his illustrious presence.[85] In Cola Petrarch quite likely saw the end of his long career of "servitudo"—or at least a relatively palatable servitude attached to a brilliant position.

Divorce

Sometime during the summer or fall of 1347 Petrarch made up his mind to leave Avignon for good and to return to Italy. In Eclogue 8, called "Divortium," he expresses this desire to Cardinal Colonna. Alternately obsequious and hostile, this work presents a dialogue between the elderly shepherd Ganymede and his servant Amyclas—that is, the cardinal and Petrarch. It is not certain that his patron ever received or read the poem. It may have been composed after a definitive break had occurred between the poet and the cardinal, and it most likely dates from late 1347, along with several other eclogues that present political allegories, including an obscure one written to Cola.[86]

Ganymede initiates the pastoral conversation by asking, "Where now would you lead my fat lambs and their mothers? / Can you so soon forget both me and what's mine, you ingrate? [Quo, pastos, abigis cum matribus agnos, / Ingrate atque oblite mei rerumque mearum?]" (*Bucolicum Carmen*, pp. 114–15). Amyclas explains that his shepherding has not been going well; his sheep are unhealthy, the grass is poor, the air is unpleasant, and the water is bad (pp. 114–17). In addition, Amyclas appeals to his own desire for freedom, that universally acknowledged value:

> Triste senex servus! Sit libera nostra senectus.
> Serva iuventa retro est; servilem libera vitam
> Mors claudat.

> Slavery's sad in old age; I would spend my last years in freedom,
> Leaving youth's bondage behind me. I beg that a lifetime of service
> End with the death of a freeman. (pp. 116–17)

When Ganymede bluntly asks Amyclas who has drawn him away from their friendship, Amyclas describes the beautiful mountains, valleys, rivers, and springs of Italy, which draw him home. While visiting that rare locale during the preceding summer, Amyclas made friends with Gillias,[87] who invited him to be his "comrade" and "leader" (pp. 118–19). And finally, Amyclas confesses that he has been held in unwilling service by "vicious habit," Ganymede's love, and the beauty of a girl, once compelling (pp. 122–23). But now he desires his liberty, and "the love of liberty surely / Cannot give cause for offense [nulla est iniuria iustus / Libertatis amor]" (ibid.).

Not completely persuaded by this reasoning, Ganymede asks, "Whom will you find, hapless one, to hear your song with approval? / Who will inscribe your verses on the light and delicate laurel? [Ah! miser. Et merita quis te cum laude canentem / Audiet, aut levi describet carmina lauro?]" (pp. 124–25). But Amyclas points out that his current audience has grown tired of his voice, and that he hopes to find a new audience in Italy. He is uncertain of the future, but he says to his old patron and friend:

> fortuna vaga est, et protinus, inter
> Quamvis pressa manus, ceu lubricus effluit anguis.
> Nil habet ista magis tua nunc opulentia certi
> Quam mea paupertas.

> fortune's a slippery thing to handle,
> Seize it as fast as you can it will yet slip your grasp like a slimy
> Serpent. Those riches of yours are no more secure than my wretched
> Poverty. (ibid.)

The determined, if cautious, attitude toward fortune expressed in this poem offers a sharp contrast to the bitter disappointment and sense of dejection pervading book 2 of the *Secretum*. Amyclas anticipates an upturn of his fortunes when he arrives in Italy. Even if fortune itself is unpredictable, Amyclas acknowledges a certain control over the future—a degree of freedom of the will—especially for those willing to grasp the slimy serpent.

At this explanation Ganymede expresses a sense of betrayal, of having been used; his own fate, he says, was to "shape things useful to others." If, however, Amyclas insists on leaving, Ganymede predicts that he will die in poverty (pp. 126–27). Amyclas, not surprisingly, gets the last word. He closes with a description of the poet's pastoral paradise, from which the need for money and other forms of support—including Ganymede's—is conspicuously absent. The fantasy of poetic freedom, again cast in pastoral terms, recalls the ending of Petrarch's hortatory letter to Cola and the Roman people, where the poet describes sitting by a spring and making his music:

> Ipse per estatem mediam, vel colle virenti,
> Valle vel umbrosa, nitidique in margine fontis
> Solus apollinea modulans sub fronde sedebo,
> Lanigerumque gregem pascam, et loca florea circum
> Mellificas imitabor apes. Te dives habebit
> Silva, sed urentes turbabunt otia cure.

> I for my part through midsummer, under the leaves of Apollo,
> Seated upon a green hillside or in the deep shade of a valley
> Hard by a crystalline fountain all alone shall pour forth my music,
> Tending my sheep the while. And in such flowery recesses
> After the style of the bees I shall live, while you in your fertile
> Woodland, though rich, will yet find burning cares to trouble your
>   leisure. (pp. 126–27)

Bishop calls this poem "an unpleasant leave-taking from a kind master," as well as "an unpleasant end to a friendship that had filled half Petrarch's life."[88] Also sympathizing with the patron rather than the patronized, W. Leonard Grant calls Eclogue 8 "a justification of the poet's extremely shabby return for the invariable generosity, patience, and understanding of his patron, Cardinal Giovanni Colonna."[89] The apparent ingratitude of this eclogue is particularly striking, however, in the context of the poem's homoeroticism—the mutual though now embittered love of the two shepherds, the rivalry of Gillias for the loyalty of Amyclas, the title "Divortium,"[90] and, of course, the name "Ganymede," cupbearer (i.e., servant) and beloved of Jupiter.[91] In some sense the homoerotic dimension of Petrarch's "Divortium" is conventional, insofar as poems of shepherds' love are as old as the pastoral genre itself.[92] Also, as Thomas Bergin notes in his edition of the *Bucolicum carmen*, "Ganymede, the mortal carried off to Olympus to join the gods, seemed to the poet an appropriate name to designate Cardinal Colonna, exalted to the pomp and luxury of the College of Cardinals" (p. 232). However, the love between Ganymede and Amyclas also represents social relations under the patronage system, the dependence of a less affluent man on a wealthier one; its homoerotic dimension is not exclusively a pastoral convention, but also a reflection of medieval power relations between men, relations that were themselves eroticized. As Luce Irigaray and Eve Sedgwick have argued, patriarchal economies (medieval or modern) are fundamentally homoerotic, insofar as all exchanges (women, money, goods, signs) are made between men and represent the bonds between men.[93]

What is intriguing, then, about "Divortium" is not its homoerotic overtone, but the ambivalence of the love between Amyclas and Ganymede. To accuse Petrarch of ingratitude toward his benevolent patron Cardinal Colonna is to miss the point—namely, that ambivalence on both sides would be a likely by-product of such a relationship. Indeed, Amyclas insists throughout the poem that he has served Ganymede well and that Ganymede has been generous with him. Nevertheless, their long and amicable relationship belies the inequity of their resources—an inequity that is represented as both natural (Amyclas does not critique the institution of patronage per se) and, at the same time, productive of enormous resentment on both sides (Amyclas resents his dependence; Ganymede resents the ingratitude of Amyclas).

In this version of the myth of pastoral humanism, the marketplace has infiltrated not only the geography but also the relationships of the poem's arcadian setting. Petrarch introduces the economic problems and inequities of the pastoral valley, only to attempt to transcend the marketplace by representing Ausonia (Italy) as infinitely more hospitable in its geography and its patrons. Once again, Petrarch poses a choice between good and bad pastoral. In Ausonia, Amyclas claims, he will live happily "after the style of the bees." In other words, Petrarch further mystifies the patronage system to be found in Italy through the fantasy of being self-supporting (like the bee) and having control over his patronage options (as the bee chooses his own flowers).[94]

In Petrarch's writings of the summer and early fall of 1347, several versions of the perennial freedom/determinism debate emerge. This debate is also at the heart of the *Secretum*, where Francis and

Augustine analyze the will and its limits in particular detail. Although it is possible to read the treatment of will in the *Secretum* as primarily theological or philosophical, it was freedom and bondage in the economic sense that apparently concerned Petrarch the most in the mid-1347 writings, in the *Secretum*, and, for that matter, throughout his life. Petrarch's deepest dreams of humanist mastery—of the completion of his epic poem, the *Africa*, of the leisure time to undertake new projects, and of the glorious role of poet laureate that he longed to assume at *Roma instaurata*—hinged on his escape from servitude in Avignon and the patronage system that held him there. Unfortunately, Petrarch's intense hopes of escape and freedom were short-lived.

The Slimy Serpent Fortune

Petrarch's few extant letters to Cola chart the rise and fall of the humanist's hopes for the tribune, for the city of Rome, and for himself. In his hortatory letter to Cola and the Roman citizens, Petrarch optimistically—and "unmedievally"—describes Cola as the new Brutus who has dared to restore the liberty of the people.[95] In his next extant letter to Cola, written about one month later, Petrarch confesses to the tribune his anxiety about the fate of the new regime. Cola's letters to the pope are being circulated widely, and Petrarch urges him to be cautious and to persevere. The eyes of the entire world are upon the tribune, and "never will the present age . . . never will posterity cease to speak of you [nunquam te praesens aetas . . . nunquam posteritas silebat]."[96]

Still another month later, toward the end of August, Petrarch confesses to Cola his having alienated many of his former allies in Avignon by defending the tribune. The humanist also indicates the degree of his involvement in the Romans' struggle: "for I do not regard your affairs from afar as if I were absent. On the contrary, I feel as if I were in the very center of the battle line, as if I were destined to conquer in the great struggle or be conquered by it [neque enim ut absens et de longinquo finem spectans, sed in acie media praesens sum, vel victurus ingenti praelio, vel vincendus]." Petrarch states that he is obsessed with the fortunes of Cola and writes about his feelings day and night. He has trouble sleeping. However, he describes a waking dream in which he pictures Cola enthroned on a high mountain and surrounded not only by the living, but by all future generations. This multitude awaits the fate of Cola, "because of whom, as you see, not only the earth, but the very sky and stars have lost their peace [de quo, ut vides, non terra solum sed coelum ipsum atque astra dissentiunt]."[97] Apparently Petrarch himself had lost his peace of mind, as he saw his dreams of empire begin to evaporate. Quite possibly the apocalyptic tone of letters such as this one fed both the megalomania and the fear of Cola di Rienzo, who had just crowned himself tribune and was announcing his candidacy for the emperorship of Rome.

Petrarch left few records documenting the collapse of Cola's regime during the fall of 1347.[98] But by November he had decided to leave Avignon for good, and many have conjectured that his primary reason for returning to Italy was to advise Cola di Rienzo against the perilous course he had taken. Petrarch received from Pope Clement VI two official excuses for leaving the court—he was to be formally installed in the canonry of the cathedral at Parma, an office he had received during the previous year, and he was to serve as an official envoy to Mastino della Scala in Verona, whom the pope was asking to block the movement of Louis of Hungary into Italy.[99]

On November 20—the same day the Colonna forces attacked the city of Rome—Petrarch left Avignon. Just two days into the journey, Petrarch wrote to his friend Laelius of his despair at the Roman situation. In this letter he describes his fears not only for Italy (facing a devastating invasion by Louis of Hungary), but also for himself, because the collapse of Cola's government would spell the end of his own hopes for escape, financial independence, and "pastoral" freedom.

I recognize the fate of the fatherland, for wherever I turn I find reason and occasion for grief. Once Rome is torn to pieces what will happen to Italy? Once Italy is disfigured what would my life be? [Roma enim lacerata, qualis Italie status? Italia deformata, qualis mea vita futura est?] In this sorrow, which is both public and private, some will contribute wealth, others bodily strength, and still others power and advice. I see nothing that I can contribute except tears.[100]

In this letter Petrarch reveals much about the status of the humanist in the early modern state. Having placed his oratorical and intellectual skills at the disposal of the powerful—the papacy, the
Colonna family, and then Cola di Rienzo—Petrarch here appears
stunned to find that he has no power of his own. These last lines of
the letter convey above all Petrarch's sense of political impotence.
By his own admission, he is not even a real player in this controversy; thus tears are his only option.

While Petrarch's hopes for the new empire and his place in it
were rapidly fading, the humanist wrote to his friend Lodewyck
Heyliger, nicknamed Socrates, about the virtues of Horatian mediocritas. The argument of this letter, written on November 25, the
day Petrarch arrived in Genoa, bears a striking resemblance to the
discussion of mediocritas in book 2 of the *Secretum*. Here, too, Petrarch disingenuously proclaims his lack of ambition: "I have never
been a seeker of great fortune, whether because of modesty, petti-
ness, or, as some great men prefer to conceive it, magnanimity." Petrarch then launches into a discussion of mediocritas, the golden
mean, for which he has always striven. If good fortune should
chance to come his way in the form of some position of middling
status, so be it; however, any office of greater status than that he
would summarily reject:

Si optata michi mediocritas, quam iure Flaccus auream vocat, ut pridem
promittebatur, obvenerit, est quod grata intentione suscipiam, et perliber-
aliter mecum agi dicam; sin invisum illud et grave maioris officii honus im-
ponitur, renuo, excutio. Pauper esse malim quam solicitus.[101]

If my desired moderation which Horace rightly calls golden, should come
to me as it was promised long ago, I accept it with gratitude and I shall admit that it was done for me in a most liberal way. But if that hateful and
heavy burden of a major office is imposed upon me, I shall refuse it and push
it away. I would rather be poor than upset.

Petrarch also asks his friend to spread this news of the modesty of
his ambitions around Avignon. If indeed Petrarch had planned to
join Cola in Rome, then it would seem that by late November he
was beginning to reconsider that option (thus, perhaps, the marked
lack of interest in a "major office").[102] Here he seems to be protest-

ing too much, fatuously announcing the innocuousness of his plans for the future. Perhaps he hoped that not all bridges to his patron, Cardinal Colonna, had been completely burned.

The theme of the golden mean seems to have been a favorite with Petrarch, especially during 1347, that year of upheavals. It occurs in the *De otio religioso*, presumably written after Petrarch's visit to the Carthusian monastery of Montrieux earlier that year. Petrarch rather gratuitously advises the ascetic monks to avoid temptations such as worldly success and the desire for wealth, and in general to seek a middle course.[103] In the letter quoted above, however, Petrarch describes mediocritas not in biblical but in Horatian terms. The humanist's renewed interest in Horace is also indicated by his purchase, shortly after his arrival in Genoa, of a tenth-century manuscript of that poet's works, which he would later fill with enthusiastic marginalia.[104] Petrarch's reference to Horatian mediocritas at the end of 1347 suggests another clue to the dating of the *Secretum*, or at least the above-described portions of book 2, where references to Horace abound. In contrast to the mood of Petrarch's November 1347 letter to Socrates, however, the discussions of avarice, ambition, and accidia in the *Secretum* project a sense of overwhelming disappointment, besiegement, and loss. This fact supports the idea that Petrarch wrote, or perhaps redrafted, that section of the book sometime after his final break with Cola di Rienzo, and after he relinquished his personal ambitions regarding the short-lived empire of Rome.

The rupture with Cola came only four days after Petrarch wrote to Socrates of his middling ambitions. With what seems to have been a sudden change of heart, Petrarch wrote to Cola on November 29, explaining why he had changed his mind about joining the tribune in Rome. Copies of Cola's letters to Avignon had been sent to Petrarch as he traveled from Provence to Italy, and he did not like what he had been hearing about the situation in Rome. Perhaps he had received word of the uprising there and of the deaths of several members of the Colonna family. In any case, Petrarch angrily derides Cola for his arrogant and dangerous behavior. He also reflects on the apparent change of fortune afflicting not only Cola, but himself: "Can the stars have so suddenly changed against us and God have become so hostile?" Later he again invokes the theme of the will in bondage to fate:

Why however do I become so upset? Things will always go as eternal law decrees. I cannot change them, but I can flee from them [ibunt res quo sempiterna lex statuit; mutare ista non possum, fugere possum]. You have therefore freed me from a considerable task: I was hastening to you with all my heart, but I am changing direction for I certainly shall not see you as another person.[105]

Here Petrarch vacillates between two positions on will. The first is that men—and Cola in particular—are free to control their actions and their destinies; thus humans are accountable for their morality and their political choices. The second, in contrast, is that "eternal law" or "the stars" determine the course of human events, and that there is no point in raging or struggling against what cannot be changed. Petrarch's adaptation of the free will / determinism dialectic seems as much rhetorical as philosophical. After all, it is not so much "the stars" as it is Cola whom Petrarch struggles to change.

Yet by invoking a predestinarian worldview (here as a rhetoric of attack), Petrarch claims to have ransomed his own will, for he discovers that he has the power to flee. This power, Petrarch says, has been liberated by Cola himself. This final extant letter to Cola offers a clear example of how predestinarian arguments, far from precluding human action or power, can instead be construed as liberating (their utopian dimension), extending to the believer an alternative form of mastery. In this case, the mastery is Petrarch's freedom to reject a former friend and to attempt to salvage his career and reputation.

Unfortunately, Petrarch's would-be mastery, the power to flee, was at that point still severely compromised by the worsening political crisis in Rome. Finally, then, it was not Cola or Rome that Petrarch was worried about, but himself: "Wherefore, if (as I hope is not the case) you are perhaps overlooking your reputation, at least consider mine. You know what a tempest is hanging over my head and how great would be the crowd of censurers who would conspire against me if you begin to collapse."[106] By the end of November

1347, Petrarch knew that his fortunes were precarious precisely because he had bound them to Cola's. In so doing, he had severed his ties to the Colonna family, his bread and butter for nearly two decades. What Petrarch tries rhetorically to reverse throughout the letter is his own sense of powerlessness at this predicament.

The Politics of Expedience

Why Petrarch's reputation was not undone by the Cola debacle remains an interesting question. By the beginning of the next year he had assumed his position as canon of the cathedral; in August Clement VI awarded him the position of archdeacon in that same diocese. As his biographer Morris Bishop tells it, Petrarch became well-off for the first time in his life, having a house, secretaries, servants, and an undemanding job that afforded him much leisure time.[107] To what did Petrarch owe this surprising good fortune, instead of the political and economic reprisals he expected in the wake of the Cola di Rienzo affair?

In part, Petrarch's reputation seems to have been helped, paradoxically, by the advent of the Black Death. The plague had arrived in Sicily in the late fall of 1347 and would work its way through Europe during the next year. By January of 1348, Avignon had been hit, and eventually some three-quarters of the city's population were killed.[108] It is not a coincidence that Petrarch received his archdeaconate during that summer, at a time when the dying were sometimes buried alive, when bodies were dumped in the Rhône, and, in short, when the social order of Avignon and of most of Europe was collapsing.

During this time Petrarch proved himself a master of the politics of expedience. He wrote, for example, an absurd letter of condolence to his former patron, Cardinal Giovanni Colonna, sometime in the early part of 1348. In that letter he expresses his profound regret that the cardinal's brothers, nephew, and cousins have been killed; he neglects to mention, however, the circumstance of certain of their deaths—the November 20 battle in Rome, when the Colonna forces clashed with the militia of Cola di Rienzo at the gates

of the city.[109] Nor does Petrarch mention his earlier role in inciting
the Roman people to rise up against those ravening wolves, his patron family. Instead, he emphasizes his almost filial obligation to his
patron:

Because I was brought up by you since my youth, grew up under you and
was educated by you so far as the malevolence of intervening misfortunes
or the mediocrity of my talent allows [sub te nutritus a iuventute mea, sub
te auctus atque eruditus sum, quantum vel intercurrentium casuum malig-
nitas vel ingenii mediocritas passa est], it is only right that I must persist in
directing this pen, this hand and my mind, however humble, to the conso-
lation and solace of your mind.

Petrarch claims to have been thunderstruck by the news of the deaths
in the family, which took some time to reach him. In his deep pain,
Petrarch says, he found it difficult to write the cardinal: "How often, having succeeded in standing, I tried to write something! [Quo-
tiens, assurgere nisus, scribere aliquid volui!]"[110] Nevertheless, he
eventually managed to overcome his mediocrity (another version of
that favorite theme), to collect himself and to write his condolences.

   As in previous texts, Petrarch uses the rhetoric of fate to intriguing effect—here, to exculpate himself of any blame, however
indirect, for those deaths. Never does he mention the human causes
of the Roman bloodshed or, for that matter, the question of moral
responsibility—his own, for example. Instead, he talks about the inevitability of death: "[Death] cannot be avoided, it can only be
scorned [(Mors) vitari non potest, sperni potest]." But, as always,
the best men will transcend the blows of fate through their stoic
courage, and Cardinal Colonna is such a man: "Those who live
among us and those who shall be born after us will have reason to
admire you, to praise you, to hold you up as an example, and to admire the strength of your mind unbroken despite misfortunes and
your noble dignity worthy of the true Roman spirit [generosam vere
romani spiritus maiestatem]."[111] Everything that goes around, comes
around: at this juncture, then, it is Cardinal Colonna who is endowed with genuine "romanitas." Fortunately for Petrarch, his ex-
patron had the good grace to die of the plague in April of 1348,
sparing the humanist the embarrassment of further sycophancy.[112]

Notes on the Redating of the *Secretum*

I have argued that many of Petrarch's writings of 1347 reflect the humanist's preoccupation with poetic, intellectual, and political freedom, which he casts in pastoral terms; with the "servitudo" of his dependence on Cardinal Colonna and on the patronage system; and with the overwhelming ambitions he felt for Cola di Rienzo, for the new Rome, and for himself as poet laureate of the reborn republic. A question remains, however: do parts of the *Secretum*—specifically, the debates on avarice and accidia in book 2—actually date from this period and indeed reflect these preoccupations?[113]

Both Rico and Baron maintain that the *Secretum* was drafted early in 1347, shortly after the *De otio religioso*. They suppose that Petrarch completed his first draft of the *Secretum* sometime in the spring of that year, and though both critics believe that Petrarch revised the *Secretum* several times, neither considers the possibility that parts of it might have been written in response to the Cola di Rienzo affair; Rico holds, in fact, that there is no way to determine which specific portions were written in 1347 and which in 1349.[114] The exclusion of Cola di Rienzo from these critics' philological and biographical considerations is puzzling, but there are two possible explanations.

First, both Rico and Baron interpret Petrarch's crisis of 1347 in primarily philosophical, rather than (or in addition to) political, terms.[115] Rico concludes that Augustine and Francis represent two phases of the humanist's spiritual and ethical development—the former his "desired future" and the latter his "past overcome." Rico also concludes that the dialogue analyzes the conflict between Stoicism and Aristotelianism, positions that Augustine and Francis embody.[116] Baron argues simply that Augustine represents the humanist's conscience, that in 1347 Petrarch experienced an identity crisis and wondered "what kind of activity would allow someone with his humanistic values and occupations who also longed for a profound experience of the divine to live in both worlds."[117] Second, Rico and Baron recuperate the somewhat unflattering portrait of Francis in the *Secretum* because Petrarch remains for them an admirable and sympathetic humanist. Francis represents for Rico the humanist's former ("transcended") self, and for Baron the humanist struggling to maintain his own version of piety and virtue in a rapidly changing world.

The less idealizing counterclaim of this chapter is that in defense of his class privilege (and, at times, nonprivilege), Petrarch invented several key ideologies of humanism. This claim rests, in part, on a possible redating of the *Secretum*, on the idea that Petrarch began work on his dialogue in the spring of 1347 and continued adding to it throughout the year. Indeed, nothing would have prevented him from adding some reflection of his anxieties regarding the Cola di Rienzo situation during the late summer and fall. Furthermore, the desperate tone of the discussions of avarice and accidia in book 2 of the *Secretum* suggests that those confessions may very well have been written after Petrarch made a definitive break with Cola—that is, in December of 1347 or perhaps early the next year. Possibly the siege imagery in the accidia section reflects Petrarch's anxiety over the invasion of Italy by Louis of Hungary. Also, the discussion of mediocritas and other Horatian themes throughout the second book accords with Petrarch's renewed interest in Horace during the second half of 1347, as reflected in his allusions to that poet in contemporaneous works and in his acquisition of a new manuscript of Horace's collected works late in November.

Any attempt to redate a Petrarchan text is inevitably controversial, because it relies on multiple conjectures that are difficult, if not impossible, to prove, regardless of one's critical perspective. Certainly, though, it is possible to argue against the conjectures of other critics in defense of one's own. For example, Baron asserts that Petrarch was completely free of ambitio in 1347, "when he was living in the 'silvarum recessus et silentia rura' of the Vaucluse," and that therefore the discussion of ambitio in book 2 must have been written at a later date. Actually, Petrarch's letters to Cola, his eighth eclogue, and other writings of that period suggest just the opposite. Baron also contends that most of the discussions of avarice and accidia date from 1353, after Petrarch had been lured back from Italy to Avignon in 1351 by the promise of a high curial office.[118] Baron assumes that the discussion of a "primus locus" (*OL*, pp. 148, 150) for Francis pertains to this possibility. However, the possibility of such a high position—namely, that of poet laureate of Cola's Rome, or perhaps some still more prestigious job there—also existed in 1347.

Baron hypothesizes that the denunciations of city life in the accidia section refer not to Avignon, but to Milan, where Petrarch lived in 1353 and after. Strangely, he assumes that Petrarch would not have had cause to denounce life in Avignon in 1347 because he was primarily residing in the Vaucluse. However, one does not have to be in a city to dislike it. In addition, Baron assumes that Petrarch could not have written nostalgically about the Vaucluse in 1347 because "he was at the high point of his life" there. However, the pastoral ideology of humanist leisure that Augustine outlines in the avarice section does not necessarily represent Petrarch's life in that valley, or, for that matter, conflict with his great dissatisfactions at his "servitude" to Cardinal Colonna and, perhaps, with his guilt or regret at the desire to leave. Finally, it is conceivable that Petrarch wrote of the loss of an arcadian paradise when he left France at the end of the year to improve his fortunes in Italy.[119]

Though it is certainly possible that parts of the *Secretum* were added in 1349 and 1353, as Rico and Baron hold, it is plausible that the original draft of those parts of book 2 discussed at length in this chapter dates from 1347 and reflects the political turmoil of the latter half of that year. As Kenelm Foster has recently noted, no other political event of Petrarch's lifetime had an effect on him comparable to that of Cola di Rienzo's rise to power.[120] It seems likely, then, that this major event would have left its stamp on a work begun in 1347 and revised periodically thereafter.

Once again, however, any attempt at dating Petrarch's works remains problematic—especially works with as many interpolations as the *Secretum* seems to contain. For that reason it is important to defend a second case, one that does not hinge on the dialogue's reflecting Petrarch's involvement in the Cola di Rienzo affair during the summer and fall of 1347. A reading that is less historically specific but still in keeping with the critique of humanist ideology offered here would hold that the *Secretum* represents the humanist's conflicted dreams of grandeur, of escape from the "servitudo" of the patronage system as he had long experienced it in Avignon, and of wealth and social status. Thus, even if the *Secretum* was not written in 1347 or if the events vaguely described in book 2 do not reflect Petrarch's response to the Cola situation, we can still draw similar conclusions about his financial predicament as a humanist in pursuit of free time—for example, that he generally desired to escape from the political economy governing his relative privilege and, in his mind, deprivation.

Humanist Mythologies of Will

Whether one reads the *Secretum* as, in part, a treatment of the Cola di Rienzo incident or as a palimpsest of Petrarch's ruminations on his economic and social situation, it is possible to conclude that its debate on will reflects the humanist's desire to transcend the marketplace. Petrarch's articulation of alternately voluntarist and determinist points of view has often been taken as indicating uncertainty about the status of the will. Though in one sense that may be true, it is also plausible that the rhetorics of free will and of fate are two sides of the same coin, two forms of appeal serving to ransom the humanist's will from some form of non-mastery.

In the *Secretum*, as in many letters and poems dating from 1347–48, Petrarch articulates theories of will that include both voluntarist and predestinarian elements. Though it is possible to read these texts as elaborations of specific theological or philosophical positions, the economic and political registers of these theories of will are also components of Petrarch's desire for mastery.

The rhetoric of freedom in the works discussed above very often coincides with elements of pastoral—specifically, the fantasy of pastoral escape. The image of arcadian living, whether in the country or in the city (as in the hortatory letter to Cola), serves as a call to freedom. This fantasy of escape hinges on the possibility of not only living in an earthly paradise, but also avoiding or transcending an earthly hell, the marketplace (Avignon, Babylon, etc.)—that is, the political economy that tangibly constrains the humanist's will to leisure. Augustine suggests that it is this freedom from the market-place that makes possible the humanist's poetic freedom. Thus Petrarch's pastoral myth of economic freedom ransoms the poet's will from the bondage of the marketplace by attempting to recuperate his ineluctably damaged sense of personal autonomy (often thought of as "modern" selfhood). The voice of Augustine in the *Secretum*, as well as Petrarch's pastoral letter to the Roman people and his Eclogue 8, might be read as expressions of that desire for freedom.

Augustine insists on a radical freedom of the will, suggesting that the troubled humanist need only wish hard in order to experience true freedom. "And so, after I committed my will fully, I was instantly able to act and with amazing and blessed swiftness I was a changed man," he insists (*S*, p. 48). By such sheer power of will, Augustine argues, Francis can leave the world of economic and political struggle behind and return to a self-sustaining world of pastoral innocence and pleasure. True morality, he suggests, depends precisely on severing one's ties to the world of kings and generals and renouncing one's quest for social status and financial gain. What Augustine would have Francis renounce is the nascent capitalist economy of France and Italy, in conjunction with the courtier politics of the late medieval papacy. In its stead, Augustine envisions a humanist's paradise outside of and free from the contaminations of this foul marketplace of the greedy and powerful. The problem with this ideology of free will is not that pastoral retreats per se are a bad idea, but rather that humanist practice cannot be and has never been anything other than a product of the economies producing it. In other words, to ransom the will from the marketplace of the social order is to deny or obscure the humanist's place within that marketplace.

Terry Eagleton has suggested that "crisis and the humanities were born at a stroke," along with capitalism. He writes, "The very idea of constructing a certain privileged enclave called the humanities, relatively marooned from the common activities of social life, in which the most precious values of that life might be nurtured and contemplated, is part of the problem rather than the solution." In other words, the idea of a transcendent humanism is one aspect of the political economies that have always framed the discourse and practice of that humanism:

Historically speaking, the idea of the humanities, at least in the modern period, arises at a point where certain kinds of positive human values are felt to be increasingly under threat from a philistine, crassly materialist society, and so must be marked off from that degraded social arena in a double gesture of elevation and isolation. How *could* the humanities not be in crisis in social orders where it is perfectly clear, whatever their own protestations to the contrary, that the only supremely valuable activity is one of turning a fast buck?[121]

Humanists' problem, Eagleton suggests, is their nonrecognition or denial of their degree of entrenchment in the political economy that they hope to transcend. Though humanists may feel besieged by the materialist culture in which they find themselves, Eagleton argues that there can be no escape from that culture.

Thus only in an ideological sense can the humanist ransom the will from its bondage to the marketplace. The utopian component of any ideology is precisely the way in which it appears to ransom the will of the believer from the constraints he or she experiences. For the humanist—in this case, the "first humanist"—such constraints are multiple; the *Secretum* focuses on those pertaining to "fortuna," a word laden with theological, philosophical, and, of course, economic significance. Petrarch's recurring dreams of pastoral represent a liberation from the constraints of fortune in all of these senses.

Elsewhere in Petrarch's writings, and even in the *Secretum*, "fortuna" is precisely what one cannot escape. Yet Petrarch's discussions of fate, fortune, the stars, and eternal decree also have a liberating (utopian) aspect. As argued in Chapter 1, a predestinarian argument can function as mastery, just as a voluntarist argument can. Nonmastery has a liberating side, to the extent that it transfers "freedom" from one register to another, such as from the power to transcend one's place in a social system to the power to explain one's "predestined" place within it. Petrarch attempts to justify his own actions and social position by representing them as that which could not be otherwise; in this sense the rhetoric of nonfreedom readily serves as a justification of the status quo.

So, for example, when Petrarch writes to Cardinal Colonna about the inevitability of death, he obscures his own role in the Roman republic's war against the baronial families. Or, in the *Secretum*, when Francis insists upon the impossibility of personal transformation, he justifies his previous actions—such as the pursuit of fame, wealth, and prestige—by suggesting that various forces of the universe mandated them. Such determinism also legitimates Petrarch's relative economic privilege vis-à-vis most of medieval society; by representing human destiny as being in a state of constant flux because of the unpredictable turns of "fortuna," Petrarch obscures the reality of a relatively stable social hierarchy, as well as the humanist's status within it.

This is not to say that Petrarch never sincerely complains about fortune—his own or anyone else's—or that he does not actually feel a servitude of the will. Viewing determinism as an aspect of the humanist's self-justifying ideology does not preclude some genuine resentment of fortune or of political hierarchies on Petrarch's part. Certainly the rhetoric of the will in bondage to fate has many applications.

The Crisis of Humanism and the Fortunes of Theory

To define Petrarch as a humanist is to locate in his works a certain set of ideals or ideologies, depending on one's critical sympathies. The myth of pastoral transcendence and of the personal freedom usually thought to go with it is both an ideal for any humanist in pursuit of leisure time and an ideology, a means of naturalizing and thereby decontextualizing the privilege of such leisure—subject though that ideology may be to co-optation by still more powerful classes. It is possible to trace in Petrarch's humanist ideologies the "dynamics of endurance," the cultural reproduction of value legitimating the competences and privilege of educated elites—humanists by profession or by avocation.

To define Petrarch as the *first* humanist is to locate in his works a certain enduring and originary value. As argued, à la Barbara Smith, at the beginning of this chapter, the reproduction of a classic text hinges not on claims for its intrinsic value (originality, complexity, or sublimity) but rather on its extrinsic value: what generations of readers find in that text that reifies and legitimates their own masteries (their good taste, discriminating judgment, or position as certain kinds of readers). If Petrarch is the first humanist and modern man, it is largely because his works appear to confirm the humanism and the modernity of his audiences, in addition to certain overarching notions of academic freedom or bondage to the marketplace. In other words, one finds in Petrarch the many ideologies of humanism that best serve the needs of professional humanists (here I speak of academic readers of Petrarch, though conceivably there are others). Certainly Petrarch can be read as justifying the contemporary humanist's relatively privileged class position and somewhat obscured relation to the capitalist marketplace, in which it is still necessary to scramble for the modern benefices of grants and time off. Likewise, Petrarch can be read as confirming the professional humanist's uncanny abilities to read obscure texts of the early modern age.

Yet perhaps this account of Petrarchan value as culturally reproduced by generations of humanist readers does not do justice to the appearance of origin that so many have discovered in that fourteenth-century personage. It is hard to believe, in other words, that we are solely responsible for our own myths of cultural origin—that we make them up as we need them. Indeed, this book is (at least sometimes) predicated on the belief that significant transformations—social, economic, cultural—actually originated in the early modern period and, for that matter, that we can identify the distinct features of a period called the early modern, conceivably falling between Petrarch's lifetime and Galileo's. According to those basic assumptions, it is reasonable to think of Petrarch as an originary figure of some sort. Or perhaps both possibilities—that of origin and that of contingency—are valid. "Can it be," writes Albert Ascoli, "that 'history' always has this hybrid form: the form of a past which imposes figures of itself on the present to which it gave rise and of a present which decomposes and recomposes the past to conform to its own needs and understandings?"[122]

To pose Ascoli's question in a different way, and to return to the problem of method discussed toward the beginning of this chapter:

Can two presumably antithetical modes of reading obtain at the same time? The answer to this question will also clarify the framing concern of this chapter: namely, the relation of humanism to poststructuralist thought. In asking it, we confront again the crisis of theory, a crisis both in the modern sense of "extremity" and in the ancient sense of "deciding" or "determining"—here, the outcome of theory's quarrel with humanism.

A poststructuralist (or a more ethically preoccupied post-poststructuralist) critique of Petrarch would analyze the obfuscations of humanist ideology (as, indeed, this reading does). Such a critique would insist on its distance, and *difference*, from Petrarch's ideological representations of his own subjectivity, which, though not uniformly redolent of Old Mastery, nevertheless extend to Petrarch and to subsequent generations of humanists a belief in the possibility of ransoming one's will from one's own culture. It is this fantasy of individualism and personal autonomy with which the politically oriented versions of recent theory would be likely to take issue.

Nevertheless, in at least one key way, the many forms of poststructuralism have not rejected humanism, but instead have incorporated it; humanism, as I have said, is the unconscious of contemporary theory. Humanism and poststructuralism converge not in their differences, of course, but in their desire for difference from the past. Humanist readings of the past, not surprisingly, bear the markings of that individualism taken to characterize the early modern, because humanism itself teaches that originality, creativity, and, above all, personal difference are possible. Likewise, poststructuralist readings of the past also stress difference, if not precisely in these terms. Recent psychoanalytic theory, feminisms, neo-marxisms, the semiotics of culture, reader-response theory, relativisms, and sociological critiques—all of these partake of that fundamentally humanist gesture of difference, and of mastery. Even deconstruction, the most equivocal of these theoretical frames, partakes of, if not an epistemology of difference-as-progress, then certainly its rhetoric.

Petrarch offers us an important paradigm of the rhetoric of difference. He was last seen standing, you may recall, on the threshold of "a more propitious age":

> But if you, as is my wish
> and ardent hope, shall live on after me,
> a more propitious age will come again:
> this Lethean stupor surely can't endure
> forever. Our posterity, perchance,
> when the dark clouds are lifted, may enjoy
> once more the radiance the ancients knew.

"I'm not one of them," he yells across the abyss to future generations of critics. "I'm one of you!"

CHAPTER 3

Theology

Will and Bondage in Martin Luther, Ignatius Loyola, and Teresa of Avila

The rhetoric of difference in the early modern age was not unique to humanism. The theological discourses of the Renaissance, Reformation, and Counter-Reformation also relied on the trope of difference from the past, a difference enabling the recovery of a more distant past unsedimented by degenerate custom. Early modern theology also shared the individualism of humanist discourse in that religious movements or reforms were frequently bound up with the conversion narratives of their founders. To participate in such a movement often meant following the path of spiritual metamorphosis marked out by certain masters, ancient or contemporary. Moreover, the individual was a microcosm of the larger religious movements of the age, a theater in which daily dramas of difference and recovery were enacted. For it was within the individual that the signs of religious change (such as genuine *imitatio Christi*, justification by faith, or mystical favors) were scrutinized, evaluated, and either confirmed or rejected.

The marks of personal transformation, of conversion in the broad sense of redirected spirituality, betokened a certain authority on the part of the convert, whose distance from past error—personal, cultural, or doctrinal—confirmed that person as a legitimate founder or member of a religious community and licensed the individual to speak or to write, most authoritatively about his or her spiritual changes. It is not a coincidence that the genre of autobiography was reborn in the early modern age, frequently taking the form of the conversion narrative.

Petrarch's *Secretum* was among the first of these narratives of conversion—another fact suggesting that humanist and theological discourses were by no means mutually exclusive. Yet the author of the *Secretum* explored the problematic of personal transformation and the will from a position somewhat different from those of later, theological writers of confessions. Although he was tonsured and had probably taken minor orders, Petrarch wrote less as a professional member of the clergy than as a professional and in some sense secular intellectual.[1]

Theological writers tended to use their narratives of conversion to explain and authorize their positions as leaders of religious reform movements. In this chapter I will examine three such narratives of mastery in the context of the theological debates on will that framed them. Martin Luther, radical theologian and father of the Protestant Reformation, confessed the details of his conversion throughout his works, but perhaps most pointedly in the 1545 Preface to his complete Latin writings. Ignatius Loyola, founder of the Jesuit order and leader of the Catholic Counter-Reformation, dictated the story of his conversion to a scribe; that text, composed in 1553–55, survives as the *Acta quaedam*, or *Autobiography*. And Teresa of Avila, founding mother of the Spanish Discalced Carmelites and first female "Doctor of the Church,"[2] tells the story of her midlife mystical conversion in the remarkable *Libro de la vida* (ca. 1560–66).

Though Luther's theology is overtly predestinarian and Loyola's and Teresa's ostensibly voluntarist, one cannot assume a straightforward opposition between these Reformation and Counter-Reformation theories of will. Such an assumption does not do justice to the complex interrelation of sixteenth-century theologies of grace, justification, and human agency. Moreover, it proves faulty when one explores the common features of the rhetorics of these writers. The confessions of Luther, Loyola, and Teresa share a rhetoric, if not a theology, of the will. For the rhetoric of spiritual conversion is necessarily one of mastery, a representation of the writer's will as ransomed from one or more forms of "predestinarian" bondage. All of these narratives thus thematize, either directly or indirectly, the ransoming of the will. I will analyze their rhetorics of liberation in relation to the theological conceptions of freedom or nonfreedom espoused by their authors.

In the 1545 Preface to his complete Latin works, Martin Luther describes his break with the Roman church, as well as the evolution of his views on justification and grace. Ironically, the bondage of the will represented in the Preface is not that of Luther's predestinarian theology, the incapacity of the will to make competent moral choices and to effect its own salvation. In fact, Luther's theology of predestination functions rhetorically in the Preface as a mastery, by means of which Luther claims to liberate himself from other forms of bondage of the will that are far more threatening to him—namely, degenerate custom and death itself.

The *Acta quaedam* of Ignatius Loyola likewise relies on a rhetoric of mastery. Loyola represents the ultimate exercise of the will's freedom as complete obedience, voluntary bondage. Paradoxically, the liberating claim of Ignatian rhetoric, paradigmatically presented in Loyola's story of conversion, is the claim that obedience frees the believer from the world's bondage to disorder and to moral uncertainty. But to obey—to master one's own will and thereby to ransom it from disorder—one must also master a language for determining the divine will. The *Acta quaedam* relates the history of Loyola's discovery and mastery of that mantic language.

The Counter-Reformation writings of Teresa of Avila contain an implicit theory of predestination particular to the subject position of their author. As a woman descended from Jewish converts to Christianity (conversos), Teresa experienced a form of servitude not faced by Luther or Loyola—namely, subjection to the misogyny and anti-Semitism of Counter-Reformation Spain. It was these forms of bondage that Teresa sought to overcome, however obliquely, through her writings, as through her religious practices. The *Libro de la vida* manifests a unique rhetoric of mastery through which Teresa in part recuperates this bondage to the authoritarian church and state of sixteenth-century Spain.

Few topics were as hotly debated in early modern theology as the status, powers, and limits of the will. But it was invariably through the rhetoric of mastery that religious writers sought to establish their claims to spiritual and institutional authority—authority, for example, to explain the freedom or nonfreedom of the human subject. The uniqueness of each narrative, then, lies not in its claim to mastery (which underlies the very structure of confessional writing), but rather in its individual strategies for ransoming the will, and in its particular configurations of bondage.

Martin Luther

The Theology of Justification and the Bondage of the Will

On September 4, 1517, one Franz Günther, student at the University of Wittenberg, completed the requirements for the degree of Bachelor of Holy Scripture by defending a set of theses. Later called the *Disputatio contra scholasticam theologiam* (Disputation against scholastic theology), the theses were written by the dean of the faculty of theology, Martin Luther (*WA*, 1: 221–28). They presented in germinal form the idea of the will's bondage to sin, upon which foundation Luther was then constructing his theology of justification by faith.

Thesis 5 states: "It is false to state that man's inclination is free to choose between either of two opposites. Indeed, the inclination is not free, but captive. This is said in opposition to common opinion" (*LW*, 31: 9). In a similar vein, thesis 39 asserts: "We are not masters of our actions, from beginning to end, but servants. This is in opposition to the philosophers" (*LW*, 31: 11). The "common opinion" of the "philosophers" attacked here is that of scholastic theologians, who, in Luther's view, attributed altogether too much authority to the human will by assigning it even limited autonomy in making moral choices.[3] Luther proposes, in contrast, not only that the will is not free, but that without divine grace it is necessarily inclined toward evil. As thesis 7 claims, "without the grace of God the will produces an act that is perverse and evil" (*LW*, 31: 9).

On the eve of the Reformation, Luther and others in his circle had begun to recover and to elaborate upon a predestinarian theology inchoate in the thought of Augustine.[4] The political and eco-

nomic implications of Luther's theology of non-mastery, of the servitude of the will, fueled a bitter controversy over the sale of indulgences just a few weeks later, when, as legend has it, he posted his
Ninety-Five Theses on the door of the Wittenberg cathedral on the
last day of October.

The papal practice of granting indulgences remitting or com-
muting the punishments of sinners had by Luther's day become a
vast international trade.[5] During the Middle Ages, certain theological developments regarding the sacrament of confession, formally
instituted as an annual requirement by the Fourth Lateran Council
(1215), had contributed to the rise of indulgence selling.[6] For example, medieval theologians came to distinguish between what an
effective confession could accomplish (absolution of guilt and satisfaction of the sinner's eternal punishment) and what it could not (satisfaction of the sinner's temporal punishment on earth or in Purgatory).[7] An indulgence could remit temporal punishment,[8] and by the
late Middle Ages indulgences were widely issued, as persons hoping
that they and their dead could escape the flaming torments of Purgatory increasingly ignored the subtle restrictions and caveats that
theologians had placed on papal intercession for the dead and the
living. In 1517 Albrecht of Brandenburg, archbishop of Mainz and
Magdeburg and bishop of Halberstadt, collaborated with the Medici
pope Leo X to sell indulgences throughout Albrecht's sees and other
parts of Germany. Albrecht financed the venture through the bank-
ing house of Fuggers, and for their efforts in the fund-raising campaign, those two parties were to receive half the profits (*LW*, 31:
22).[9] Though Luther did not know the particulars of this arrange-
ment at the time, his Ninety-Five Theses critiqued the practice of indulgence selling, which he and others found reprehensible.

At this juncture Luther's emergent theology of justification began to converge with a progressively more stringent and public critique of ecclesiastical authority. As we have seen, Luther's theology
was founded on the idea that the human will is not free. Rather, he
argued, all of men's good acts and the forgiveness of their evil ones
depend exclusively on the grace of God, a grace unearned and profoundly unmerited by any human being. Because human will alone
is utterly unfree to choose the good, Luther contended, no works

performed by the individual could result in anything but evil, unless the gift of divine grace had already liberated the will from its tendency toward sinfulness. Justification, the Pauline term that Luther defined as God's forgiveness of a person's sins, is completely independent of that person's penance, piety, and other good works; the true Christian is justified by faith alone. "Justification," Jaroslav Pelikan notes, was for Luther "the very antithesis of merit."[10]

Thus the concept that buying indulgences was a form of good work that could remit divine punishment was for Luther not only incorrect, but arrogant.[11] In his Ninety-Five Theses, Luther attacked particularly the papal claim to be able to absolve guilt and cancel the punishments of sinners.[12] As he elsewhere explained in greater detail, no man, not even the pope, has this power, which necessarily resides with God alone.[13] Furthermore, an individual's contrition does not effect or influence God's forgiveness of sin, but is itself a function of grace already received.[14]

The predestinarian implications of this theology are spelled out explicitly in Luther's 1525 *De servo arbitrio* (On the bondage of the will), which he wrote in response to the irenic *De libero arbitrio diatribe sive collatio* (Diatribe or discourse on the freedom of the will) by Desiderius Erasmus, published the preceding year.[15] Condemning as heretical Erasmus's defense of a very limited freedom of the will, Luther expounded in the *De servo* a predestinarian theology founded in part on the counter-Pelagian writings of the later Augustine. Throughout the *De servo* Luther insists that the notion of free will has no scriptural basis,[16] whereas one can find abundant biblical evidence of the bondage of the will. God's foreknowledge and foreordaining of the fate of Esau (Gen. 25:21–23) and the hardening of Pharaoh's heart (Exod. 4:21), for example, cannot be contested (*LW*, 33: 164–75, 195–202). Moreover, God foreordained the crime of Judas before his birth. At this realization that a merciful God would damn one of his own creatures, Luther confesses his own fear and horror: "I myself was offended more than once, and brought to the very depth and abyss of despair, so that I wished I had never been created a man [ut optarem nunquam esse me creatum hominem]" (*LW*, 33: 190; *WA*, 18: 719). Luther argues, though, that despite such despair, one cannot deny the necessity of human actions or humanity's utter dependence on divine grace for salvation. There is no middle ground ("mediocritam") in the dilemma, for to ascribe to the will a modicum of independent power to choose the good is the same as ascribing total power to it (*LW*, 33: 245; *WA*, 18: 755).

Luther describes the nonfreedom of the will with a brutal metaphor of human moral incapacity. The will is like a passive animal, controlled either by God or by the devil:

Thus the human will is placed between the two like a beast of burden. If God rides it, it wills and goes where God wills, as the psalm says: "I am become as a beast [before thee] and I am always with thee" [Ps. 73:22–23]. If Satan rides it, it wills and goes where Satan wills; nor can it choose to run to either of the two riders or to seek him out, but the riders themselves contend for the possession and control of it. (*LW*, 33: 65–66)

Erasmus, for one, found this view of human will rather bleak, with disturbing social implications concerning human responsibility. For that matter, so did Matthias Flacius, Philipp Melanchthon, and other of Luther's successors, who sought to mitigate the Manichaean echoes in Luther's more extreme statements on the bondage of the will.[17]

But however oppressive this vision might have seemed to some of his contemporararies, it remained for Martin Luther and for thousands of others a liberating theology. As argued in the preceding chapters, any apparent non-mastery—for example, that of being a mute and passive beast before God and the devil—can nevertheless function as a mastery. One liberating dimension of Luther's predestinarian theology was its decentering power. Like many latter-day "non-masteries," Luther's theology of grace had the singular value of gradually dislodging a dominant worldview and establishing another in its place. It freed its subscribers from countless authoritarian constraints of the precursor theology; indeed, its persuasive power hinged on its promises of liberation—its utopian component. This is not to argue that Protestantism in any of its forms was categorically less authoritarian than Roman Catholicism, but rather that the reformers' attacks on ecclesiastical structures were frequently experienced as liberating by those persuaded by the new theologies.[18]

Luther writes in the 1520 tract *De libertate christiana* (The freedom of a Christian) that "a Christian is a perfectly free lord of all, subject to none. A Christian is a perfectly dutiful servant of all, subject to all [Christianus homo omnium dominus est liberrimus, nulli subiectus. Christianus homo omnium servus est officiosissimus, omnibus subiectus]" (*LW*, 31: 344; *WA*, 7: 49). In this exuberant explanation of the meaning of faith, Luther elucidates the paradoxically liberating implications of his conception of human nonfreedom. Christians are categorically not free to effect their own salvation or that of others through good works, but they are free from the demand to perform such works. "It is clear," Luther argues, that "a Christian has all that he needs in faith and needs no works to justify him; and that if he has no need of works, he has no need of the law; and if he has no need of the law, surely he is free from the law. It is true that 'the law is not laid down for the just' [1 Tim. 1:9]" (*LW*, 31: 349). Luther does argue that the believing Christian will *want* to do good works,[19] but the rhetoric of liberation is clear here; the Christian is in some sense above the law, understood not simply as the Pauline opposition of the letter to the spirit, but also as the institutional authority of the Roman church.

Faith liberates the believing Christian not just from the law, but also from other constraints, such as fear, sin, and death:

Who would have the power to harm or frighten such a heart [of the Christian]? If the knowledge of sin or the fear of death should break in upon it, it is ready to hope in the Lord. It does not grow afraid when it hears tidings of evil. It is not disturbed when it sees its enemies. This is so because it believes that the righteousness of Christ is its own and that its sin is not its own, but Christ's, and that all sin is swallowed up by the righteousness of Christ. . . . Death is swallowed up not only in the victory of Christ but also by our victory, because through faith his victory has become ours and in that faith we also are conquerors. (*LW*, 31: 357–58)

Thus, Luther's theology denies one type of human freedom yet insists on another, more radical sort: freedom from the believer's worst fears. Interestingly, the possibility that a believer might not be one of Christ's elect does not surface as a problem here. Though he does not state that the believer knows he or she will be saved, Luther adopts a rhetoric of certainty when speaking of death and salvation. And while he cannot claim the authority of knowledge of the presence of grace and still remain consistent with his own theology, he uses that rhetoric to its full effect. As Heiko Oberman has noted,

Luther rarely qualifies his assertions with the scholarly "ni fallor [if I am not mistaken]"; instead, he frequently opts for the more emphatic "immo [certainly]."[20] But Luther, like de Man in the twentieth century, might have drawn a distinction between the rhetoric of mastery and an epistemology of mastery, thereby qualifying the degree of authority his language seems to claim.

Luther's Conversion and the Rhetoric of Mastery

Near the end of his life, Luther wrote of the liberating force of the idea of justification as he had originally experienced it. In the short, autobiographical Preface to the first volume of his complete Latin works, issued in 1545,[21] Luther left the only record of a decisive event in his life, a conversion experience culminating in his reinterpretation of Paul's Epistle to the Romans.[22] Recalling the early years of the Reformation, his former theological errors, and his struggle for liberation from the Roman church, Luther adopted a striking rhetoric of mastery, representing his rereading of Romans as a hermeneutic triumph over the problem of justification and grace, and as the pivotal breakthrough that made the Reformation possible.

As Heinrich Boehmer once remarked, Luther's theological works are often viewed as the "fragments of a great confession."[23] Indeed, the extent to which Luther's theology of justification was a personal one, bound up with his own experience of conversion, has preoccupied countless students of the Reformation and of Luther himself.[24] As Luther makes clear in the Preface and elsewhere, his authority to write, to teach, and to reform was founded on the literal and self-evident meaning of the Bible.[25] Yet although Luther claims that biblical meaning—specifically, the idea of justification by faith—is plainly available for all to see, he also contends that virtually no one had noticed that particular meaning before he himself did. Thus, although Luther claims only the authority of a reader of the Bible, an authority that remains in a profound sense not his own but God's, the 1545 Preface nevertheless offers a tale of mastery, of how Luther came to formulate his revisionary biblical hermeneutic after a long and painful struggle.

Interestingly, the problem of biblical interpretation is mirrored in the Preface by another problem that Luther broaches—namely, that of the reception of his own texts. Luther says that he has come to recognize the political import to posterity of his life, a life that would be represented by the immense body of his written works. He claims he is publishing these works in order to defend himself from at least one potentially subversive group of readers—namely, future editors. Luther expresses his dread of those men, sympathetic or otherwise, who might influence the way in which posterity receives his books:

Persuaded by these reasons, I wished that all my books were buried in perpetual oblivion, so that there might be room for better ones. But the boldness and bothersome perseverance of others daily filled my ears with complaints that it would come to pass, that if I did not permit their publication in my lifetime, men wholly ignorant of the causes and the time of the events would nevertheless most certainly publish them, and so out of one confusion many would arise. (LW, 34: 327–28)

If others in Luther's absence might publish his books haphazardly, better that he himself exert some control over the process. With the disclaimer that he has been forced by necessity to edit his works, he pleads with the reader to interpret them favorably: "But above all else, I beg the sincere reader [pium lectorem], and I beg for the sake of our Lord Jesus Christ himself, to read those things judiciously, yes, with great commiseration [cum iudicio, imo cum multa miseratione]" (LW, 34: 328; WA, 54: 179). This passage raises interesting questions about Luther's theology—specifically, that of the status of persuasion within his predestinarian system, in which such linguistic efforts might be considered as ineffective as any other kind of good work.

Luther goes on to describe his former incriminating connection with the papacy; so drunk had he been with its dogmas, he says, that he would have been happy to murder anyone and everyone as an act of obedience. He asks the reader's forgiveness for the younger Luther who, before his conversion, wallowed in the error of papal obedience. His contradictory concessions to papal authority in the first days of the conflict were due, he admits, to his own inexperience, as well as to the confusion of the times. Even then, however, from the depths of his heart he longed to be saved (LW, 34: 328). The irony of Luther's seeking to persuade the reader of his good intentions in the days of his subservience by asserting his desire for salvation is that according to his theology, the desire to be saved or to acquire grace counts for nothing with God. Moreover, the positive, if illusory, willfulness suggested by Luther's wish for salvation is retracted in his next explanation of the conflict: "I got into these turmoils by accident [casu] and not by will [voluntate] or intention. I call on God Himself as my witness" (LW, 34: 328; WA, 54: 180). Suggesting that he in no way contrived to bring about the events of 1517 and thereafter, Luther implies the inevitability of his role in the indulgence conflict, into which he was drawn by chance rather than by choice.

In fact, Luther's Preface alternates between the rhetoric of "casus" and that of "voluntas," emphasizing his intention or willfulness only where appropriate. Implicit in this rhetorical dichotomy are the conflicted impulses of the author: though Luther insists on God's foreordaining of the Reformation and of his own role in it, he also appropriates that rebellion to himself. The narrative continually suggests that God's will has been executed through the agency of Luther, but it is his own agency that calls for the recognition and approval of the reader.

Luther's voluntarist rhetoric emerges even more clearly in the discussion of custom and necessity that follows. He writes that it was not easy for him to fight against the long-confirmed errors of the church (LW, 34: 333–34). He recalls the proverb "it is difficult to change habit [difficile est consueta relinquere]," to which he adds the authority of Augustine (significantly, the Augustine of the Confessions): "If one does not resist custom, it becomes a necessity [Consuetudo, si ei non resistitur, fit necessitas]" (LW, 34: 334; WA, 54: 183). To verify the compelling nature of custom (here, blind obedience to the church), Luther enumerates his already impressive spiritual and intellectual accomplishments at the beginning of the conflict—his seven years of public and private teaching of Scripture, which he had nearly memorized, his then-incipient theory of justification sola fide, and his public defense of the proposition that the pope does not govern the church by divine right—only to show that he somehow had not yet reached the conclusion that "the pope must be of the devil [scilicet papam necessario esse ex diabolo]," because "what is not of God must of necessity be of the devil" (LW, 34: 334; WA, 54: 184).

Luther derives the idea that custom unresisted becomes necessity from the discussion of will in book 8 of Augustine's *Confessions*. There Augustine describes the perversity of his own will as he resists conversion:

The enemy held my will in his power and from it he had made a chain and shackled me. For my will was perverse and lust had grown from it, and when I gave in to lust habit was born, and when I did not resist the habit it became a necessity [voluntate perversa facta est libido, et dum servitur libidini, facta est consuetudo; et dum consuetudini non resistitur, facta est necessitas].[26]

Augustine describes this habit as the bondage of his spirit to sensuality, but Luther modifies it to signify the world's bondage to Rome. What appears to be an analogy is actually a trope on Augustinian servitude; the internal vice for which Augustine takes responsibility is transmuted to the climate of vice that Luther discovers in the world around him, and that remains in large part external to him. In fact, Luther recasts the Augustinian version of necessity—the tendency of human nature toward expedient and evil choices—in a turn that accentuates his own rebellion against necessity. However, it remains indeterminate *which* necessity he struggles against: the decadence of the Roman curia, the preordained necessity of his rebellion, or the need to defend his position with the example of his precursor Augustine.

Reverting to his predestinarian argument that God has determined his choices, Luther writes: "Having been drawn into these disturbances by force and driven by necessity, I had done all I did: the guilt was not mine" (*LW*, 34: 335). As he narrates the episode of his conversion, Luther attests to the workings of Providence in the events that led to his hermeneutic breakthrough regarding the righteousness of God and justification by faith. He describes his earlier difficulty with the Epistle to the Romans:

I had indeed been captivated with an extraordinary ardor for understanding Paul in the Epistle to the Romans. But up till then it was not the cold blood about the heart, but a single word in Chapter 1 [verse 17], "In it the righteousness of God is revealed," that had stood in my way. For I hated that word "righteousness of God" [Iustitia Dei], which, according to the use and custom of all the teachers, I had been taught to understand philosophically regarding the formal or active righteousness, as they called it, with which God is righteous and punishes the unrighteous sinner.

Though I lived as a monk without reproach, I felt that I was a sinner before God with an extremely disturbed conscience. I could not believe that he was placated by my satisfaction. I did not love, yes, I hated the righteous God who punishes sinners, and secretly, if not blasphemously, certainly murmuring greatly, I was angry with God [non amabam, imo odiebam iustum et punientem peccatores Deum, tacitaque si non blasphemia, certe ingenti murmuratione indignabar Deo], and said, "As if, indeed, it is not enough, that miserable sinners, eternally lost through original sin, are crushed by every kind of calamity by the law of the decalogue, without having God add pain to pain by the gospel and also by the gospel threatening us with his righteousness and wrath!" (*LW*, 34: 336–37; *WA*, 54: 185)

In this remarkable passage Luther describes once more his blameless but overscrupulous conscience.[27] He confesses his hatred of God for crushing him with guilt and fear, after having already created him with the unbearable burden of the knowledge of his original sin. However, God is not to blame for human misunderstanding of the gospel; Luther asserts that hermeneutic custom had obscured the meaning of Paul's letter.

Luther then discovers that Romans actually conveys the mercy rather than the severity of God. As he continually meditates on its significance, the meaning of the verse "He who through faith is righteous shall live" is gradually revealed to him, "by the mercy of God [miserente Deo]." Luther begins to understand that the righteous live by "the gift of God [dono Dei]," that is, by faith (*LW*, 34: 337; *WA*, 54: 186). He then explains the actual sense of Paul's words: "The righteousness of God is revealed by the Gospel, namely, the passive righteousness with which the merciful God justifies us by faith, as it is written, 'He who through faith is righteous shall live' " (*LW*, 34: 337). The active and menacing righteousness attributed by custom to God gives way in Luther's interpretation to a passive form of righteousness evinced by God's gratuitous gift of grace to man. At this revelation, Luther says, "I felt that I was altogether born again and had entered paradise itself through open gates" (ibid.). The gates of Paradise are the Scriptures, or rather, one word ("iustitia") from Romans, on whose shifted significance hinges the conversion of the entire text of Scripture, and thus of Luther himself. "There a totally other face of the entire Scripture showed itself to me [Ibi continuo alia mihi facies totius scripture apparuit]," he says of that transformation (*LW*, 34: 337; *WA*, 54: 186).

Luther represents the conversion of the text partly as the transmogrification of his own memory. For within his memory he held not only the entirety of Scripture, but the misleading associations of hermeneutic consuetudo. After his breakthrough, Luther confesses that he ran through the Scriptures from memory and was able to draw a string of analogies: "I also found in other terms an analogy, as, the work of God, that is, what God does in us, the power of God, with which he makes us wise, the strength of God, the salvation of God, the glory of God" (*LW*, 34: 337). As he presses the meaning of each word that before had been problematic, his memory is liberated from its bondage to the letter—not simply to a lower or literal order of meaning, but to false and arbitrary signification. The "work of God," for example, like the righteousness of God, does not mean *God's* work (i.e., what God does), but what he allows to happen in men. After this textual conversion, Luther can reinterpret Scripture in terms of the spirit and not the letter—that is, in terms of liberating faith rather than menacing law. And he falls in love with the word he had previously hated (ibid.).[28]

A paradox emerges from this narrative of conversion. Though the phrases "miserente Deo" and "dono Dei" suggest that God foreordained Luther's hermeneutic discovery, Luther seems by his reinterpretation of "iustitia Dei" to ransom his own will from its bondage to fate. When understood as the righteousness of a legalistic God threatening an ineluctably evil humanity, the phrase only reinforced Luther's sense of helplessness and doom. But when understood as a passive form of righteousness, it prompts in Luther the recovery of something very much like the will. By allowing man to be justified by faith, God demonstrates his own passivity, and thereby, in a paradoxical way, the activity of man (although man's faith is subsequent to the gift of divine grace).

Luther's assertion of the passive righteousness of God remains, however, a peculiar distinction within his predestinarian theology. For whether God threatens man with the law or allows him to believe himself the recipient of grace, the will of man remains in utter bondage, and God's passivity is relative at best. Yet the Preface implies a transformation or reincarnation of the will in man's capacity for faith—or specifically, in Luther's own capacity for faith. No longer the victim of his own self-hatred and despair, Luther experiences in his conversion an apparent freedom; the rhetoric of his text, if not its theology, suggests that to believe in one's salvation somehow effects it. Luther's knowledge of the captivity of his will recedes behind his certainty of a predestined escape from damnation.

The apparent cognitive certainty of deliverance and the sense of freedom it generates have a definite bearing on Luther's rhetorical presentation. We have seen that Luther relies on the rhetoric of willfulness as he describes his role in the indulgence controversy. Drawing the Preface to a close, Luther again emphasizes the significance of his intellectual and spiritual persistence, which would be of indeterminate value in a strictly predestinarian theology:

> I relate these things, good reader, so that, if you are a reader of my puny works, you may keep in mind, that, as I said above, I was all alone and one of those who, as Augustine says of himself, have become proficient by writing and teaching. I was not one of those who from nothing suddenly becomes the topmost, though they are nothing, neither have labored, nor been tempted, nor become experienced, but have with one look at the Scriptures exhausted their entire spirit. (*LW*, 34: 338)

Luther insists that he did not get his interpretation out of the blue, but arrived at it after a long struggle (as did the Augustine of the *Confessions*). Luther stresses his own contribution, the will to understand, rather than the gift of illuminating grace empowering the will. However, within Luther's theological system, such intellectual effort may mark the presence of grace, but its representation of personal freedom must also of necessity be an illusion.

Luther concludes: "Farewell in the Lord, reader, and pray for the growth of the Word against Satan" (ibid.). He prays for the fortification of just men against the devil, referring specifically to precursor misinterpretations of the New Testament. Within the just, however, the Word of God expands in its true significance under the paradoxical illusion of discovery known as reading.

Luther ends his prayer with a request for the completion of God's work in him, or the completion of his own work—that is, for the correct interpretation of his writings, as well as their ethical or political fulfillment: "But may God confirm in us what he has accomplished and perfect his work which he began in us, to his glory,

Amen" (*LW*, 34: 337). Luther hopes this imperative can be partly accomplished by his justificatory Preface, which is intended to inspire the good faith of every reader. By seeking to establish a context for his writings, he hopes to influence the manner in which his choices will be understood. But once again Luther's rhetoric seems to exert an influence that, according to his own theology, remains illusory.

The disjunction between Luther's predestinarian theology and his voluntarist rhetoric has not passed unobserved. Indeed, theologians and historians often take pains to explain away what might be construed as an inconsistency on Luther's part. Marilyn Harran, for example, notes that although "Luther's primary concern was to effect a return, indeed a conversion, of the church back to its source, the Word," Luther understood that "the church, like the individual, is converted or reformed only through the work of God. For this reason, Luther seldom referred to himself as a reformer, although he often spoke of himself as an instrument of the Word."[29] In a related vein, Heiko Oberman makes a distinction between the term "Reformation" and the more limited notion of "betterment":

> Where the Gospel is preached, Satan's destructive assaults can be survived. Where Christian teachings tear the authorities from the clutches of the Antichrist, the world can once again come into *its* own. Luther regarded this emancipation of the world, the restoration of its secular rights and its political order, as both necessary and possible. But for this dimension he used the sober, secular, practical, temporal and above all relative term *betterment* rather than the glorious *Reformation*. In short: Reformation is the work of God, betterment the task of Adam and Eve.[30]

Each of these historians seeks to clarify the problem of agency in Luther's predestinarian theology, in effect by separating political practice from theological belief.[31] My goal here is not to prove that Luther's language was genuinely inconsistent with his theology, but rather to point out that the rhetoric of voluntarism, of mastery, that characterizes the 1545 Preface and other of Luther's works is precisely the utopian element of his predestinarian theology. Every rhetoric of mastery posits one or more forms of "predestination" to be overcome. What is particularly interesting about the rhetorical voluntarism of Martin Luther, though, is that the bondage to which it appeals is not the most apparent one in Luther's theological system—namely, the concept of the nonfreedom of the will to effect its own salvation. Instead, the bondage over which Luther would triumph is both the past and the future: the degenerate custom of Roman Catholicism, decentered by Luther's theology of justification, and a necessity more compelling than custom, namely, death. Luther's rhetoric in the Preface offers itself as the corrective of death, just as his theology does, for he hopes it will preserve an immortal Luther, impervious to the fluctuations of fortune, the misunderstandings of assorted *impii lectores*, and the ravages of editors in the far-distant future.

Ignatius Loyola

Freedom, Obedience, and the Counter-Reformation

Questions of justification and human will were among the first orders of business addressed by the Council of Trent, the assembly that launched the Catholic movement of counter-reform by clarifying doctrinal ambiguities. During the second half of 1546, theologians debating these questions strove to navigate between the Lutheran doctrine of justification, which was based on the idea of the inefficacy of individual will, and Pelagian theologies of freedom, which denied or de-emphasized the necessity of divine grace in human salvation. By January 7, 1547, the council had approved a decree on justification. One of its essential points, as Hubert Jedin notes, was that human will cooperates with divine grace before the process of justification takes place. Thus, in contrast to Lutheran theology, the Tridentine decree on justification asserts the possibility of human merit.[32] Moreover, while asserting its modified version of the freedom of the will, the council anathematized both Lutheran and Pelagian theologies of will.[33]

Members of the newly established Society of Jesus attended those debates on freedom and grace, which took place over several months. The Jesuit Diego Laínez made an influential contribution by strenuously attacking Lutheran influences in the theologies of will under discussion and by defending the rights and authority of the Roman church.[34] This watchdog role was, in fact, to become a trademark of the Jesuits. Ignatius Loyola, founder and first general of the Order, made it the primary commitment of the Jesuits to disseminate the teachings of the Catholic church and to defend its institutional practices. In the "Rules for Thinking with the Church," appended to his *Spiritual Exercises* (Exercicios spirituales), Ignatius stressed the need for obedience to the church and conformity to its doctrines. Number 13, perhaps the most famous of these rules, asserts:

> If we wish to be sure that we are right in all things, we should always be ready to accept this principle: I will believe that the white that I see is black, if the hierarchical Church so defines it [debemos siempre tener, para en todo açertar, que lo blanco que yo veo, creer que es negro, si la Yglesia hierárchica assí lo determina]. For, I believe that between the Bridegroom, Christ our Lord, and the Bride, His Church, there is but one spirit, which governs and directs us for the salvation of our souls, for the same Spirit and Lord, who gave us the Ten Commandments, guides and governs our Holy Mother Church.[35]

Here, as throughout his writings, Loyola insists on the principle of obedience to God, to the church, and to one's superiors. In these same rules for "sentido verdadero" (right thinking or feeling), Loyola points out the problems and dangers of making theological assertions—on the topic of predestination, for example. In Rule 15 he recommends that persons not make a habit of discussing that troublesome issue. In Rule 17 he says that one may discuss problems of faith, "but, in these dangerous times of ours, it must not be done in such a way that good works or free will suffer any detriment or be considered worthless" (*SE*, p. 141).

There are several points to be made about these rules in relation to Ignatian theology. First, Loyola was not greatly inclined to tackle theological dilemmas on his own; he preferred to leave such judgments to the authority of the church. Second, Loyola, along with the post-Reformation church, promulgated a limited version of freedom of the will, and as we shall see, his writings describe in several ways a set of practices based on that theory. Third, Loyola's theology revolved around the concept of obedience, which would ideally ce-ment the Jesuit order in a stable hierarchy. The relation of Loyola's notions of obedience to his theology of free will bears further analysis, if only because these concepts might seem at first glance to be mutually exclusive. I shall argue, however, that obedience paradoxically embodies Loyola's strategy for overcoming his own experience of bondage of the will and constitutes for Loyola the right exercise of free will. Loyola developed this strategy, he reveals in his autobiography, during the years following his conversion from courtier and worldly soldier of fortune to ascetic founder of the Jesuits and devout "soldier" of the Counter-Reformation church.

In Loyola's conversion narrative, as, indeed, in the Tridentine decree on justification, there remains some confusion as to the division of labor between a free-willing mankind and a foreknowing, forewilling God who determines the fate and actions of humanity. Thus it is possible to identify within Loyola's autobiography what might be called predestinarian elements—namely, the operations of Providence, or divine will, which induce profound uncertainty, confusion, and sometimes despair in the converted Loyola. Yet Loyola seeks, paradoxically, to do the will of God by making his own will conform to that of his divine master. Loyola's autobiography explains how he overcame his uncertainty and confusion, which are necessary conditions of all contingent, human activity, first by determining the divine will and second by obeying it. Loyola's theology is ultimately voluntarist, because the passive obedience of the servant— taking orders from God, from the pope, and from superiors—is defined as an empowering and authoritative act, a decisive consent that manifests, in the will to serve, the ultimate freedom of the will. Ironically, the liberating and utopian promise of Ignatian rhetoric is the call to obedience. For it is by and through obedience that Loyola hopes to reorder the world, a world in bondage to multiple forms of chaos.

One of these forms, Loyola suggests, is the political and social disarray caused by the Protestant insurrection and by other occasions of disobedience, momentous or mundane. But disorder cannot be fully externalized; it extends, more profoundly and more subtly, into the daily life of the obedient believer. In his writings Loyola explores this more personal chaos, an anxiety induced by the state of

moral uncertainty or unknowing; every moment of daily life requires
decision making, and Loyola seeks to determine, for himself and for
others, correct choices, choices fully conforming to the will of God.
The goal of these determinations is not simply obedience, but also
the continual creation of order in one's own life, as in the outside
world.

Roland Barthes has argued that Loyola envisioned a new language of prayer, unique in its "technical elaboration of an inter-
locution" aimed at eliciting specific answers from God. Barthes calls
this form of prayer a "mantic art." It is "comprised of two codes:
that of the question addressed by man to the Divinity, that of the response sent by the Divinity to man." Loyola's mantic prayer aims at
eliciting from Providence "semiophanies" that, once the obedient
servant learns how to interpret them, resolve the practical difficulties of his vocation. If, as Barthes argues, the *Spiritual Exercises* presents the "code of demand," and the *Spiritual Diary*, in which Loyola noted his own receipt of mystical favors, offers the "code of response,"[36] then the *Autobiography* is essentially the history of the
discovery of that language. In narrating his conversion, Loyola, like
Luther, describes his past bondage (to an ungodly lifestyle, however,
rather than to Catholic consuetudo). He also describes the anxious
bondage of his unknowing and his constant pursuit of a corrective—
namely, providential semiophanies that direct him out of his uncertainty, though they do not fully alleviate it (because there are always
more choices to be made). In the *Autobiography* Loyola recalls the
stages in his development of that language and the ransoming of his
will from the captivity of confusion.

The *Acta quaedam*

The narrative of Loyola's life has come to be called an autobiography only in this century.[37] This is not surprising, because Loyola did not actually write the story of his conversion, but dictated it
to an amanuensis over the course of several months. As he ap-
proached the end of his life, Loyola was persuaded by his fellow Jesuits (particularly his colleague and friend Jerome Nadal) to leave a
record of his own history and that of the Order—both of great importance to the relatively new Society of Jesus. After hesitating for

some time, Loyola ultimately began to tell the story of his conversion and of the foundation of the Order in early September 1553 (according to his Portuguese scribe, Luis Gonçalves da Câmara), but he stopped after three or four more sessions during that month (*A*, pp. 16–17). Reluctant to continue, Loyola pled illness or business whenever da Câmara reminded him of his promise to finish this work. They began again on March 9, 1555, but soon Loyola refused to dictate.[38] When plans were made to send da Câmara on a mission to his native territory, he urged Loyola for the last time to finish the narration, whereupon the elderly man summoned him to hear further dictation just before his departure.[39] The extant versions of the narrative that da Câmara composed from these scattered sessions begin with the wounding of Loyola at Pamplona in 1521 (erroneously reported as having occurred in his 26th year) and conclude with certain 1538 events in Rome preliminary to the formal organization of the Jesuit order.[40]

Da Câmara describes the dictation process as follows: He would listen to Loyola without making notes until the end of each session. Then, retiring to his own quarters, he would make short notes of what he had heard. Finally, dictating to his own scribe, he would formulate an expanded version of these notes. Da Câmara recorded the *Autobiography* in Spanish, except for the last quarter of the text, which continues in Italian. The linguistic shift is due to da Câmara's having left Rome with only his unfinished notes from the final session. He attempted to complete these at the earliest opportunity, which was in Genoa at the end of December. When he could not locate a Spanish scribe there, he settled for an Italian one (*A*, p. 18).[41]

Da Câmara states that he faithfully wrote down everything that he heard, but he also claims that Loyola "began to tell me about his whole life and his youthful escapades [travesuras], clearly and distinctly and with all the circumstances" (*A*, p. 16; *FN*, p. 358). Because these "travesuras" are only vaguely summarized in the first sentence of the *Autobiography*, it is likely either that da Câmara did not record them or that some later editor suppressed them; we cannot prove the latter theory but have good reason to suppose it.[42]

The odd *fortuna* of the *Autobiography* was further complicated by its suppression by Loyola's Jesuit successors for many years after its initial circulation. Pedro de Ribadeneira, disciple and eventual biographer of Loyola, complained to Father Nadal in 1567 that the defects of the text marred the fidelity of those parts that were written more completely.[43] He requested that copies of the text be taken away from those members of the Society in possession of them. Appeal was made to the father general, Francesco Borgia, and at his order during the same year the copies were recalled. Next a number of biographies of Loyola were produced by Ribadeneira, Juan Antonio Polanco, Juan Pedro Maffei, and other Jesuits.[44] Not until 1731 did the first printed Latin translation of the *Autobiography* appear. Until the end of the nineteenth century no other translation existed, and the original Spanish and Italian version was not published until 1904, when the Jesuit editors of the *Monumenta Ignatiana* published the first variorum edition. Only in this century has the *Autobiography* been widely translated and to a certain extent popularized.

We turn now from this peculiar history to the text itself. Because the *Autobiography* narrates the development of Loyola's choice of a way of life, and because a significant aspect of Loyola's theology concerns the making of right choices through the "discreción de espíritus [discernment of spirits],"[45] it is useful to ask how the saint ultimately decided to confess his past. Or rather, we should ask why this was such a difficult choice for him to make.

Loyola's associates had pressed him for some time to allow his followers to benefit from his conversion experience. The future success of the Order depended in part on the continued influence of its founder, whose spiritual example was of great consequence to his followers. The knowledge of the spiritual history of one who abandoned the life of a courtier and soldier for less worldly pursuits would interest his companions; more importantly, it might induce others to make a similar choice of vocation. The significance of Loyola's example of conversion and model of spiritual obedience in the light of post-Tridentine Catholicism must not be underestimated. As his friend Nadal observed to da Câmara, "the Father could do nothing of greater benefit for the Society than this and . . . this was truly to found the Society" (*A*, p. 17).

Because Loyola recognized the political and religious impact his confession would have, its most persuasive and effective telling must have weighed heavily on the aging Jesuit, whose spiritual gifts seem to have outweighed his literary ones. Yet Loyola determined to make his confession, da Câmara relates, after referring to divine authority, as he customarily did when making decisions of importance:

> While Master Polanco and I were eating with him, the Father said that Master Nadal and others of the Society had often asked a favor of him, but he had never decided about it. But that after having spoken to me, when he retired to his room, he had a great desire and inclination to do it, and (speaking in a manner that showed that God had enlightened him as to his duty to do so) he had fully decided to reveal all that had occurred in his soul until now. (*A*, pp. 15–16)

Here Loyola alludes to his practice of putting questions before God through prayer to determine the correct course of action. Loyola's act of obedience is twofold: he decides not only to confess (that is, to perform his "duty"), but also, in a unique act of submission, to turn the control of his own history over to an interpreter—albeit a predictable one, who announces in his preface that he has devoutly adhered to the sense of Loyola's words in rephrasing the confession.

The uniqueness of Loyola's method of self-representation becomes clearer when viewed in the context of his theology of free will and obedience. A section of the *Constitutions*, the set of laws governing the Order, epitomizes Loyola's theology of the will, the freedom of which he paradoxically defends with the following simile: "Everyone of those who live under obedience ought to allow himself to be carried and directed by Divine Providence through the agency of the superior as if he were a lifeless body which allows itself to be carried to any place and to be treated in any manner desired [come si fuese un cuerpo muerto, que se dexa llevar adondequiera y trattar comoquiera]."[46] Here the figure of the cadaver graphically suggests what Loyola says elsewhere about the right disposition of the will toward authority, either divine or mortal—namely, that a person must at all costs strive to maintain the indifference of one dead to the desire of one option over another (riches versus poverty, honor versus dishonor, a long life versus a short one).[47]

Loyola provides a less graphic model of obedience in the *Spiri-*

tual Exercises, where he speaks of the three varieties of men. The third, and the most worthy of emulation, is the kind of man who, having acquired 10,000 ducats "not purely, as [he] should have, for the love of God" (*SE*, p. 77), decides to save his soul. This he does by desiring to free himself from material attachment, but in such a way that "[his] inclination will be neither to retain the thing acquired nor not to retain it, desiring to act only as God our Lord shall inspire [him]" (*SE*, p. 78). Both paradigms of Ignatian indifference describe a will neither paralyzed nor apathetic, but simply inert until Providence directs it. Unlike the corpse, however, the kind of man described in the *Spiritual Exercises* chooses his own inertia. Paradoxically, this surrendering of freedom represents for Loyola the greatest exercise of the freedom of the will and the supreme choice that it can make.

Loyola's confessional strategy is analogous to the cadaver-like obedience he advocates elsewhere. As author and subject he allows his words and experiences to be interpreted by another voice; thus his very manner of writing—or dictating—is an example of passive choice. The founder of the Jesuits submits his will in obedience—not, finally, to the authority of his scribe, but to Providence, which governs the medium of exposition (defined both as the written word and as the writer). Loyola's submission demonstrates his faith in the conveying power of writing and in its ultimate right interpretation or reading. This submission is an ideal confessional strategy for both the tentative writer and the man of prodigious faith.

The Loyolan model of the obedient will has applications on the semiotic level as well as the administrative. Familiar dualistic assumptions such as the subservience of body to spirit and that of man to God, fixed in a stable hierarchy by loving obedience, apply to the theory of language implicit in the *Autobiography* as well as to its method of composition; Loyola's insistence on rigid obedience to spiritual authority as the ideal state of the will has its analogue in a semiotics of obedient signs. Just as spiritual obedience remains an ideal for the Order, semiotic obedience is the ideal of language. But though Loyola implies that language is the servant of intellect and written language the servant of the spoken, he also suggests that there are good and better servants.

According to da Câmara, Loyola would have liked to avoid making his confession altogether rather than present it through the unreliable medium of language. But faced with the inevitability of becoming a text (a story, an impression, a figment of his former self), he decided to assert some influence over the destiny of that text by confessing. Yet the decision that on the one hand represents an attempt to control fate is on the other a means of allowing control by Providence. Loyola must rely on God to inspire obedience wherever it is lacking: in the teller of the story; in the scribal encoder forging the signs for one who surrenders his will, cadaverlike, to Providence (da Câmara is a forger in the sense of being a creator, as well as an impostor); and finally in the reader, the ultimate interpreter of the signs.

In his intriguing biography of Loyola, W. W. Meissner offers a psychoanalytic analysis of the saint's fascination with obedience—his own, as well as everyone else's. Though Meissner's discussion of aggressivity, authority, and obedience constitutes only a small part of his argument, it is useful to relate this discussion to the Ignatian hermeneutics of obedience. "It is characteristic of the authoritarian character," Meissner writes,

to see himself as governed by fate, rationalized as destiny, natural law, duty, or the will of God. The essential factor is that there be a higher power to which he can only submit. The authoritarian does not lack courage, activity, or belief. But the root of his existence in powerlessness transforms these characteristics. Activity becomes action in the name of something higher than himself. To suffer is the highest virtue. *His heroism is to submit to fate, not to change it.*[48] (my emphasis)

How is the submissiveness of this type of individual related to his desire to dominate others? The authoritarian personality, Meissner argues, admires and generally obeys authority. However, he also identifies with authority, wishes to *be* that authority and to have others submit to him. Meissner's analysis suggests certain psychological dimensions to the voluntary bondage—in the case of the *Autobiography*, a bondage or submission to language—that typifies much Ignatian discourse on will. On the one hand, the frustration and anxiety generated by subjection to the medium and processes of communication, which one *knows* one cannot master, are offset by the projection of divine authority into language, an authority to which it is deeply gratifying to submit. On the other hand, this offsetting requires similar obedience or subjection on the part of the reader, who ideally must acknowledge the conflated authorities of God and his servant Loyola. Thus the bondage of the writer is predicated on that of the reader. And implied by the voluntary bondage of Loyola to the text of his life as encoded by da Câmara is a paradoxical mastery of divine language.

La vida es signo

Implicit in the *Autobiography* is an opposition between the unreliable language of humankind and the mystical language of divine imperatives that Loyola eventually masters. The narrative opens with Loyola's first inklings of such a language, as he comes to recognize the signs of his vocation. Wounded at Pamplona and later by his doctors, who brutally rebreak his leg bones after setting them badly, the dying soldier is told on the vigil of Saints Peter and Paul that he does not have long to live. But because of Loyola's devotion to Saint Peter, God wills that he should begin to be healed that very night (*A*, p. 22).

What follows is an account of how Loyola learns to "read" the divine semiophanies calling him to a new life. "He was much given to reading worldly and fictitious books [libros mundanos y falsos], usually called books of chivalry," da Câmara writes (*A*, p. 23; *FN*, p. 370). However, no romances are available in the house of his brother, where he is recovering, so Loyola is given the *Life of Christ* and a book of saints' lives (ibid.).[49] Rather taken with this new literature, Loyola alternates between chivalric fantasies concerning a certain noblewoman and saintly daydreams of going to Jerusalem barefoot and eating nothing but herbs. "What if I were to do what St. Francis did, what St. Dominic did?" he wonders (*A*, p. 23). Gradually he realizes that whenever his worldly thoughts of the noblewoman subside he remains unhappy ("quedaba triste"), whereas the other thoughts leave him happy ("de otros alegre"). In this way he begins to differentiate between the signs of God and those of the devil (*A*, p. 24). A vision of the Virgin carrying the infant Jesus confirms forever his correct discernment of and reactions to these signs, and he is greatly consoled. From that day forward

Loyola never consents in the least to the things of the flesh (A, pp. 24–25).

When Loyola leaves his sickbed, he sets out to pay homage to the new mistress of his affections, the Blessed Virgin. He travels by mule to Montserrat, site of a renowned shrine to the Madonna. On the way there occurs one of the confession's most interesting episodes, which more than any other justifies Miguel de Unamuno's comparison of the saint to Don Quixote,[50] and is also the perfect parable of Loyola's obedient quest for a providential semiophany.

On the way to Montserrat, Loyola encounters a Moor riding in the same direction. The two begin to discuss the virgin birth, whereupon the Moor observes that "it seemed to him that the Virgin had indeed conceived without a man, but he could not believe that she remained a virgin after giving birth. In support of this he cited the natural reasons that suggested themselves to him" (A, p. 30). When the Moor realizes that his views do not sit well with his fellow traveler, he hurries off down the road. As Loyola contemplates these blasphemies, he cannot decide whether he should catch up with the Moor and kill him or patiently overlook the insults. When he arrives at a junction where a narrow road runs off the broader one taken by his enemy, Loyola decides to submit the decision to God: If his mule turns off the better road, away from the Moor, that will be a sign from God to leave him alone. Fortunately for all, the mule takes the road less traveled.

Loyola's decision to let his animal become the arbiter of his decision raises an interesting question—namely, why the mule should become the vehicle for a divine message. After all, there are dozens of possible conveyors of the mantic yes or no that Loyola seeks in the world of binary choices (clouds, cracks in the road, butterflies), so how does he decide upon his mule?

In fact, Loyola's deferral tropes on several texts, among them books of chivalry and the Bible—notably the story of Balaam, who was chastised by an angel for not listening to his animal (Num. 22–23).[51] Where Balaam fails to listen and understand, Loyola anticipates a semiophany to avoid chastisement. He asks for the sign, submitting his judgment to Providence. Nor can he be charged with creating or determining the language of the sign, because he acts in keeping with an established biblical precedent.

Loyola's tropes on profane texts have made some of his devotional critics uncomfortable, presumably because those tropes seem
to problematize Loyola's claims to communicate with God. Significantly, Pedro de Ribadeneira's *Vida*, the first official biography of
Loyola, excludes the episode with the Moor.[52] More recent critics
have shown uneasiness about the next segment of the *Autobiography*, where Loyola explicitly confesses the secular origins of his concept of performing a vigil over his arms. After the encounter with
the Moor, Loyola recalls the romance of Amadís of Gaul and others like it, whereupon he decides to perform a vigil over his arms before the altar of the Virgin at Montserrat.[53] As the editors of the
Fontes narrativi remark, the saint may have had in mind the vigil of
arms performed by Esplandían, the son of Amadís, in book 4 of that
romance.[54] Other readers have been suspicious of Loyola's chivalric
obsession and have attempted to disprove his statement that he had
a profane vigil in mind when he planned his own.[55] However, Jesuit
critic Pedro Leturia argues that influence by profane models of devotion should not be construed as undermining the authenticity of
Loyola's piety. Like almost every other Spaniard of his day, Loyola
was immersed in the chivalric fantasies of his culture, but he sub-
sumed these into his own idiom of sainthood.[56]

Nevertheless, the semiotic conversion of a gesture from the romance of Amadís, like the conversion of any infidel, raises the suspicion of force among some devotional readers. The persuasive force
of Loyola's history, its call to obedience, depends on his establishing
the authenticity of the language of interpellation through which he
communicates with God. Perhaps the occlusion of the *Autobiography*—its missing parts, its censorship, its infrequent translation—is
due to the fact that over the centuries many readers have perceived
it to be a disobedient text, unfaithful to the history of the *fundador*.
Or perhaps we should think of Borgia, Ribadeneira, and later cen-
sors of the text as disobedient readers.

The Language of Mystical Favor

Devotional critics have been more receptive to the next part of
the *Autobiography*, where Loyola describes his development of the
Spiritual Exercises. For example, Antonio de Nicolas contrasts the
saint's sometimes suspect interpretations (as in the mule episode) to

the legitimate hermeneutics of the *Exercises*.[57] While staying at a monastery in the town of Manresa, Loyola undergoes a kind of internship in the "discernment of spirits." Like Martin Luther, Loyola is overwhelmed by his sense of sinfulness, by scruples that arise from unsatisfying confessions, and by his failure to represent his sins adequately and thereby rid himself of them. These problems threaten to bring him to despair. He perseveres with daily confession and communion but gains no satisfaction from penance, because forgotten sins flood into his mind after each confession. Seven-hour prayer vigils fail to reassure him; instead, temptations of suicide overcome him, and he briefly considers throwing himself into a large pit in the next room (*A*, p. 35).

Tortured by memory but also aided by it, Loyola recalls the story of a saint who fasted until God granted him something that he wanted very much.[58] He too decides to fast "until God took care of him or until he saw that death was indeed near" (*A*, p. 36). He does this for a week, but his confessor immediately orders him to desist. For two days Loyola is freed from scruples. They return on the third, but later that same day he is mysteriously liberated from them. Da Câmara writes, "From that day forward he remained free of those scruples and held it for certain that Our Lord through his mercy had wished to deliver him" (ibid.). However, Loyola also emphasizes his own volition in overcoming his scruples—namely, the volitional hermeneutic exercise of determining the will of God. Spiritual obedience for Loyola entails exercising his will to understand that of God, and by a painful process of trial and error he begins to communicate with the Divinity in search of a response.

Finally purged of his obsessions, Loyola progresses to a new stage of spiritual development. The *Autobiography* gives an intriguing account of the visions and illuminations that come to the ascetic in his remaining months at Manresa. For example, one day when Loyola is reciting the hours of our Lady, "his understanding began to be elevated so that he saw the Most Holy Trinity in the form of three keys [teclas]" (*A*, p. 38; *FN*, p. 402). The word "teclas" may refer to the keys of a musical instrument or possibly to a chord, suggesting Loyola's synesthetic apprehension of the persons of God. Also, many times while praying, Loyola sees with "inner eyes [ojos interiores]" the humanity of Christ: "The form that appeared to him was like a white body, neither very large nor very small, but he did not see the members distinctly" (*A*, pp. 38–39; *FN*, p. 402). Thus he is many times led to think that "if there were no Scriptures to teach us these matters of the faith, he would be resolved to die for them, only because of what he had seen" (*A*, p. 39). Loyola's proclivity for visionary experience, a semiophany of images, must be contrasted with the humanist hermeneutics of certain of his contemporaries. Luther and Erasmus had proclaimed that Christ lived and breathed within Scripture far more than in the Eucharist or any other visible sign of his presence.[59] In contrast, the untranslatable and inhuman language of mystical revelation conveys far more to Loyola than the language of man or of Scripture.

Of the two languages (mortal/scriptural and visionary/mystical), Loyola overwhelmingly favors the latter. Its signs, the mystical images, render their contents (such as the humanity of Christ) in a manner entirely different from that of normal language. Loyola implies that nothing is lost in the translation from vision to understanding, and he intimates that he has discovered a paradigmatic language of perfectly obedient signs. He indicates that there is an immediacy of what is communicated within the medium of God's language, and a condition of understanding that must be considered to possess the integrity of unfallen language. Having at his disposal only human language, Loyola can only describe approximately what he has experienced in his visions. However, human language also aspires to the ideal it imitates through the Loyolan model of obedience—obedience on the part of the dictator, the scribe, and the reader.

Loyola goes on to describe an even higher order of communication. During his months at Manresa he happens on one occasion to pass by the Church of Saint Paul, about a mile from the town. Sitting beside the river Cardoner he begins to perform his devotions, and the eyes of his understanding are opened. This time he sees nothing but understands a great deal. For his entire life he remembers the impact of the "ilustración" (still a visual metaphor) on the banks of the river:

Though there were many, he cannot set forth the details that he understood then, except that he experienced a great clarity in his understanding. This was such that in the whole course of his life, through sixty-two years, even if he gathered up all the many helps he had had from God and all the many things he knew and added them together, he does not think they would amount to as much as he had received at that one time. (A, pp. 39–40)

Loyola intimates that he has experienced a language wholly perfect— that is, a language without signs, and therefore without mediation— which he was privileged to understand only once in his life. However, he cannot describe the communication at all, and even what he learned remains obscure within his memory. He can only recollect his response to that illumination: ecstasy.

Having experienced this transfiguration of language, Loyola attempts to translate his ineffable illumination of spirit into a practice, a moral imperative. He becomes a pilgrim and a beggar, allowing Providence to determine his every action. He begs daily only for what he needs to survive, and he relies on Providence to bring him to the Holy Land in spite of seemingly insurmountable obstacles. It is there that Loyola hopes for an overwhelming encounter with Christ's presence, the traces of which are preserved in situ in paradigmatic and historic semiophanies.

Loyola is especially fascinated by the footprints of Christ, mysteriously imprinted on Mount Olivet at his ascension. Despite the constant danger of Turkish attacks, Loyola returns to that place and bribes the guards to let him in again to study the directions of the footprints, because the first time "he had not clearly noticed on Mount Olivet in what direction the right foot was pointed nor in what direction the left" (A, p. 51). Loyola is a man obsessed by the visual, perpetually impressing on his own memory images of divinity that confirm his volition to serve. This episode also reveals the nature of his lifelong quest: the search for an order in the world that transcends the chaos generated by malevolent Turks, blasphemous Moors, heretical Protestants, and, perhaps most important, Loyola's own state of unknowing.

By the end of his pilgrimage Loyola has acquired a kind of fluency in the language of mystical revelation expressing the will of Providence, but he is still far from persuading others of the practical applications of his conviction (that is, of the virtues of a lifestyle of spiritual obedience). He therefore spends over ten years in several major universities in Spain and France, where he strives to acquire the rhetorical and theological apparatus, as well as the contingent of followers, enabling a transition from the private realm of mystical cognition to the ethical and communal one.[60] The actual narrative of the saint's life ends abruptly with the report of certain events of 1538, after Loyola and his companions have arrived in Rome. Da Câmara then closes by describing his last session with Loyola. When the aging Jesuit concludes his story, the scribe asks him how he came to write the *Spiritual Exercises* and the *Constitutions* (A, pp. 92–93). Loyola responds that he assembled his *Exercises* gradually, whenever he recognized that some aspect of his own self-examinations might be of benefit to others.

As for the *Constitutions*, Loyola recounts to his scribe the nature and frequency of his communications with God, which helped him determine the structure and laws of the Order. Of Loyola's most recent communications, da Câmara writes:

His devotion, that is, his ease in finding God, had always continued to increase and now more than in his whole life. Each time and hour that he wanted to find God, he found Him. Now he also had visions very often, especially those mentioned above in which he saw Christ as the sun [di veder Cristo come sole]. This often happened while he was speaking of important matters, and it came to him as a confirmation.[61]

In this way da Câmara describes his leader's facility in petitioning God for confirmation of important decisions and in interpreting the signs of Providence as answers to the questions posed.[62]

Next Loyola reads to da Câmara a portion of a journal describing the spiritual favors he had received in confirmation of certain rules of the *Constitutions*. Da Câmara thereby learns of the frequency of Loyola's visions of the persons of the Trinity and the Virgin. To prompt these visionary responses, Loyola would pray while saying mass, always with copious tears, over the decision to be made.[63] Intrigued, da Câmara begs in vain to see all the pages or drafts relating to the *Constitutions*: "I wanted to see all those papers relating to the constitutions, and I asked him to let me have them a while, but he did not want to" (A, p. 94).

This curious episode of denial can be understood as a parable of interpretive obedience. We do not know why the elderly Loyola refuses to show the scribe the text he prefers only to read to him. But whatever his reasons, Loyola insists on the trust, or rather the obedience, of the narrator of his mystical revelations. The example of Loyola's obedience, both in the narrative that he has dictated and in the very process of dictation, manifests its imperative force in this final scene, which has a semiophanic quality of its own. We might think of this demand for obedience as a secondary paradigm for Ignatian right reading. In the narrative, the living Loyola overrides (and overwrites) his own texts, which would, according to the norms of that semiotic universe, be vulnerable to the interpretive distortions of a da Câmara. Through this scene of withholding, which is likewise a scene of revelation, Loyola seems to will the hermeneutic conformity of his scribe and future readers to his meaning and his world historical mission.

Implicit in this call to obedience is a chain of command that Loyola made explicit to those joining the Order. The early biographer Ribadeneira describes how the founder regularly addressed the members of the Society on the value of obedience. Ribadeneira excerpts many of Loyola's thoughts on the subject, among them the following: "There are three ways to obey. The first is when they command me by virtue of obedience, and that is good. The second is when they order me to do this or that, and that is better. The third is when I do this or that, sensing some signal of the Superior, although he does not command me or order me, and that is much more perfect."[64] As always for Loyola, the choice to serve one's superiors (God, the pope, the general of the Order, and others) is the true mark of personal freedom. Obedience also expresses the desire that one's own act of submission generate an ordering power extending beyond the self as a "señal"—a sign, but also a signal to others. It is this señal of obedience and of order that Loyola extends beyond the pages of his *Autobiography*.

Teresa of Avila

Freedom and Bondage in the Nonmoral Sense

It is a paradox of Renaissance and Reformation thought that those who espoused the nonfreedom of the will claimed to be liberated by their bondage—a claim that may be the mark of every negative hermeneutic—while advocates of doctrines of human freedom tended to subscribe to some notion of servitude of the will. It is worth bearing in mind who framed these paradoxes of the will, either in the most abstract terms of human identity or in more concrete terms of social and political hierarchies. Most of these authors were men, and we detect in their writings the usual dogmas of patriarchal culture—for example, the natural right of men to govern women, animals, and Nature "herself." Indeed, those men who made pronouncements on freedom or its limits enjoyed a degree of freedom and privilege not available to most of their female contemporaries. Clearly early modern debates on will and mastery did not pertain to women's lives in the same ways as to men's, if only because women and men inhabited different cultural spaces. That is not to say that women's writing (what there was of it) was automatically less patriarchal than men's,[65] but rather that of necessity women experienced their culture in a different way—generally from the vantage of the margin.

Rather than documenting the effects of theories of will on the lives of early modern women, a task worthy of volumes, my goals here are to consider the situation of one sixteenth-century woman writing on freedom and servitude, and to raise questions about "female" mastery in relation to the other masteries considered in this book. The notion of female authority was as problematic for Teresa of Avila, the Spanish Carmelite, as it was for most men and women of her age, though Teresa's uniquely productive career as a theologian, writer, and religious reformer might seem to belie the notion that mastery was primarily a male fantasy and opportunity. Certainly the modes of authority available to the women of Teresa's day were severely circumscribed, but the roles of nun and mystic were traditionally popular, as witnessed by the number of *beatas*, or holy women, during the Spanish Counter-Reformation.[66] What is most striking about Teresa's writing is that she acknowledges her own religious authority and mystical favors while simultaneously undercutting them with a rhetoric of female inferiority. In other words, she asserts several types of female mastery but at the same time states their impropriety or virtual impossibility.

Teresa's *Libro de la vida* bears witness to the strong misogynist tendencies of Renaissance thought, according to which women were weak-willed, morally feeble, intellectually defective, and otherwise inferior.[67] Teresa herself seems to have internalized this view. "The very thought that I am a woman is enough to make my wings droop," she writes; "how much more, then, the thought that I am such a wicked one!" (LT, p. 123).[68] Teresa sees "female" sin as different from "male" sin such as that of Augustine, for in her own sinfulness general evil converges with the evil of woman.

In Teresa's writings the concept of servitude, of nonfreedom, assumes an entirely different configuration than it does, for example, in Martin Luther's. Servitude implies for her a more literal bondage of the will—namely, the political and psychic effects of being female in sixteenth-century Spain. The rhetoric of her autobiography might be thought of as a conflict between her will to conform to her culture's demands of non-mastery and her will to circumvent those demands. Teresa's Vida and other works do not present a feminism in the modern sense of the word, but they do confront the peculiar situation of a woman—and presumably many women—struggling against a culture that considered female inferiority to be gospel. The Vida demonstrates that notions of mastery are, among other things, gendered.

A Double Alterity: Teresa's *Converso* Ancestry

We can begin to understand the conflicts and contradictions of any era by studying its ideas of otherness, its marks of political, sexual, and racial difference. The Renaissance of Jacob Burckhardt and his heirs, an age idealized with metaphors of human dignity, psychic freedom, and the rebirth of ancient learning, gives way to other readings and other legacies if one explores these signs of difference.[69] Woman and Jew—both popularly thought to embody the contraries of dominant moral and cultural values—are two figures of alterity in the Renaissance. Although their stereotypes are not interchangeable, they overlap in significant ways. Throughout Renaissance and Reformation texts, with some exceptions, woman and Jew stand for multiple modes of inferiority: mental and physical weakness, guile, cunning, sensuality, and vanity, among others.

Teresa of Avila, self-proclaimed Magdalen turned mystic, and

granddaughter of a converso, embodied both of these strains of alterity. How then was it possible for her to become not only a saint
after her death, but, perhaps more surprisingly, a political and religious authority in her lifetime? Moreover, what kind of sanctifying
forgetfulness made possible the "discovery" in this century of
Teresa's Jewish origins, origins for which the editors of the recent
Obras completas feel compelled to apologize (thereby proving that
the converso stigma lives on in some places)?[70] Was it in spite of her
otherness or because of it that Teresa was vindicated after death by
the very groups that suspected or persecuted her during her lifetime?

In a convoluted way the *Vida* offers an index of the change in
how Teresa was perceived by herself and others, a change catalyzed
in part by the actual writing of the autobiography. In other words,
the *Vida* describes Teresa's otherness even while prompting a reval-
uation of it; thus her mastery has much to do with the act of persuading, of confronting and recuperating her alterity (her femininity, that is, but not her Jewish ancestry). Teresa's identity evolved in
her own mind and in the minds of her contemporaries from that of
a stigmatized and dangerous *alumbrada*, that notorious species of
heretic so vexing to the Spanish Inquisition, to that of a politically
powerful visionary, in both senses of the word. Without a doubt,
Teresa's writing contributed to her acceptance as a legitimate mystic and thereby to her temporal authority, though it was not until
her death in 1582, or really until her canonization in 1622, that the
charge of *iluminismo*, the scourge of women and conversos, was
once and for all dismissed. Let us look closely, then, at the curious
metamorphosis of Teresa of Avila, and at the *fortuna* of her texts
in the context of the culture that produced them, in order to better
understand the marginal position from which Teresa wrote, what
that position meant in the culture of Counter-Reformation Spain,
and how, in this particular case, one writer made the best of her alterity.

To understand Teresa's vulnerable position as a woman of converso origins, we must understand something of the complicated history of Spanish anti-Semitism and the origins of the Spanish Inquisition in the late Middle Ages. The era of rabid anti-Semitism that
culminated in the expulsion of the Jews in 1492 and the persecutions

of the inquisitor Torquemada just a few years before the birth of Teresa, contrasts with centuries of relative pluralism in medieval Spain (though there was never a time in Spanish history when Jews escaped discrimination).[71] Anti-Semitism had become extreme by the end of the fourteenth century, and the year 1391 was marked by massacres of the Jewish communities throughout Andalusia and Castile. In Seville, Cordova, Toledo, Madrid, and other major cities the Christians razed synagogues or turned them into churches and killed or baptized Jews en masse.[72] Pogroms also took place throughout Aragon during the same year. At this point Jewish communities in Spain were on the verge of extinction, and an unprecedented number of conversos, Jews baptized mainly by force or necessity, attempted to escape the stigma of their former religion by joining the ranks of Christians. However, conversos faced at least as much hostility from so-called Old Christians as the remaining Jews did, because the mass conversions of the fourteenth and fifteenth centuries intensified rather than alleviated political and economic rivalries.[73]

By the mid-fifteenth century the hatred of Jews and conversos had reached another crescendo. In 1458 Franciscan monk Alfonso de Espina, an esteemed theologian and the confessor to Henry IV of Castile, produced one of the key anti-Semitic documents of his century, the *Fortalitium fidei contra Judeos* (Fortress of the faith against the Jews). This document, reprinted several times over the next 70 years, helped disseminate the mythology of Jews being sources of every evil. Espina identified Jews as traitors, homosexuals, regicides, murderers, killers of Christian children, poisoners, and usurers, for example.[74] The rabid friar attempted to give historical evidence for his accusations, citing, among others, a then-recent case of the murder of a Christian child, whose heart was reputedly cut out by Jews for their diabolical rites.[75] Ironically, Espina, who drew most of his knowledge of Jewish practice from the writings of converso apologists,[76] did not spare the conversos his rage. He despised them for supposedly continuing to practice Jewish rites in secrecy and for blinding the authorities to their need for punishment. Espina proposed the establishment of an Inquisition in Castile to punish these crimes against Christianity.[77]

Twenty years later Ferdinand and Isabella, "los reyes católicos,"

spearheaded the movement to crush the conversos by founding the
Spanish Inquisition in Castile and reactivating it in Aragon.[78] In 1483
they appointed the brutal Dominican Tomás de Torquemada, also
of converso origins, to the post of inquisitor general.[79] Under his
aegis there commenced several decades of violence against Jews and
conversos, who were invariably accused of Judaizing—that is, of secretly practicing their former religion—and of molesting authentic
Christians. When it so desired, the Inquisition succeeded in extract-
ing confessions of bizarre crimes—outrages derived primarily from
the subliterature of Espina's *Fortalitium fidei* and the like, and from
the imaginations of the torturers.[80]

This history of persecution was of great relevance to Teresa and
her family. Teresa's paternal grandfather, Juan Sánchez, a prosper-
ous merchant in Toledo, was one of the hundreds of conversos
brought to trial in the mid-1480's. To escape a more severe punishment Sánchez came forward in June of 1485 and confessed to having committed "many serious crimes of heresy and apostasy against
the holy Catholic faith."[81] During the autos-da-fé held in February,
April, and June of the next year, a total of 2,400 conversos, including Sánchez, were "reconciled" to the Catholic church.[82] Teresa's father, Alonzo, then still a child, was "reconciled" along with his father. Sánchez was publicly sentenced and forced to march in a hu-
miliating parade of penitents. Along with two hundred other
reconciliados, he was also made to wear the *sambenitillo con sus
cruces*, the garment of reconciliation, during his auto-da-fé and for
six successive Fridays.[83]

The significance of the sambenitillo as a punishment should not
be underestimated. The Spanish, obsessed with *honra*, or reputation,
dreaded infamy sometimes more than death, because the loss of
honor doomed entire families and future progeny to disgrace. The
Inquisition, desirous of perpetuating the shame of those they pun-
ished, would hang the offenders' sambenitillos on display in their
churches. As these garments decayed over the years, they were customarily replaced with new ones bearing the names of the original
owners.[84]

The reconciliados faced other penalties besides disgrace, however. For the rest of their lives they were forbidden to wear fine

clothes or to hold certain public offices. They gave a fifth of their wealth to the monarchy, then waging war on the Moors in Granada. And they lived in fear of the stake, to which they would be sent if they failed to carry out their penances or if they reverted to any form of "Judaizing."[85] The threat of the stake was very real, and thousands of "unreconciled" conversos were burned in Toledo and other cities in the Inquisition's purges.

Juan Sánchez changed his name to Juan de Cepeda, the name of his wife's family, and by 1493 he had moved with his clan to Avila, one of the few relatively tolerant cities in Spain. A few years later he won a *pleito de hidalguía*, a legal procedure through which one established a claim to nobility and therefore exemption from taxes.[86] But though he and his family prospered, they nevertheless lacked the full social acceptance of Old Christians. As Rosa Rossi, Jodi Bilinkoff, and others have argued, Teresa must have felt the impact of belonging to a family of "tainted" blood. It was not a coincidence that, contrary to custom, Teresa later refused to require proof of *limpieza de sangre*, or "purity of blood," from nuns seeking admission to her "reformed" convents.[87]

I have outlined some versions of the alterity attributed to Jews and conversos, alterity generally construed as subversive of Old Christian values. Each generation understood Jewish alterity in slightly different ways, however, and by the time of the Counter-Reformation the ideology of the stain had begun to take on a different configuration. Not surprisingly, Spanish Protestants, alumbradas, and other heterodox persons of the mid-sixteenth century were suspected of being, among other things, Jews—that is, of converso lineage—and the cult of limpieza de sangre grew more obsessive.[88]

Two examples show that conversos still faced repression and brutality during Teresa's lifetime. In 1547 the Estatuto de limpieza de sangre was issued in Toledo and later in other cities; this edict made access to prestigious social positions contingent on one's *hidalguía*, or nobility, and also on one's genealogical limpieza. In 1559, the year of the first papal Index, the Spanish Inquisition held a great auto-da-fé at Valladolid; there several members of the prominent Cazalla family and those in their circle were burned as Lutherans. Not surprisingly, those burned were, for the most part, conversos.[89] It is obvious why Teresa never mentioned her ancestry, and recent biographers have shown the degree to which her career and indeed her life were threatened by the Inquisition, both because she was a woman making theological pronouncements and because it was always possible that her converso origins might be used against her.[90]

Certainly Teresa's double alterity, the fact that she was a female of converso origins, made an impact on her theology of will and mystical servitude. Teresa's notions of mastery are gendered and, in a nearly invisible way, "raced." Let us examine the possible effects of these strains of alterity on her conversion and on the formation of her mystical theology, as described in her autobiography.

The Rhetoric of Self-Mortification

Teresa's *Vida* begins with a chronologically structured account of her life from childhood to her second conversion at the age of 40, then evolves into a narrative form difficult to classify.[91] Like the last four books of Augustine's *Confessions*, the major portion of the *Vida* constitutes what might be called an autobiographical theology. Teresa's confession is also unusual in that it was produced in conjunction with the Catholic sacrament of confession; she wrote at the express command of her confessors. Thus the rhetoric of self-mortification characterizing the *Vida* derives, in part, from that of its penitential model. However, Teresa's rhetoric seems to respond to more than the stated purpose of her writing—which is to explain her mystical experiences to her spiritual counselors—and it suggests certain other motives for that writing.

The circumstances that prompted Teresa to compose the *Vida* were difficult ones. After approximately twenty years in the convent, she had begun an entirely different phase of her religious life and was experiencing strange phenomena, such as voices and visions, during her meditations. Troubled by these events, Teresa turned to her confessors and to other men for spiritual advice. Gaspar Daza, Teresa's sometime confessor, together with Francisco de Salcedo, a respected Avilan and confidant of the saint, concluded that the "favors" she had been receiving actually came from the devil (*LT*, p. 226). Their extreme doubts about her experiences intensified her own and caused her to embark on a long search for a spiritual director who could allay these fears. In 1560 a supportive confessor, the Dominican Pedro Ibáñez, encouraged her to provide her spiritual directors with written clarification of the mystical phenomena she had described in order to facilitate their investigation (*LV*, p. 13).[92] By 1562 she had completed a draft for another Dominican confessor, García de Toledo. In 1565, still slightly tentative about her mystical gifts and encouraged by inquisitor Francisco de Soto Salazar, Teresa prepared a final version for the scrutiny of Juan of Avila, famed ascetic and discerner of spirits (ibid.). Thus the *Vida* was gradually assembled over a five-year period.

Initially, at least, the writing of the *Vida* represented Teresa's struggle to determine the validity of the mystical favors she had been experiencing since her early forties. That Teresa was afraid of these graces and that several of her spiritual advisors believed she might be possessed by demons were entirely consistent with the mood of Counter-Reformation Spain. At the time of Teresa's writing, the Inquisition's purges of heretics were in full swing. The efforts of the monarchy and the Inquisition to enforce orthodoxy generated no small terror among many religious figures, particularly those of converso origins. The Inquisition also scrutinized female forms of heterodoxy, namely, the ecstatic piety of certain beatas, who were frequently suspected of illuminism, Lutheranism, or deception by Satan.[93] In this highly charged atmosphere of fanaticism, suspicion, and fear, Teresa was anxious to determine whether or not her mystical experiences were genuine, and she was terrified at the possibility of self-deception (*LT*, pp. 219–28).

However, Teresa finished the *Vida* years after the initial negative conclusions of her advisors Daza and Salcedo. Her motives for writing therefore could not have been simply to satisfy her confessors or to gain assurance from them of the validity of her mystical favors. Teresa claims to search for confirmation of her mysticism, but at the same time she announces her absolute certainty of it. Given her apparent certainty as to the source of the graces she had been receiving, if not as to her authority to explain them to her examiners in theologically acceptable terms, Teresa's constant self-deprecation in the *Vida* calls for careful analysis.

Perhaps the most striking feature of Teresa's confession is her rhetoric of self-mortification, which is both more pronounced than and qualitatively different from the self-scourgings of the male autobiographers considered in this chapter. On virtually every page Teresa announces her immorality or stupidity, as well as her unworthiness of the spiritual gifts that God has decided to bestow on her. Rarely is she specific about her sins, though she insists that few people actually recognize them: "However wretched and imperfect my good works have been, this Lord of mine has been improving them, perfecting them and making them of great worth, and yet hiding my evil deeds and my sins as soon as they have been committed. He has even allowed the eyes of those who have seen them to be blind to them and He blots them from memory" (*LT*, pp. 82–83). Not only does Teresa declare herself a terrible sinner, she does not seem to anticipate a time when she will not be one. Even though she has begun a "vida nueva" since her mid-life conversion, she claims she has not really changed her former ways:

I beg anyone who reads this account of my life to bear in mind how wicked it has been—so much so that, among all the saints who have been converted to God, I can find none whose life affords me any comfort. For I realize that, once the Lord had called them, they never offended Him again. I however, became worse, and not only so, but I seem to have studied how to resist the favours which His Majesty granted me. (*LT*, p. 64)

Mindful of the effects of such rhetoric on her readers, Teresa has her audience take note of her abasement, her badness: "I know well that nobody will derive any pleasure from reading about anyone so wicked, and I sincerely hope that those who read this will hold me in abhorrence, when they see that a soul which had received such great favours [tantas mercedes] could be so obstinate and ungrateful" (*LT*, p. 108; *LV*, p. 37). These are but a few samples of self-flagellation from a text that is riddled with statements about the author's sinfulness, even as Teresa asserts herself to be the recipient of "tantas mercedes." How should we interpret these statements and the rhetoric of self-mortification as an autobiographical strategy, conscious or unconscious?

Luis de Leon, editor of the 1588 edition of the *Vida*, took these apologies to be signs of an overscrupulous and saintly nature.[94] That impression has been reinforced by devotional readings of Teresa's work over the last several hundred years. Few have questioned the sincerity of what appear to be Teresa's pious guilt and self-loathing. It is commonly accepted that this rhetoric of self-mortification is proof of Teresa's saintly disposition, her overscrupulous character, and her humble drive for greater spiritual perfection.

That reading is problematic for several reasons, one of which is that it accepts female self-hatred as normative. Indeed, the sincerity of Teresa's singularly negative presentation of her life and personality is beside the point. What matters is the expectation—then, and also now, among certain devotional readers—that self-mortification is a sign of humility in the female saint or ascetic. One might argue that Teresa's campaign for reform hinged on her being taken seriously as an obeisant, overly modest, self-loathing character. Female authority in the Counter-Reformation church was virtually an oxymoron, but such authority might be gained or underpinned by the *via negativa* of a rhetoric turned against its user. We must remember that most contemporary accounts of Teresa describe her as a charming, intelligent, and strong-willed character, and that the undermining rhetoric of the *Vida* is countered by its bold assertions of unique spiritual powers. Teresa's verbal self-mortification did not completely mitigate or conceal her claims to a knowledge of mystical theology, as her several brushes with the Spanish Inquisition over the *Vida* attest.[95]

In a recent book on Teresa's rhetoric, Alison Weber examines her self-deprecation in the *Vida*, along with the apparent spontaneity, sincerity, and homespun quality of her writing. Weber draws a distinction between the idea that Teresa wrote like a woman and the idea that she wrote "as she believed women were *perceived* to speak." Weber also challenges the prevailing view that Teresa actually considered herself a wicked and degenerate female and argues instead that Teresa used a "rhetoric of femininity"—that is, a conscious strategy of manipulating stereotypes of woman's character and language to her advantage. "Teresa concedes," Weber writes, "women's weakness, timidity, powerlessness, and intellectual inferiority but uses the concessions ironically to defend, respectively, the legitimacy of her own spiritual favors, her disobedience of *letrados*, her administrative initiative, her right to 'teach' in the Pauline sense, and her unmediated access to the Scriptures."[96]

Weber analyzes Teresean rhetoric in terms of a theory of the double bind, which might loosely be described as the condition of having to respond to mutually exclusive demands. One double bind that Teresa faced was having to defend her authority while at the same time demonstrating her absolute humility and unworthiness. Teresa successfully resolved this double bind, Weber argues, by means of three strategies: first, by responding to the contradictory demands with paradoxes or contradictory claims of her own; second, by redefining the dependency of her binding relationship with authority; and third, by "metacommunicating"—that is, talking about the double bind, in effect explaining its mechanisms. One example of the first strategy within the *Vida* is the way in which Teresa explains her past; the force of her descriptions, Weber notes, is confessional, but the rhetorical effect is defensive.[97]

The argument that Teresa's self-reproaches made her claims to power less threatening to the patriarchies of church and state does not mean, however, that she herself had not internalized her culture's negative vision of femininity. Arguably, then, her confessions of wickedness function both as a strategy for gaining authority in the extremely misogynistic and racist climate of mid-sixteenth-century Spain and as an acknowledgment of her particular servitude to the prevailing conceptions of gender and racial identity.

It might be objected that male religious autobiographers from Augustine to Loyola also dwell on their wickedness, their past and present sins. But those accounts differ from Teresa's in a significant way: they tend to represent the temptations and corruptions of the world of the flesh as feminine. It is through their (and their cultures') gendering of the world-to-be-transcended that these men attempt to maintain a distance from sin. Teresa, in contrast, cannot imagine transcending the world of the flesh in exactly the same way, because she embodies that world by virtue of her femininity;[98] woman's identity under Counter-Reformation patriarchy remained ineluctably endowed with the negative qualities attributed to things female. As Donald Weinstein and Rudolph M. Bell note,

While male saints often were gifted with a special form of clairvoyance that enabled them to sniff out the faintest odor of sin in their fellows, it was woman's part to root out the evil within herself rather than to act as champion of morality and censor of the hidden sins of others. In the world of the spirit as in the world of the flesh, men and women were different and unequal.[99]

In a climate of undeniable misogyny, sixteenth-century Spaniards declared, with humanist Juan Luis Vives, that "woman's thought is rash and, for the most part, inconstant, rambling, and alien." Or, with Luis de Leon, Teresa's first editor, that "woman of her own invention bespeaks weakness, and inconstancy, fickleness, baseness, and little worth." Or, with Teresa herself, that "women's nature is weak, and the self-love which rules in us is very keen." Statements such as the last suggest not simply Teresa's strategic concession to the bigotries of her culture, but also her internalization of them.[100]

Teresa's Teoloxía Mistica and the Rhetoric of Ambivalence

Teresa's response to her own identity as constructed within her culture might best be described as ambivalent; she seems both to embrace and to struggle against the misogyny and racism of sixteenth-century Spain. Not surprisingly, that ambivalence extends beyond women and conversos to various authority figures, as her oblique criticisms of her father and her confessors imply.[101] But perhaps the most interesting suggestion of Teresean ambivalence within the *Vida* emerges in her account of her dealings with God, to her the most loving, but also the most demanding, father of all. At the heart of the *Vida* Teresa explores the ultimate double bind: that the mystical favors from God that function as the ultimate mark of her distinction among other humans simultaneously require of her a profound physical and emotional abasement, a servitude of the will that is figured both as tender love and as metaphoric rape.

In chapter 20 and indeed throughout the *Vida*, Teresa states that the effects of the mystical raptures and other favors she receives from God are not entirely pleasurable—at times, they are far from it:

One of them is the manifestation of the Lord's mighty power: as we are unable to resist His Majesty's will, either in soul or in body, and are not our own masters [no somos señores], we realize that, however irksome this truth may be [mal que nos pese], there is One stronger than ourselves, and that these favours are bestowed by Him, and that we, of ourselves, can do absolutely nothing. This imprints in us great humility. Indeed, I confess that in me it produced great fear—at first a terrible fear. (*LT*, pp. 191–92; *LV*, pp. 78–79)

Here Teresa describes her particular experience of bondage of the will—that of the enraptured soul powerless to struggle against the "mercedes" bestowed on it and terrified by that powerlessness. Though not as blatant a confession of ambivalence as Martin Luther's "I did not love, yes, I hated the righteous God who punishes sinners" (*LW*, 34: 336–37), this discussion of mystical favors in terms of a fruitless struggle to avoid or stop them suggests some resentment toward God on Teresa's part. She complains that "mal que nos pese" ("in spite of ourselves" or, as Peers translates it, "however irksome this truth may be"), "no somos señores" ("we are not our own masters") (*LV*, p. 79; *LT*, p. 192). The line is an ironic one to the extent that "señores" connotes not only divinity and divine mastery, but also masculinity and social rank.[102]

Of resistance to such mystical favors Teresa writes, "It is a terrible struggle, and to continue it against the Lord's will avails very little, for no power can do anything against His" (*LT*, p. 191). Intriguingly, the context for this statement is an account of Teresa's being held down on the ground by other nuns during mass while a rapture takes place. The sexual freight of this narrative of a struggle both bodily and psychic or spiritual would not have been lost upon Teresa's contemporaries; it was recognizable as a highly significant component of her rhetoric of submissiveness.

In no sense did Teresa invent this language of non-mastery, fraught with implications about gender, class, and race; one might point, for example, to the vast precursory tradition viewing humanity and the church as female (the bride) in relation to God or to Christ.[103] Indeed, it was precisely the familiarity of Teresa's metaphors that made them disarming. Thus Teresa's representation of her acceptance of divine favors as the capitulation of a woman to a male master does not obviously challenge sixteenth-century patriarchal relations between the sexes, but instead appears to reify them further. Arguably Teresa's many descriptions of being overcome or mastered by God have a dual function; using Weber's terms, we might say that the force of such statements confirms women's powerlessness and humility in often violently eroticized language, while their effect confirms Teresa's authority as a genuine mystic.

Teresa's stated resistance to mystical gifts and her declarations of pain, uncertainty, and fear concerning them also have a dual rhetorical function. Pursuit of such gifts with open arms might have suggested to the sixteenth-century reader a certain inappropriate (sexual) pleasure or hubris on Teresa's part, inconsistent with the non-mastery and humility she proclaims. And conceivably Teresa may have used these figures to express her dislike of both mystical and nonmystical servitudes of the will—a dislike that conveniently remained invisible in a culture where such female reluctance and deferrals to male force were considered the norm.

The Rhetoric of Joyful Dismemberment

Throughout her exposition in the *Vida* of the four levels of mystical prayer, Teresa uses progressively more exuberant and erotic language to convey the pleasures of such prayer. At the same time, she adopts metaphors of pain, punishment, and dissolution to explain the sublime value and validity of her favors from God. For example, she writes that at the early levels of prayer, the novice generally experiences certain frustrations and aridities. She confesses that she herself would rather have done the severest penance than practice "recogimiento [recollection]" to begin her prayer of union. That recogimiento should be unpleasant and depressing, however, Teresa attributes to the interference of the devil as well as to the bad habits of the person attempting to pray.[104]

In the second stage, the "prayer of quiet," when certain supernatural graces become more plentiful, the fear of failure and loss of favor begin to subside. At this point in her account, Teresa describes in greater detail the psychology of mystical prayer. The powers of the soul begin to disband; its three faculties—memory, reason, and will—are dissociated from one another as it begins to ascend the heights of mystical contemplation. The will alone is occupied as it consents to make itself the captive of God (*LT*, p. 149). However, memory and intellect, marooned in a helpless state, attempt to dis-

tract the will from the union it enjoys. When this happens, Teresa
enjoins the initiate to force the will to ignore the commotion caused
by the other faculties.[105] Nevertheless, the bewilderment of the neglected faculties at this disintegration of the normal organization of
the soul may result in a distress so great that sometimes it is necessary to stop praying for a time.[106]

But despite these potential problems, Teresa insists on the many
bounties of prayer, which she attempts to clarify in her description
of the third level. Mentioning that she had attained this level some
five or six years earlier, Teresa writes:

> O God, what must that soul be like when it is in this state! It would fain be
> all tongue, so that it might praise the Lord. It utters a thousand holy follies,
> striving ever to please Him Who thus possesses it. I know a person who,
> though no poet, composed some verses in a very short time, which were full
> of feeling and admirably descriptive of her pain: they did not come from her
> understanding, but, in order the better to enjoy the bliss which came to her
> from such delectable pain [sabrosa pena], she complained of it to her God.
>
> She would have been glad if she could have been cut to pieces [se de-
> spedazase], body and soul, to show what joy this pain had caused her. (*LT*,
> p. 165; *LV*, pp. 65–66)

Here Teresa refers to herself in the third person as one who would
gladly be dismembered in order to prove exactly how joyful her suffering really is. Psychic dismemberment, Teresa continually suggests,
is an aspect of mystical experience paradoxically generated by
recogimiento, the gathering or recollection of the faculties of the
soul, and by union itself.

In the fourth and most perfect degree of prayer, the soul experiences the highest level of union, which Teresa calls "arrobamiento
[rapture]"; she uses the word "rabto" much less frequently. Again
she employs the language of dismemberment to convey what the soul
would suffer as a testimony of its profound happiness: "The soul is
left so full of courage that it would be greatly comforted if at that
moment, for God's sake, it could be hacked to pieces [la hiciesen
pedazos por Dios]" (*LT*, p. 181; *LV*, p. 73). Teresa reports that once
during union God himself spoke to her about the fragmentation of
her soul in rapture: "It dies to itself wholly [deshácese toda], daughter, in order that it may fix itself more and more upon Me; it is no

longer itself that lives, but I. As it cannot comprehend what it understands, it is an understanding which understands not" (*LT*, p. 179; *LV*, pp. 72–73). The sense of "deshacer" is a broad one, which might be glossed as "to be consumed, destroyed or annihilated."[107] In addition, the word "deshacer" implies that the loss or confounding of identity in union is also an undoing or dissolution, for its connotations as a transitive verb include "to take apart" and "to cut to pieces," and as a reflexive one, "to be crippled" and "to be grievously mistreated." Teresa says here that God himself adopts the metaphor of dismemberment in order to present the mystery of the annihilation of self at the culmination of prayer.

During rapture the soul's transport normally inspires fear; therefore Teresa encourages the person who is proficient in prayer to be unafraid when the soul is carried off to an unknown place. The utter passivity of the soul is in fact what differentiates union from rapture, in that during the latter all powers of resistance are gone. Before it can attempt to help itself, the soul feels itself carried off by something like a cloud or an eagle. Teresa confesses that she is anxious to resist, doing everything in her power to forestall rapture whenever it happens in public (or sometimes even in private). Nevertheless, resistance is impossible: the soul is borne aloft, and at times even the body is lifted off the ground (*LT*, pp. 190–91).

The saint reveals a certain discomfort with levitation, a gift reserved for a very few, but extremely frightening nevertheless. Levitation causes her enormous consternation; it is the aspect of rapture that she feels most inclined to resist. Yet there are dangers to resistance: "When I tried to resist these raptures, it seemed that I was being lifted up by a force beneath my feet so powerful that I know nothing to which I can compare it, for it came with a much greater vehemence than any other spiritual experience and I felt as if I were being torn apart [ansí quedava hecha pedazos]" (*LT*, p. 191; *LV*, p. 90).[108] The feeling of being sundered, Teresa implies, arises from her resistance to the force lifting her off the ground; the aftermath of resistance is physical pain. But in another sense the "pieces" she is torn into are the body and the soul, which she can no longer control, and which seem radically separated from one another. The distress caused by detachment is occasionally so severe, she writes, that sometimes she falls unconscious. Witnesses have described to her the symptoms of her racking torment in this state: her pulse almost stops, her hands become stiff, and her bones seem completely disjointed.

Teresa's rhetoric of violent dismemberment plays a complicated role in what some have called "nuptial mysticism" or "spiritual marriage."[109] Teresa describes her relations with God as supremely blissful. However, her rhetoric of dismemberment bears close examination, if only because it is too often recuperated by her interpreters as yet another mark of the soul's "marriage" to the divine master. To sublimate the erotic and disturbing aspects of Teresa's metaphors is to ignore or obscure her relation to the patriarchal authority of her culture.

Several points can be made about Teresa's erotic and violent rhetoric, specifically her depictions of certain overpowering mystical experiences as akin to figural rape or dismemberment. First of all, Teresa's ambivalent responses to "despedazamiento" and the like function rhetorically as "appropriate" female resistance to divine mastery of her body. Conceivably, those protestations might also be taken seriously as suggestions that Teresa does not entirely enjoy the figural rape and other forms of servitude that she must, as a bona fide mystic, experience. Yet this ironic and possibly unconscious dimension of her rhetoric inevitably remained invisible to her contemporary audience, for whom such protestations indicated not only humility, but also appropriately submissive feminine sexuality. At a time when the Inquisition increasingly condemned mystical favors to women for their sexual and often "demonic" content, Teresa's erotic mysticism survived Inquisition scrutiny—in part, one must suspect, because it was suitably contained by her rhetoric of reluctance and resistance.

Second, we might wonder why Teresa adopted physical and often sexual metaphors to represent divine favors, when those metaphors were potentially problematic both for her and for the Inquisition. For that matter, why did Teresa experience rapture, levitation, and other forms of communication with God both as ecstatic love and as violence against her person? It might be argued that Teresa's mysticism was framed in these terms precisely because those were the terms her culture validated for women's experience of the Divinity. Throughout the early modern period, women more than men tended to represent their experience of God in bodily terms—often, though not exclusively, emphasizing physical suffering.[110]

Third, the rhetoric of dismemberment in Teresa'a *Vida* reflects a certain ambivalence not only toward the Maker (or Unmaker), but also toward Teresa herself, unmade or undone by mystical favors. As a woman and as the descendant of conversos, Teresa certainly experienced a profound ideological violence against her person. The *Vida* obliquely represents that cultural violence directed at her and at others like her, against which she could not easily or directly struggle. Significantly, Teresa's conception and representation of God is violent. But the loving violence wrought by her Divinity is, unlike that of her culture, transforming. If Teresa is undone by the ultimate master, she is at the same time elevated (literally, she claims), remade, and authorized to speak. Such violence redeems her gender and her converso origins, perhaps punishing her for both at the same time, but nevertheless conferring legitimacy on her experiences and on her person.

The Harrowing of Hell

Teresa's complicated attitudes toward the mystical loss of will emerge in her curious description of her visionary descent into Hell (chapter 32). She recalls that at one point during prayer she was fortunate enough to see what her wickedness actually merited. By God's will she was allowed to visit Hell and to see the place that some devils there had been preparing for her. She entered a dark and fetid tunnel to arrive at a tiny space, potentially her final home: "The entrance, I thought, resembled a very long, narrow passage, like a furnace, very low, dark and closely confined; the ground seemed to be full of water which looked like filthy, evil-smelling mud, and in it there were many wicked-looking reptiles. At the end there was a hollow place scooped out of a wall, like a cupboard, and it was here that I found myself in close confinement" (*LT*, p. 301).[111] The horror she saw, however, was pleasant in comparison to what she felt: "To say that it is as if the soul were continually being torn from the body is very little, for that would mean that one's life was being taken by another; whereas in this case it is the soul itself that is tearing itself to pieces [el alma mesma es la que se despedaza]" (ibid.; *LV*, p. 131).

The metaphor of dismemberment, familiar from her descriptions of rapture, seems surprising in the context of her descent into Hell. Here Teresa once again suggests her ambivalence toward rapture or its aftermath by pointing out that damnation and rapture have something in common. However, we may also observe a slight turn in her use of the metaphor. In this case, "el alma mesma es la que se despedaza"—the soul tears itself to pieces. To describe damnation she borrows the metaphor of distress and passivity to explain what the soul inflicts on itself. The saint disguises her ambivalence toward rapture, which she has again disclosed through the description of infernal "despedazamiento," by figuring infernal dismemberment as self-inflicted punishment. Intriguingly, Teresa describes the will of the damned soul (herself, in this scenario) as active, whereas that of the enraptured soul is passive. It is striking that the nonpassivity of the soul is figured here as damnable and *self*-violating. Perhaps Teresa could not represent the active will of the conversa in any other way.

Nevertheless, Teresa's writing of the *Vida* and her search for earthly confirmation of her mystical authority suggest precisely the lack of passivity that is figured both as the cause of her harrowing of Hell (it is her "wicked"—that is, insubordinate—will that temporarily lands her there) and as the effect of Hell (punishment as auto-dismemberment). Certainly Teresa does not overtly regard her writing in this way, given that she begins a writing career with the *Vida* and pursues it relentlessly until her death. However, the ambivalence that emerges in her analysis of the state of the will in rapture ultimately exposes motives for confession more complicated than the desire to facilitate the investigations of her confessors or to declare her own authority. Teresa's search for spiritual advisors through the confessional and through the circulation of the *Vida*, as well as her assertion of mystical authority in her autobiography and later writings, reveal the stamina of the will that she has partially ransomed. But Teresa's profound ambivalence toward her creative and reconstitutive willfulness surfaces continually as the rhetoric of self-mortification and attests to an unresolved psychic conflict.

I have argued that the rhetoric of conversion narratives is necessarily one of mastery—mastery of one's past life, first of all, but mastery, too, of others. In that category of "others" each of these writers prominently situates the reader. Luther addresses his Preface to "pious readers," and implicitly to impious or unfaithful readers as well. Loyola creates throughout his works an elaborate parable of obedience, which he also demands from his audience. Finally, through her *Vida*, Teresa negotiates—principally with male readers such as confessors and inquisitors—for the power to claim authority on the subject of mystical prayer. In each of these cases, the author's will, or desire for mastery, is necessarily in bondage to the reader, partly because readers, by virtue of their political power or their sheer numbers, are capable of bestowing institutional authority on authors. It is the persuasive force of such texts that enables a ransoming of the author's will from bondage to the reader.

I have also used the words "predestination" and "bondage" in other senses, however—especially to indicate what the writer of a confession cannot control, overcome, or transcend. We see in the 1545 Preface, for example, Luther's urge to ransom his texts from death and misinterpretation. A similar anxiety can be found in Loyola's *Autobiography*, to the extent that he envisions an ordered world, a phalanx commanded by God and driven by insistent obedience. Clearly this vision was at odds with the reality of the sixteenth-century world, divided by difference and "disobedience." Finally, though Teresa negotiated with the patriarchal and anti-Semitic power structure of her country, she certainly did not overthrow it, nor did she fundamentally challenge the prevalent "predestined" meanings of sexual and racial difference—a fact that helps account for the canonization of Teresa and her works. Indeed, as Alison Weber has noted, Teresa's "rhetoric of femininity, which served her own needs of self-assertion so successfully, also paradoxically sanctioned the paternalistic authority of the Church over its daughters and re-

inforced the ideology of women's intellectual and spiritual subordi-
nation."[112]

Conversion narratives, then, inevitably confess the impossibility
of mastery even as they insist on it, demanding readers' assent and
approval. A confessional writer creates a spectacle for readers—a
spectacle both in the sense of a "marvel or curiosity" and in that of
"an object or scene regrettably exposed to the public gaze."[113] Lest
we think that this double structure inheres primarily in tales of conversion, let us turn now to what might seem to be a very different
early modern discourse—the scientific, specifically as it is embodied
in the writings of Galileo Galilei. There, too, we shall find a rhetoric of will and of freedom, through which its user strives to ransom
his will from a political and epistemological bind.

Science

Galileo and the Book of Nature

⌒

Scientific Mastery

Toward the close of the first day of Galileo's *Dialogue Concerning the Two Chief World Systems* (Dialogo sopra i due massimi sistemi del mondo) (1632), the character Salviati evaluates the power of human reasoning.[1] First he explains that in relation to the divine mind, man's intellectual powers are extremely limited: "*Extensively*, that is, with regard to the multitude of intelligibles, which are infinite, the human understanding is as nothing even if it understands a thousand propositions; for a thousand in relation to infinity is zero [mille rispetto all'infinità è come un zero]" (*D*, p. 103; *Opere*, 7: 128). In defending not only the Copernican theory but also a relatively new version of scientific analysis, Salviati is careful to admit that there are limits to human reasoning. Clearly no man's mind can rival that of the Divine in terms of the quantity of what can be understood; clearly, too, Salviati is making some attempt not to rub theologians and other potential critics the wrong way with proclamations of scientific hubris.

But after announcing man's cognitive limitations, Salviati declares that those limitations are themselves limited. For in a certain qualitative sense, human knowledge can and does approach a divine state:

But taking man's understanding *intensively*, in so far as this term denotes understanding some proposition perfectly, I say that the human intellect does understand some of them perfectly, and thus in these it has as much absolute certainty as Nature itself has [e ne ha così assoluta certezza, quanto se n'abbia l'istessa natura]. Of such are the mathematical sciences alone; that is, geometry and arithmetic, in which the Divine intellect indeed knows infinitely more propositions, since it knows all. (Ibid.)

Here Salviati makes a broad assertion about the capabilities of human reasoning. In certain cases man reasons, in a word, "perfectly"—as well as God does, just not as often. More importantly, Salviati contends that some people reason more perfectly than others. Those individuals who know geometry and arithmetic are the select few who find themselves in the position to reason perfectly, because the propositions regarding which such reasoning is possible pertain to "the mathematical sciences alone." Salviati refers not to mathematics per se, but to the model of scientific reasoning that Galileo himself helped create.

As numerous historians and philosophers of science have argued, Galileo revolutionized the natural philosophy of his day by placing it on a solid mathematical foundation.[2] In the *Dialogue* Galileo advances a claim to power, both intellectual and political, for the new science—at that time a fairly novel claim, based on the authority of mathematics vis-à-vis that of theology, philosophy, and the other disciplines. Salviati, Galileo's persona in the *Dialogue*, makes very clear what sort of authority the scientist can possess: "But with regard to those few [propositions] which the human intellect does understand, I believe that its knowledge equals the Divine in objective certainty [certezza obiettiva], for here it succeeds in understanding necessity, beyond which there can be no greater sureness" (*D*, p. 103; *Opere*, 7: 129). As we shall see, the authority afforded by a knowledge of "the mathematical sciences" rests on a ground different from those of the other forms of Renaissance mastery we have considered. Galileo also makes far broader claims for scientific mastery than, say, Petrarch does for humanism. Here Galileo promises "certezza obiettiva"; he offers the votaries of science a godlike understanding of "necessity, beyond which there can be no greater sureness."

One hears in Salviati's words the echo of an earlier Renaissance mastery—that of Giovanni Pico della Mirandola, who one hundred fifty years earlier had written a similar paean to the divine potential of the human mind.³ Unlike Pico's, however, Galileo's vision of human divinity is based not on a syncretic knowledge of all the disciplines, but on a highly specialized understanding of natural philosophy and mathematics—a valuation foreshadowing the advent of physics as the master discipline of the sciences.

Whereas Pico's heaven is the mystical abode of God and the angels, Galileo's heaven is the book of divine secrets, the source of supreme and most noble knowledge. It is a book that can be read by humans. In the dedication of his *Dialogue*, Galileo describes that text to his patron Cosimo de' Medici, arguing for the importance of his field of study: "The constitution of the universe I believe may be set in first place among all natural things that can be known, for coming before all others in grandeur by reason of its universal content [universal contenente], it must also stand above them all in nobility as their rule and standard" (*D*, pp. 3–4; *Opere*, 7: 27). Galileo's dialogue is a claim not just for the Copernican system but for the powers of the new science, which, by virtue of its "universal contenente," is the most noble of "all natural things that can be known." The notion of the universality of scientific truth has been an orthodoxy for so long that it is difficult for the twentieth-century reader to imagine the novelty of Galileo's claim for his seventeenth-century audience. For now, let us say that the earth moved with Galileo, moved away from several medieval and Renaissance concepts of mastery toward a relatively new one, the scientific. This ideology of human power that Galileo helped formulate is, of course, far more widely held today. Partly for that reason it is worth considering, once again, Galileo's defense of mathematical science as the most universal, necessary, and objective of knowledges. For Galileo's persuasive rhetoric contributed enormously to the rise of modern science and its gradual establishment as the primary discourse of western culture.⁴

Because Galilean science is founded on a strong voluntarism—what I call here the will to read—it is essential to analyze the writings of Galileo and other early modern scientists in the context of the theories of freedom and predestination then current. It is possible to draw connections, for example, between Galileo's scientific voluntarism and Counter-Reformation theologies of will. Likewise, it is possible to witness the Galilean will to read as an outgrowth of that more optimistic side of Renaissance philosophy, the voluntarist humanism of Pico and of later figures.[5]

More important, perhaps, is the connection between the voluntarism of several strands of twentieth-century science, popularly expressed as a belief in technological progress, and its early modern counterpart. If there is a discourse in the twentieth century that embraces in an undiluted form a Renaissance notion of mastery, that discourse is the scientific. Those visions of human autonomy that for so long have been taken to characterize the early modern worldview typify in certain ways the dominant discourse of our own time.

But, as we have seen with other Renaissance masteries, Galileo's utopian will to read the book of Nature is undermined by an awareness of the limitations of that longed-for freedom, limitations imposed by the linguistic barriers of Nature itself. Galileo's rhetoric of freedom, sometimes swaggering, sometimes sublime, serves to counteract a genuine anxiety about the failure to interpret. For Galileo, science is first and foremost a problem of reading, and his occasional acknowledgments of the seemingly insurmountable obstacles facing the interpreter of celestial motion suggest a hermeneutic determinism at the heart of his will to read.[6]

Galileo's voluntarism, then, is both tenuous and unstable, though at its strongest moments it surfaces in the notion of linguistic mastery. This notion hinges on the existence of a perfectly literal sign system, the geometrical language of Nature. Galileo claims to decipher this language, which is utterly unique in that it *can* be mastered—that is, read definitively. Galileo's struggle to read, then, is framed by problems of the literal and figurative dimensions of language. Special cases of Galileo's struggle against the figurative—specifically, his discovery of the phases of Venus and his famous thought-experiment concerning the tower and the rock—suggest that his claims to read literally and thereby to know are profoundly complicated by intrusions of the figurative within the very language that he claims is unfailingly stable. Other genres of discovery writing, such as the theological, bear some relation to Galileo's rhetoric of discovery.

Whatever the limitations of his claim to read the language of Nature, Galileo succeeds in establishing a theory that scientific discourse is more literal and therefore better than other languages. He does so, in part, by insisting on the utopian dimension of the mathematical language of Nature, thereby writing a new chapter of an old history. In effect, Galileo situates his scientific discourse in the context of an age-old fantasy of human mastery over the figural.

If Galileo's voluntarism is based on a utopian vision of a purely literal language that he can master, then his will to read founders at the barriers of the figurative. Certain more pessimistic episodes in Galileo's texts disclose a sense of the servitude of the scientific will to read. At these moments there appears in Galilean science an analogue of the Lutheran theology of grace. This dialectical discourse on mastery and servitude is relevant to those described in the preceding chapters, and also to the contemporary discourses on freedom within the sciences and humanities.

The Figural and the Literal

There are many accounts of the cultural transformations that took place between the late Middle Ages and the Enlightenment, when the empire of Christianity was gradually and for many reasons displaced by other institutions and discourses, scientific ones in particular. What is fundamental to each of these readings of a breach between faith and reason, or more specifically between religion and science, is the idea of a separation between two modes of thought or ways of reading, an idea that dates back in part to the early modern period.[7]

Formulations of this split originate, not surprisingly, in early modern attempts to distinguish matters scientific—natural philosophy—from theology and moral philosophy. Galileo was one of the first to articulate that split. To defend and legitimize his Copernican views to the Catholic church, he identified as supreme authority not one law—one book—but two. Scripture is the first book, he argues in his 1615 letter to Cristina di Lorena, Grand Duchess of Tuscany and mother of Cosimo de' Medici, his patron; the second "book," he says, is Nature.

Though by no means the first to use the book of Nature metaphor,[8] Galileo gives it a revolutionary turn. The universe is a book "scritto in lingua matematica," he writes in *Il saggiatore* (The as-

sayer) (1623); its "characters are triangles, circles, and other geometric figures without which it is humanly impossible to understand
a single word of it; without these, one wanders about in a dark
labyrinth [senza questi è un aggirarsi vanamente per un oscuro labe-
rinto]."⁹ One might take this statement from the middle of Galileo's
career as a random metaphor, had he not invoked the figure of the
book of Nature and its mathematical alphabet throughout his life.¹⁰
Indeed, the connections between mathematical science and language
were of great significance to Galileo. E. A. Burtt, Alexandre Koyré,
and many others have argued that Galileo's radical innovation was
his insistence that the "language" of science is mathematical.¹¹ These
men do not emphasize, though, that Galileo's theory of mathematics
as the basis of the new science was also a new hermeneutic theory,
by which I mean a theory of interpretation. It is this hermeneutic
breakthrough that I wish to consider in the context of the doctrine of
scientific mastery that Galileo helped cultivate at the end of the Renaissance.

Let us examine Galileo's hermeneutics, then, and ask how
Galilean science reads the book of Nature, for the early modern split
between theology and science can be thought of as a controversy
over what and how people interpret—that is, as a rhetorical controversy. In effect, Galileo proposes two "word systems," one scriptural and figural, the other natural and seemingly literal. It is precisely Galileo's distinction between the literal and figural orders of
meaning that helped establish the terms of scientific discourse for
the next several centuries.

Since the early modern era, science has become the dominant discourse of the West because it claims for itself some version of literal
truth and is seen to back up that claim. From Galileo's time forward,
all other discourses, with the possible exception of philosophy, have
been presumed to be tainted with rhetoric, a manifestation of their
degree of remove from some notion of truth. As John Christie argues, the very suggestion that science might rely on something like
rhetoric to persuade has been automatically "ruled out of court" for
many centuries. "The field of figuration, of rhetoric, of non-literal
persuasion, is firmly fenced off, and large warning notices affixed."¹²
To understand that critical juncture when Renaissance science pos-

ited a theory of meaning distinct from that offered by theology or philosophy, let us focus on Galileo's *word* systems in relation to the *world* systems, the Aristotelian-Ptolemaic and the Copernican, that he compared throughout his life. In so doing we can begin to sketch out the complicated relation between the hermeneutics of Galileo's science and those of theology, whose differences might not be what they seem.

In 1615 Galileo was placed in the awkward position of having to defend to the Roman Inquisition his view that Scripture could be easily reconciled with Copernicanism. Unfortunately, Galileo's letter to the Grand Duchess, widely circulated in Rome, failed to persuade Cardinal Bellarmine and the Holy Office that the hegemonies of Scripture and Nature were separate but equal, and the following year the Inquisition officially condemned the heliocentric theories of Copernicus.[13] The letter to Cristina might be described as secessionist to the extent that Galileo sought to define a domain of scientific inquiry separate from that of theology. In particular, he wanted both to show that the apparently geocentric passages of Scripture, such as Joshua 10, could be reconciled with Copernicanism, and to argue that scriptural pronouncements on Nature should not interfere with scientific investigation. As noted above, Galileo uses hermeneutic terms such as the analogy of the books to frame his distinctions between the two fields of knowledge. In this letter he describes both books, Scripture and Nature, as issuing from the Word of God; the first is the "dictate of the Holy Ghost [dettatura dello Spirito Santo]," and the second is the "observant executrix of God's commands [osservantissima essecutrice de gli ordini di Dio]."[14]

Although both books are equally divine, Galileo contends, their jurisdictions do not overlap significantly. Scripture does not provide the best explanations of problems of natural science, because it is written figuratively: "It is necessary for the Bible, in order to be accommodated to the understanding of every man, to speak many things which appear to differ from the absolute truth [vero assoluto] so far as the bare meaning of the words is concerned."[15] The Bible needs to be intelligible to every mind, however humble. Thus the language of Scripture in a sense distorts the "vero assoluto" in order to be read.

On this last point Galileo's view of biblical figuration more or less squares with orthodox hermeneutics as articulated, for example, by Thomas Aquinas. In the *Summa theologiae* Aquinas defends the figurative language of the Bible against the hypothetical objection that Scripture must be understood as forgoing metaphor and other "similitudes and figures" that necessarily obscure meaning. Aquinas argues that Scripture must be intelligible to humble intellects and that because man's knowledge comes through the senses and sense experience, Scripture relies on figuration, the comparison of divine truths with material things, in order to teach man according to the capacity and function of his intellect. He adds that figuration is necessary to veil the truths of Scripture from mocking unbelievers.[16]

Post-Tridentine theologians, unlike their Protestant counterparts, continued to stress the importance of figuration and allegory in biblical hermeneutics. Of course, their allowance for the possibility of multiple meanings based on patristic precedent did not license the novel biblical interpretations of people like Galileo. As Robert Westman says of the harsh climate after the Council of Trent, "the problem was not biblical literalism but the Scholastic monopoly over theological discourse"[17]; Westman suggests that tight control over biblical exegesis was at least as important to the papacy as was the actual substance of the interpretations.

It is worth noting that against anti-Copernicans arguing for the literal reading of passages such as Joshua 10:12–13, in which Joshua commands the sun to stand still in the middle of the heavens, Galileo claims the status of the literal for his own reading of Scripture. In the letter to Cristina, Galileo argues that the text of Joshua stoops to the limited capacity of the masses by not really explaining the physics of the situation, which was that during the battle of Jericho the sun stopped turning on its axis for several hours, thereby halting the usual movement of the spheres; in that sense it stopped in the midst of the heavens.[18] In this way Galileo maintains both that Scripture is not entirely straightforward and that his own, Copernican interpretation of Joshua is as literal as that of his adversaries—perhaps more so.

In effect, Galileo revives an earlier discussion of figurality and then turns that traditional defense of biblical rhetoric on its ear by suggesting that the pedagogic purpose of metaphor makes Scripture an inaccurate guide to the natural world. The Bible, because it is intended to be read, is not constrained to be accurate. But the book of Nature does not exist to teach or to be read. For that reason, Galileo says, Nature is "inesorabile ed immutabile";

she never transgresses the laws imposed upon her [mai non trascendente i termini delle leggi impostegli], or cares a whit whether her abstruse reasons and methods of operation are understandable to men. For that reason it appears that nothing physical which sense-experience [sensata esperienza] sets before our eyes, or which necessary demonstrations [necessarie dimostrazioni] prove to us, ought to be called in question (much less condemned) upon the testimony of biblical passages which may have some different meaning beneath their words. For the Bible is not chained [legato] in every expression to conditions as strict as those which govern all physical effects; nor is God any less excellently revealed in Nature's actions than in the sacred statements of the Bible.[19]

Because no demands of readability have been placed on Nature, her text should not be interpreted through the ambiguous medium of Scripture. Galileo tropes on Thomistic theology by insisting that man's readings of the book of Nature—not of Scripture, as Aquinas held—are based on sense experience. Surely, he argues, God does not want man to forgo the use of his senses and reason, even when experience or "necessarie dimostrazioni" appear to contradict Scripture.

Like the hypothetical opponent in Aquinas's debate on metaphor, Galileo suggests that figurative language is a problem. Is he then suggesting that Nature, writ inexorably in mathematical characters, is nonfigurative? Yes, I think so; for Galileo, Nature is structured like a language, but it is not rhetorical. Unlike Scripture (or any other text, for that matter), it is bound to nonambiguity. For Galileo and for most scientists after him, Nature's abstruse text offers a stability, a lack of slippage, not found in any other discourse.[20]

That stability does not make Nature easy to read, however. Only specialists, Galileo assures the reader, can translate its language. Thus those select few who work with this text claim something of its authority. Galileo argues in the letter to Cristina that the Copernican hypothesis has been confirmed by "manifeste esperienze e necessarie dimostrazioni."[21] Though he does not actually offer any "necessary demonstrations" in the letter, he does propose that scientific discourse, based on empirical discoveries of the mathematical laws of Nature, is more authoritative on questions of physical reality than is the Bible or any other text—precisely because the language of Nature is not afflicted with figuration, with rhetoric. If reading Nature involves translating empirical data ("manifest experiences") into mathematical characters (general laws), that decoding process is still for Galileo nonfigurative.

What Galileo understood by "necessary demonstrations" and whether he believed that he had them for the Copernican hypothesis are, of course, separate issues. Most critics, however, are willing to give Galileo the benefit of the doubt; whatever his method happened to have been—and, as discussed below, there is surprisingly little consensus on that issue—his arguments continue to be understood as scientific in either a qualitative or a quantitative way. But what is early modern science? Galileo was one of the first to define it, and his elusive definition still survives: science is the nonrhetorical.

The Round and Rather Small Figure of Venus

If science is nonrhetorical, irrefutably literal, then it does not have to depend on or appeal to mere rhetoric, the apparatus of persuasion. Science is above persuasion in that it is not constrained to be intelligible, though it does persuade in a nonfigurative fashion. The truth of manifest experience, as opposed to the rhetoric of other discourses, is that which to Galileo's mind should make science compelling.

The irony of the supposed persuasive power of the literal, of course, is that (to Galileo's frustration) it cannot persuade everyone. As he writes to his protégé Benedetto Castelli in December of 1610 concerning the latter's observations of the phases of Venus:

You almost made me laugh by saying that with these manifest observations one could convince the obstinate. You know, then, that to convince those who are capable of reason and wanting to know the truth, the demonstrations brought forth earlier were enough. But to convince the obstinate, who don't care for anything but the empty approval of the stupid and dense crowd, the testimony of the very stars, descended to earth in order to explain themselves, would not be enough [non basterebbe il testimonio delle medesime stelle, che sciese in terra parlassero di sé stesse]. (*Opere*, 10: 503–4; my translation)

Here Galileo points out the nonpersuasiveness of manifest proof, "the testimony of the very stars." However, he also discusses in this letter his own "clear observations" of Venus, as if his discoveries of its phases further substantiate the Copernican hypothesis, at least for the nonobstinate: "Know then that about three months ago I began to observe Venus with the instrument, and I saw her round and rather small figure [e la vidi di figura rotonda, e assai piccola]" (*Opere*, 10: 503; my translation). It is striking that the planet is for Galileo a "figura." Though presumably he means "figure" in the nonrhetorical sense, it was precisely the "figurative" dimension of his claims that invalidated Galileo's arguments in the minds of certain of his contemporaries. Francesco Sizi, for example, argued that Galileo's telescopic sightings, publicized in the *Siderius nuncius* (1610), were nothing but illusions. One variety of telescopic illusion, he claimed, involved the substitution of a preconceived notion for the actual image.[22] Sizi described, in effect, a rhetorical phenomenon contaminating sensory experience—a form of physical metonymy, the substitution of a concept for the experience itself. In Sizi's terms, Galileo's Venus would be a figure for something not yet named or even observed, a figure that bears no necessary resemblance to the literal, unperceived reality.

Because Sizi and other critics of Galileo have long been discredited, one might be tempted also to dismiss their tropology, the possible figurative dimensions of the empirical. After all, Galileo's observations were not illusory, we believe; therefore he presumably did not substitute an idea (a figure) for a thing. Richard Westfall, however, has argued that it is likely that Galileo had not actually observed the phases of Venus when he sent his famous anagram to the court of the emperor in Prague cryptically announcing his "discovery" concerning those phases. Westfall argues that Galileo prematurely claimed to have discovered the phases of Venus only when Castelli pointed out to him the implications of such a find.[23] Thus, even if we judge Galileo right and his seventeenth-century detractors wrong, it is still possible that Galileo based one of his most interesting claims on, quite literally, a figure of Venus—that is, as Sizi said, a preconceived notion.

If Westfall's theory is true, then Galileo's hermeneutics of Nature does not necessarily work in the way he claims it does. For Galileo did not read the text of Nature "literally" if and when he initiated his discovery through the figurative—through an idea of what he expected to find, substituted metonymically for the empirical base, the "manifest experiences," that supposedly grounded his interpretation. Galileo's "word system," then, bears a resemblance to theological hermeneutics laden with figurality, for in a certain sense the book of Nature, as translated through the language of empirical data, is also complicated by figuration.

But suppose that Galileo really did move from observation to hypothesis regarding the phases of Venus, that he really studied the planet for many months and reached an astonishing conclusion that had not occurred to him before—would this order of reading be literal and nonmetonymic? One might argue that at least hypothetically there is a form of "correct reading" of the book of Nature, corresponding to the "vero assoluto." If, however, we accept Norwood Hanson's now-standard argument that all perception is "theory-laden," then there is no such thing as an unmediated perception or interpretation of Nature.[24] According to this view, there is no way to read the "text" of Nature—that is, the empirical data—without interpreting that text through whatever conceptual framework one brings to it. The very act of perception is thus metonymic, to the extent that one cannot but impose one's "figures" onto the "literal" book of Nature.[25]

Galileo's interpretations of Nature thus rely on a rhetoric of metonymy, a problem of reading that his hermeneutics does not acknowledge. There is a distinction between the literal text of Nature and the not-so-empirical figure of Nature that Galileo constructs. Though Galileo claims that the text of Nature is "chained" and unambiguous, what is it that chains his readings to the text? "Manifest experiences" and "necessary demonstrations" are not, perhaps, as literally empirical as he asserts. This ambiguity reproblematizes the split between science and theology established in Galileo's letter to Cristina di Lorena; we must ask again how scientific discovery (Galileo's hermeneutics of Nature) differs from, for example, theological "discovery."

If Galileo's natural language not only works the same way that theological language does—namely, figuratively—but *is* in some sense theological language, then we have to think of his conversion to the Copernican view a bit differently. Perhaps scientific discovery is not *like* a religious, political, ideological, or linguistic conversion experience; it *is*, perhaps, all of those.

Compare Galileo's discovery of the phases of Venus to one of the religious "discoveries" discussed in Chapter 3. In the 1545 Preface to his Latin writings, Martin Luther describes what made him look at the world/Word differently in the years immediately preceding the Reformation. He explains that 30 years earlier he had felt oppressed by the traditional interpretation of key passages of the New Testament, and that this feeling of oppression had inspired in him a hatred of God. Nevertheless, he had continued to ponder the meaning of Paul's Epistle to the Romans and eventually discovered the possibility of a very different interpretation of Romans 1:17, "In it the righteousness of God is revealed [Iustitia Dei revelatur in illo]." Luther explains that he developed his theology of justification by faith—the fundamental doctrine of the Protestant Reformation—from the idea that man is redeemed not by good works, but by the divine gift of grace. Having recognized a new way to understand divine authority and man's relation to it, Luther then describes a chain reaction of discoveries as he runs through the Scriptures by memory: "There a totally other face of the entire Scripture showed itself to me. Thereupon I ran through the Scriptures from memory" (*LW*, 34: 337). After his hermeneutic breakthrough, Luther's thinking undergoes a "paradigm shift," to borrow Thomas Kuhn's phrase, through which he is made to see "a totally other face of the entire Scripture."

We might think there are obvious differences between Luther's rhetorical discovery and Galileo's empirical one. One man looks at the "face" of Scripture and "sees" differently; the other looks at the "figure" of Venus and "really" sees differently. But what is the actual difference between the two changes in perception? Is one necessarily more empirical than the other?

Certainly there are rhetorical similarities between the two conversion scenes. One man rejoices at reinterpreting a figure of speech; the other rejoices at reinterpreting a supposedly real figure. They both recognize chains of implications for their discoveries, implications upon which entire theological and scientific systems are based. They both feel vindicated by their discoveries. Could we say that Galileo's discovery is like a religious conversion, by which I mean here a rhetorical conversion, a way of reading a trope differently?

One might even argue that Galileo adopts and recasts the rhetoric of religious conversion, an originary genre of "discovery" writing. The rhetorical continuities between religious and scientific narratives are striking. Just as Foucault claims that the insane asylum assumed the social structure once characteristic of leprosaria,[26] so might one argue that science in many ways appropriates—though not necessarily deliberately or consciously—the structures of theological discourse.

Cases of literary borrowing are always interesting, but they are especially so with Galileo, who, we remember, attempted in the letter to Cristina and throughout his life to separate scientific from theological discourse. Galileo claims for science the privilege of nonfigurality, in a sense arguing that because that language is self-evident, it is superior to (nonliteral) persuasion. Of course, the matter of evidence—of what constituted proof, demonstration, and certainty for Galileo—is precisely the focus of intense controversy among philosophers of science, as we shall see.

A Narrative of Many Figures

Let us turn now to Galileo's most extended "reading" of the book of Nature, the *Dialogue Concerning the Two Chief World Systems*, in order to understand how Galileo undertook a presumably literal interpretation of Nature. There is much debate over whether Galileo thought that he had presented a "necessary demonstration" of the Copernican theory here—that is, incontrovertible proof of the earth's movement around the sun.

There are hundreds of views of Galileo's method; I will consider here just a few of the more recent assessments. Though Galileo, unlike Descartes and Newton, did not put forward a clear account of his scientific method, Stillman Drake argues that such a method can be extracted from the early *Trattato della sfera* (1602). There Galileo suggests four components of scientific discovery: sensed phenomena, hypotheses, geometric demonstrations, and arithmetic operations (such as the calculation of tables). Drake holds that this method, though somewhat inchoate, is the mark of Galileo's descriptive and qualitative science, which was quite contrary to the approaches of most of his contemporaries.[27]

Martha Fehér argues that Galileo accepted the Aristotelian ideal of scientific knowledge, which holds that "vera scientia" consists of necessary truths "which convey that which could not be otherwise," and that knowledge gained from observation remains "opinio" unless "demonstrated from *self-evident* principles." But, she argues, Galileo swerved from the time-honored Peripatetic method of scientific proof based on the *Posterior Analytics* in that he rejected syllogistic proof of metaphysical causes in favor of reasoning based on geometric law.[28] Fehér also contends that the theory of the tides advanced in day four of the *Dialogue* constituted for Galileo precisely the geometrical demonstration of the Copernican hypothesis that he had long sought.[29] Albert Einstein makes a similar point in his foreword to Drake's translation of the *Dialogue*: "It was Galileo's longing for a mechanical proof of the motion of the earth that misled him into formulating a wrong theory of the tides. The fascinating arguments in the last conversation would hardly have been accepted as proofs by Galileo, had his temperament not got the better of him" (*D*, p. xvii).

In contrast, William Wallace has argued both that Galileo's notion of scientific demonstration was thoroughly Aristotelian and not particularly path-breaking as method, and that Galileo did not intend to offer a "necessary demonstration" of the Copernican system in his *Dialogue*. Wallace suspects that the intrepid Galileo who claimed in the letter to Cristina to possess the necessary demonstrations demanded by Cardinal Bellarmine was confident that proof of the earth's movement and the sun's immobility would soon be forthcoming. But in 1632 Galileo still lacked that proof, which is one reason he wrote his monumental defense of the Copernican system in the form of a dialogue.[30]

In a similar vein, Jean Moss has argued that Galileo did not believe he had found the kind of mechanical proof he needed to support the heliocentric theory. In a note on the flyleaf of his copy of the *Dialogue*,[31] Galileo wrote:

Take note, theologians, that in your desire to make matters of faith out of propositions relating to the fixity of the sun and earth you run the risk of eventually having to condemn as heretics those who would declare the earth to stand still and the sun to change position—eventually, I say, at such a time as it might be physically or logically proved that the earth moves and the sun stands still [col tempo, dico, quando sensatamente o necessariamente si fusse dimostrato, la Terra muoversi e 'l (Sole) star fisso].[32]

From this passage Moss argues that Galileo knew after publishing the *Dialogue* that he still did not have the proof he had hoped for, but that one day such proof would be discovered.

Clearly the Inquisition, which tried and condemned Galileo in 1633 for continuing to hold and teach "that the earth moves and the sun stands still," was less interested in what Galileo thought he had said in the *Dialogue* than what its panel of experts believed they had found there. The readers who reported to the Inquisition during the trial found that Galileo made his assertions in the *Dialogue* "in a categorical, absolute, and nonhypothetical manner" and that he used "unconditional arguments" rather than hypothetical ones.[33] "The flaw in Galileo's case for Copernicus," Moss contends, "was his own use of persuasion to fill the lacunae where proof was still not available."[34] In other words, Moss argues, it was the rhetoric of proof that got Galileo into trouble.

A still more radical theory of Galileo's rhetoric of persuasion is advanced by Paul Feyerabend in *Against Method*. Feyerabend contends that Galileo ignored the methods of scientific reasoning then prevalent in order to defend Copernicanism on grounds that were not, strictly speaking, rational. This nonmethod, which he calls counterinduction, relies on "hypotheses that contradict well-confirmed theories and/or well-established experimental results." Furthermore, Feyerabend contends that Galileo's defense of Copernicanism in the

Dialogue hinges on "psychological tricks" and a manipulative rhetoric of persuasion.[35] We will consider Feyerabend's theory in greater detail shortly.

Rejecting the pigeonholing instincts of most philosophers of science vis-à-vis Galileo's method, Maurice Finocchiaro argues that "there is evidence that Galileo was a counterinductivist, *and* an Aristotelian, *and* a Platonist, *and* an empiricist, *and* a rationalist." Finocchiaro also argues that Galileo did not claim that his *Dialogue* constituted a "necessary demonstration" of Copernicanism so much as a set of strong arguments for the earth's motion. Thus Galileo is a "hypothetical probabilist"—that is, something like a modern scientist. Rejecting Feyerabend's assertion that Galileo relies primarily on propaganda, emotional manipulation, and other rhetorical tricks to make his points in the *Dialogue*, Finocchiaro insists on the logical core of Galilean science. And although he wants to assimilate certain notions of rhetoric and aesthetics into his model of scientific reasoning, Finocchiaro seems to maintain the traditional logocentric distinction between the rational and the rhetorical.[36]

It is not remarkable, perhaps, that historians and philosophers of science disagree over what Galileo may have meant by incontrovertible proof and over whether or not he thought he had found it. What is remarkable is that science and the humanities continue to be understood as separate disciplines, given that discussions of textual ambiguity and of the status of rhetoric are central to both. Indeed, each theory of Galilean proof discussed above relies explicitly or implicitly on the notion that these disciplines are separate. Let us consider once again the borders between science and the more "rhetorical" disciplines—theology, philosophy, and, of course, rhetoric itself. Let us bear in mind, too, that Galileo was among the first to reconfigure those borders around the new science.

Ridiculing Aristotelian natural science, or at least the character Simplicio's reliance on it, Salviati says on the first day of the *Dialogue*, "It would have been better for [Aristotle] to leave these subtleties to the rhetoricians, and to prove his point by rigorous demonstrations such as are suitable to make in the demonstrative sciences" (*D*, p. 11). What Salviati seems to be advocating as "rigorous demonstration" is a kind of proof based on both mathematical deduction and empirical evidence, as opposed, most likely, to the proof afforded by Aristotelian syllogistic reasoning. Though Simplicio argues back that mathematical demonstration is not always necessary in natural philosophy, Salviati and Sagredo affirm here and throughout the *Dialogue* that the demonstrative sciences must rely on mathematical proof wherever possible. Their insistence on mathematics as the new ground of science represents a genuine shift in Renaissance epistemology—one that owes a great deal to Jesuit science of the sixteenth century.[37]

Against the "rigorous demonstrations" of the Copernicans, Salviati continually opposes the sloppy and merely rhetorical arguments of their opponents. For example, when Simplicio produces a series of questions from an anti-Copernican treatise, Salviati responds:

As to the terrestrial globe being between Venus and Mars, let me say one word about that. You yourself, on behalf of this author, may attempt to remove it, but please let us not entangle these little flowers of rhetoric [questi fioretti rettorici] in the rigors of demonstration [la saldezza delle dimostrazioni]. Let us leave them rather to the orators, or better to the poets, who best know how to exalt by their graciousness the most vile and sometimes even pernicious things. (*D*, pp. 268–69; *Opere*, 7: 293).

Here Salviati revives with Platonic condescension an ancient prejudice against the merely rhetorical, discounting the opponents of the Copernican system for their lack of rigor. Salviati also casts aspersions on their morality—and even on their masculinity, if one detects in the diminutive "fioretti" a certain "odor di femina." Further evidence of this last point might be drawn from Salviati's contrasting of these "fioretti" with "la saldezza delle dimostrazioni"; Drake's "the rigors of demonstration" might be translated more literally as "the solidness of demonstration," which has a certain manly ring.[38]

The fact remains, as Feyerabend and others have persuasively argued, that Salviati does not have answers to all of the anti-Copernican questions raised in the *Dialogue*, some of which are quite reasonable. It seems clear that Galileo relies on the flowers of rhetoric as much as his opponents do. Feyerabend suggests that Galileo relies exclusively on counterinduction and rhetoric (and that it is reasonable for him to do so), whereas Finocchiaro and most others hold that rhetoric merely supplements Galilean reason. I would like to frame the discussion a bit differently, though, by asking the basic deconstructive question: Is it necessary for modern readers of Galileo to accept his Platonic division of reality into the literally true and the rhetorical?[39] To address this question, we must consider the complicated relation of "necessary demonstration" and rhetoric.

One of the main complaints lodged by the anti-Copernican Simplicio in the *Dialogue* is that sensory evidence—"the facts"—seems to contradict the notion of the earth's diurnal motion. When one looks at the stars, it seems that they are moving around the earth, not that the earth is moving. Moreover, one cannot feel the earth's motion. If Copernican astronomers rely on sensory data—as they claim to do—Simplicio wonders how they account for a lack of the most fundamental empirical evidence, namely, some physical sense or visual proof that the earth moves. Attempting to account for why the earth's diurnal motion cannot be felt, the three dialogists discuss the famous tower argument, which goes something like this: If one drops a rock off the top of a tower, why doesn't it land somewhere behind the tower, left behind by the moving earth? Salviati answers that question by pointing out that all objects on the earth, including the rock, the tower, and the viewer, share the earth's motion, and for that reason cannot feel it: "We never see anything but the simple downward [motion], since this other circular one, common to the earth, the tower, and ourselves, remains imperceptible and as if nonexistent. Only that of the stone, not shared by us, remains perceptible; and of this our senses show that it is along a straight line always parallel to a tower which is built upright and perpendicular on the surface of the earth" (*D*, p. 163).

In defense of this idea of shared motion Sagredo offers an illustrative comparison: If one were to take a boat trip from Venice to Alexandretta, and if one were able to draw a line of the voyage with a special pen, "what trace—what mark—what line would it have left?" (*D*, p. 172). The line, Simplicio answers, would reflect the motion of the boat over the curved surface of the water—it would be a slightly imperfect and very long arc. In contrast, Sagredo argues, if a person on the boat were drawing a picture, the circular motion of the boat over the water would not affect the artist or distort the picture. Sagredo's point is that just as the artist, the pen, and the paper share the boat's motion, all occupants of the earth share its motion and are uniformly affected. Rather curiously, Sagredo says that this shipboard artist "would have been able to derive from the pen's motion a whole narrative of many figures [un'intera storia di molte figure], completely traced and sketched in thousands of directions, with landscapes, buildings, animals, and other things" (*D*, p. 172; *Opere*, 7: 198).

Here Galileo justifies his theory of motion figuratively—that is, with an example that works metonymically, substituting a description of the boat's motion for a demonstration of the earth's motion. It is also striking that Galileo's great defense of the nonfigurative language of nature and experience illustrates that language with a story of drawing a story: Sagredo describes the shipboard art as "a whole narrative of many figures." Sagredo's figure is about figurality, which is appropriate for a dialogue on two word/world systems, the figurative and the literal. These systems are not so much two ways of organizing planets as two ways of reading and two kinds of language.

Galileo wants to vindicate something that is like a language but is better than a language (in the usual sense) because it is unambiguous and nonrhetorical. That something-like-a-language persuades (at least, it persuades some persons) by virtue of its literal truth, not by the manipulations of rhetoric. Given that Galileo thus condemns rhetoric, let us consider how the sort of rhetorical reasoning used in the boat passage squares with his concept of science as both mathematical and to some extent empirical.

Feyerabend describes such passages as rhetorical tricks, as the sort of propaganda Galileo typically uses to defend the Copernican system. The description of the shared motion of the artist, the pen, the paper, and the boat does not prove the motion of the earth. Galileo surreptitiously generalizes, says Feyerabend, from the commonsense case of nonoperative motion to a larger theory of the earth's motion.[40] Also, instead of pointing out that the approach to the tower question in the *Dialogue* is radically new and contrary to experience (not to mention method), Galileo "wants to persuade us that no change has taken place, that the second [Copernican] conceptual system is already universally *known*, even though it is not universally *used*." Feyerabend dubs this rhetorical strategy anamnesis, the "remembering" of what one has supposedly known all along. In the *Dialogue* anamnesis serves "as a psychological crutch, as a lever which smooths the process of subsumption by concealing its existence. As a result we are now ready to apply the relative notions not only to boats, coaches, birds, but to the 'solid and well-established earth' as a whole. And we have the impression that this readiness was in us all the time, although it took some effort to make it conscious."[41] Feyerabend's point is not that Galileo's mode of argument is sloppy or wrong, but rather that the tower argument doesn't work the way Galileo says it does. Feyerabend believes that science works best and progresses most with this kind of unruly, rhetorical, and "unscientific" thinking. He asserts, too, that new theories necessarily go against some of "the facts," which are themselves partly ideological in hidden ways. In Galileo's case, "the facts" to be dismantled included then obvious and commonsense theories of motion. By reasoning counterinductively, by ignoring "the facts," and by imagining a vastly different universe, Galileo was able to persuade others of the great conceptual displacements implied by Copernican astronomy.

Feyerabend may be an anarchist, but he is not, ultimately, a relativist; he argues, after all, that "variety of opinion is necessary for objective knowledge."[42] Thus even for Feyerabend, reality and rhetoric seem to remain separate categories. It was in the name of some authentic, though seemingly far-flung and nonempirical, insight that Galileo tried to persuade anti-Copernicans to ignore the facts of motion as they were understood in the seventeenth century, and it was in order to get at reality and objective knowledge that he persuaded himself to think counterinductively. Feyerabend seems to retain, in spite of himself, the traditional view of rhetoric as supplemental (in the non-Derridean sense). That is, according to his reading, rhetoric, or the figural dimension of language in general, may be used to support or supplement one's understanding of the literal. For Feyerabend, what counts in science is not how you get there, but that you get there. And the "there" is real and somehow distinct from the foggy dimension of rhetoric.

I accept Feyerabend's premise that the boat example and others like it are rhetorical, and that Galileo relies on a rhetoric of persuasion rather than on empirical or mathematical proof to defend the new astronomy. I would like to make a different point, though, about the status of rhetoric in the *Dialogue* and in Galilean science in general—namely, that the distinction between science and rhetoric can be further critiqued. We have questioned the Galilean distinction (still widely held) between these two categories; now let us question the valuations ascribed to each of them.

As we recall from the letter to Cristina, Galileo explains the differences between the language of science and other kinds of language in qualitative terms. He asserts that all reality is linguistic, insofar as it is the product of the divine Word. The book of Nature has the singular advantage of being literal, of revealing the Word without the ambiguities of that other great divine text, Scripture. Galileo's description of the two books is, of course, a claim to power. The substance of his claim to a superior knowledge, science, is that science is a nonrhetorical narrative and the most reliable hermeneutic method known to man—in fact, the only reliable method, which only a select few (like Galileo) possess.

Now let us return to the second day of the *Dialogue*. In the tower discussion Galileo represents the language of experience, the realm of "rigorous demonstrations" and even of thought-experiments, in the same way that he claims in the letter to Cristina that the language of Scripture does. That is, he draws conclusions from experience by *drawing* conclusions from experience—in other words, by creating a "whole narrative of many figures." It is not just that Galileo advances a worldview through narrative, as does the Bible. What emerges from readings like Feyerabend's is that in a fundamental sense Galileo's rhetoric works the same way as Scripture— or any other interpretation, for that matter. In other words, Galileo's presentation is structured as a system of substitutions, examples that stand metonymically for the larger "whole"—the complex realities of motion that his mathematical idealizations aim to describe. There is no way that Galileo can have direct empirical or intuitive knowledge of the motion of the earth; he cannot feel it, see it, or experience it. He can only construct a theory that explains why sensory experience does not substantiate the Copernican hypothesis, illustrating that theory with the example of the tower, and in turn clarifying that illustration with the story of the shipboard artist. We might call this hermeneutic process reasoning by metonymy.

The correctness of Galileo's heliocentrism is not at stake, though, nor is its "logic," however we define it. What is at stake is the status of the language of mathematical science. The most significant feature of Galilean science is not so much the truth of its account of the natural order as its evaluative claim to a superior form of truth against which other knowledges, other "certainties," pale. Perhaps Galileo's greatest contribution to science was not his defense of the Copernican system, but his inspired strategies for writing off competing knowledges, rival epistemologies (such as theology and metaphysics), by subtly and regularly dismissing them as merely rhetorical, as less rigorous and less reliable interpretations of the divine Word—the ultimate ground of all seventeenth-century knowledges. If so-called rhetorical disciplines involve forms of argument in many ways indistinguishable from those of the "rigorous" disciplines (particularly science), then the reason/rhetoric split implied by each of the philosophers of science discussed above becomes even more problematic.

That split is questionable, of course, because Galileo argues that his "literal" interpretation of the book of Nature is qualitatively different from interpretations of Scripture and other sorts of books—books laden with the ambiguities of rhetoric and figural language. Galileo's claim for the superiority of the scientific hermeneutics is predicated on its truth—or more precisely, on its degree of truth. In the passage quoted at the beginning of this chapter, Salviati speaks of the objective certainty afforded by the mathematical sciences, a certainty that endows the human mind with a kind of divinity. In this assertion Galileo obscures a claim to power with a claim to know. Even if the claim to understand celestial motion is in any sense more necessary or universal than, for example, the claim to know how to make ice cream, the valuations attached to those claims are, to say the least, contingent. In other words, there is no absolute reason why humans should value one knowledge more than another, as Barbara Smith and Jean Baudrillard have so persuasively argued.[43]

My point is that there are vast differences between the claim that the earth moves and the claim that science provides the knower with "objective certainty," a form of knowledge necessarily better than all others. It is essential to recognize the political implications of Galilean hermeneutics, which offers a powerful ideology of mastery still very much in effect in western technocracies. For Galileo's understanding of the book of Nature, his Picoesque insistence on the will to know and to embrace the "divinity" conferred by such understanding, offers the promise of power/knowledge still vaunted by the sciences.[44] We see in Galileo's writing the extraordinary optimism we have come to think of as Renaissance. That hopefulness is founded on a voluntarism, on the idea that knowledge and control are attained by the will to know. And Galileo's utopian notion of mastery rises from his theory of language, a Platonic fantasy of an escape from rhetoric.

Given that Galileo in effect discredits writing except in its purified and nonfigurative form (the geometric language of the book of Nature), it is quite striking that he chooses to end the first day of the *Dialogue* with a paean to the invention of writing. When Salviati proclaims again the divinity of the human mind, with its remarkable capabilities, Sagredo then confesses that he feels inadequate, not just in relation to God, but in relation to other humans—specifically, Michelangelo, Leonardo, and Raphael. Discussing the various accomplishments of artists, poets, architects, and navigators, Sagredo proceeds to praise the creator of writing:

But surpassing all stupendous inventions, what sublimity of mind was his who dreamed of finding means to communicate his deepest thoughts to any other person, though distant by mighty intervals of place and time! Of talking with those who are in India; of speaking to those who are not yet born and will not be born for a thousand or ten thousand years; and with what facility, by the different arrangements of twenty characters upon a page.

Let this be the seal of all the admirable inventions of mankind and the close of our discussions for this day. (*D*, p. 105)

In this utopian description of that "admirable invention," Galileo suggests that human mastery is demonstrated most definitively through writing. Writing, more than the other example of the creative will, confers a sort of immortality on the communicator. Interestingly, this vision of writing admits of no erosions of meaning, no ambiguities, no historical contingencies, for here the will to speak across spatial and temporal voids is triumphant.

Clearly Galileo circumscribes his model of scientific inquiry with a theory of the will to master language, to read and to write. Still, Sagredo sounds a note of anxiety in this passage; after all, his paean gives an account of what he himself is not—a great artist, a poet, or the sublime inventor of writing. Arguably Galileo speaks of his own creative belatedness here—where does science fit in with the prior human achievements listed by Sagredo? Still, though Galileo himself cannot claim to have invented language, he certainly claims to have reinvented it, or to have discovered its true potential. Galileo professes to have mastered the most perfect language of all, one unfamiliar to these artistic precursors.

Utopian Language Theory

Galileo's notion of the book of Nature as mathematical is yet another version of the utopian hermeneutics that crops up from time to time, advertising a mode of reading without loss or slippage. His notion of scientific language bears some resemblance to earlier Renaissance theories of language before Babel—that is, originary language.[45] Just as Renaissance linguists thought that through divine inspiration Adam conferred ideal names on the objects he encountered in Paradise, names that embodied the essences of the things named, Galileo advances a language of Nature that reflects an ideal similitude between the signifiers (circles, triangles, and other mathematical characters) and the signified (the hidden workings of Nature). But according to these Renaissance theories of language, the unities of Adam's language were all but destroyed after Babel, lingering only in fragments within the Hebrew tongue. In contrast, Galileo implies that the unities in scientific language have yet to be fully elucidated. Galileo updates the utopian hermeneutics of earlier centuries and removes them from their theological setting.

The difference between Galileo's theory of signs and any earlier one is, of course, that most people still believe in Galileo's theory, or something like it. Science survives as the dominant discourse because it claims a hermeneutic authority presumably lacking in other discourses. Its relation to the history of theological writing, and its problematic relation to the question of figurality in general, must remain veiled if its utopian quality—the source of the persuasive power of any discourse—is to remain intact.

And to whom does Galileo address this utopian appeal? Who reaps the benefits of this unfallen language, the pristine and unmediated vocabulary of mathematical characters? Galileo implies throughout his works that the entire world stands to profit from a greater understanding of the divine language of science. In the letter to Cristina he writes: "Who indeed will set bounds to human ingenuity [e chi vuol por termine alli umani ingegni]? Who will assert that everything in the universe capable of being perceived is already discovered and known?" The flavor of this passage is decidedly Picoesque, in that Galileo, like his utopian precursor, sees virtually unlimited potential for "umani ingegni." How could the Vatican establishment disapprove, he suggests, when Scripture itself teaches in a hundred passages that "the glory and greatness of Almighty God are marvelously discerned in all his works and divinely read in the open book of heaven [divinamente si legge nell'aperto libro del cielo]"?[46] Here Galileo transmutes the book of Nature into "the open book of heaven," a book that magnifies the Divinity. How can men and women, then, refuse to read?

As Fredric Jameson has argued, "the effectively ideological is also, at the same time, Utopian,"[47] which is to say that theories justifying the interests and privileges of a particular class must necessarily, as proof of "collective solidarity," represent those interests as universal and universally beneficial. Let us consider the utopian dimension of Galileo's language theory in the context of the specific class interests it represents—in other words, in terms of a more pragmatic understanding of the will to read.

Galileo's fight with the Catholic church over intellectual freedom (as he casts it in the letter to Cristina, for example) must also be viewed as a struggle between classes—or, in this case, between more and less empowered factions of the cultural elite. Galileo vaunts the language of Nature (that is, of science) as a universal language, a utopian language bound to the "vero assoluto." Tactfully, though not tactfully enough for his adversaries, Galileo represents the interests of his subclass—the Lincei and other wellborn, educated, but in some ways unempowered men—as universal ones.

At the same time, he identifies the opponents of these interests in his letter to Cristina, in the *Dialogue*, and in virtually all his other writings. Galileo's hermeneutics, meant to empower him and others who subscribe to it, exists differentially; it also serves to undo the hermeneutic theories of his rivals. Explaining the utopian dimensions of ideology further, Jameson states, "In a fragmented social life—that is, essentially in all class societies—the political thrust of the struggle of all groups against each other can never be immediately universal but must always necessarily be focused on the class enemy."[48] It was precisely the class enemies of Galileo—most Jesuits, the Holy Office, academics of the old school—who moved to silence him when he articulated his interests against theirs. The outcome of that struggle we know well: Galileo lost, though only in the short run.

It is the nature of ideological conflict to stress difference rather than similarity; thus the connections between seventeenth-century science and theology seem obscure, particularly from the temporal remove of several centuries. Yet these discourses overlap in significant ways, both in terms of how they claim authority (their narratology), and in terms of what authority they claim. In other words, Galileo's science and the theologies of his day in many ways share the rhetoric of mastery, as well as an interest in the kinds of mastery claimed by that rhetoric. They share, too, an awareness of the limitations on human power to know the world, truth, or the mind of God. At the risk of appearing to collapse very substantial distinctions between what we take today to be radically different types of knowledge or belief, I wish to examine the common ground between Galilean science and the theologies discussed in the previous chapters. Not surprisingly, twentieth-century critical theorists in certain ways share this interest, which concerns a theory of human volition, its powers and its limits.

Predestinarian Science

In the *Dialogue* Galileo addresses the question of will obliquely, and generally in a nontheological context. Still, it is possible to dis-cern in certain of his statements elements of a "predestinarian" science—that is, a determinism governing not just the functions of the physical world, but also man's will to discover those functions. These elements might seem to contradict the orthodox Catholic beliefs usually attributed to Galileo, as well as the voluntarist rhetoric that permeates his work. But such contradictions typify every theory of will we have considered so far. Let us examine how Galileo's theories of will are bound up with the masteries of early modern science, for these theories resonate with other (humanist, theological, feminist) accounts of volition, and they clarify many related assumptions about will in this century.

On the first day of the *Dialogue*, Salviati contrasts the humanities with the sciences, the merely rhetorical with the true, the contingent with the necessary:

If what we are discussing were a point of law or of the humanities, in which neither true nor false exists, one might trust in subtlety of mind and readiness of tongue and in the greater experience of the writers, and expect him who excelled in those things to make his reasoning most plausible, and one might judge it to be the best. But in the natural sciences, whose conclusions are true and necessary and have nothing to do with human will [l'arbitrio umano], one must take care not to place oneself in the defense of error; for here a thousand Demostheneses and a thousand Aristotles would be left in the lurch by every mediocre wit who happened to hit upon the truth for himself. Therefore, Simplicio, give up this idea and this hope of yours that there may be men so much more learned, erudite, and well-read than the rest of us as to be able to make that which is false become true in defiance of nature. (D, pp. 53–54; *Opere*, 7: 78)

What is particularly striking about this passage is the way Galileo links will to rhetoric in order to assert the limits of both. As Derrida and other deconstructors of philosophy have argued, discrediting rival knowledges by asserting that they are mere rhetoric is hardly a novel strategy. Here, predictably, Salviati separates the power to make true or false statements from the powers of rhetorical persuasion, "subtlety of mind and readiness of tongue." Science is set up as the authentic arena for investigations of the true (theology, notably, is not a contender). We have seen a related version of this strategy to separate rival epistemologies into camps of the rhetorical and the true in Galileo's letter to Cristina (only there theology is marked as both rhetorical and true—how, indeed, could Galileo have argued otherwise?). But at this point in the *Dialogue* Galileo does not offer a "separate but equal" argument, and Salviati dismisses the "rhetorical" disciplines peremptorily.

Bruno Latour cites this passage as an archetypal example of the way science dismantles a certain variety of counterargument— namely, the "argument from authority." After quoting the passage, Latour says:

This argument appears so obvious at first that it seems there is nothing to add. However, a careful look at the [Demosthenes] sentence reveals two completely different arguments mixed together. Here again the two faces of Janus . . . should not be confused even when they speak at once. One mouth says: "science is truth that authority shall not overcome"; the other asks: "how can you be stronger than one thousand politicians and one thousand philosophers?" On the left side rhetoric is opposed to science just as authority is opposed to reason; but on the right, science is a rhetoric powerful enough, if we make the count, to allow one man to win over 2000 prestigious authorities![49]

Latour's point seems to be that science can only make claims to power by means of rhetoric, and furthermore, that one of science's most powerful rhetorical devices is to claim that it is above rhetoric. Significantly, Salviati denies both the rhetorical elements of his own presentation and his own desire to persuade. Instead he asserts that the scientist need not depend on rhetoric, will, or even intelligence to arrive at the truth. Or, more accurately, Salviati asserts that those who do possess rhetorical skill, the will to persuade, and "subtlety of mind" have no advantage over the scientist. For in the natural sciences, "conclusions are true and necessary and have nothing to do with human will," Salviati says, somewhat overemphatically. He seems to imply that truth is not altered or affected by human interpretation and, perhaps, that truth defies human interpretation, in which case the will to read does not in itself suffice to open the book of Nature.

We can extend Latour's Janus metaphor by pointing out that the tone of Salviati's argument is both overconfident and uneasy. The note of anxiety in the passage is unmistakable: why is the "mediocre wit" besieged, in this fantasy, by "a thousand Demostheneses and a thousand Aristotles," who seem to be hydralike extensions of the main problem—the authority of the one and only Aristotle, who, after all, wrote not on just the humanities or law, but on science? It is as if, to limit the persuasive power of Aristotelian thought (here magnified considerably), Galileo presents science in predestinarian terms. Here Nature (as opposed to, say, the mind of God) is that constant over which human will has no influence. The will to interpret Nature according to one's own desires or interests, the desire to persuade others of the legitimacy of one's interpretations—these have no place in science, just as the desire to perform good works and the will to stay out of Hell have no place in Lutheran theology.

We can see that this "predestinarian" science has its empowering aspects: with it Galileo is able to displace the authority of "a thousand Demostheneses and a thousand Aristotles" onto Nature. The privileging knowledge is thus placed outside of mere "arbitrio umano," which consists not only of will, but also of intelligence and persuasive power. Galileo, like Luther, is attempting with such rhetoric to dismantle a two-thousand-year-old tradition by which he personally feels oppressed. But what is the status of Galileo's own "mediocre wit" vis-à-vis Nature? Does the displacement of his own will to know and to persuade appear to cause him anxiety, or does this determinist assertion somehow not apply to the insights of the "mediocre wit"? Does Galilean science offer the equivalent of grace to the will in need of ransoming?

Indeed it does. According to Salviati's reasoning, the scientist is liberated from the demands to possess "subtlety of mind" and to flaunt it with "readiness of tongue." Likewise, in Luther's terms, the soul in the state of grace is freed from the demand to do or to will good works. In a certain sense, the scientist does not have to explain or defend his discoveries, the ways he happens to "hit upon the truth for himself," any more than the soul predestined for salvation has to account for the gratuitous gift of grace.

The scientist's grace, which might be dubbed the luck of insight, is not unlike the elect's sense of justification by grace. Yet just as the saved soul might lack absolute certainty of its salvation,[50] so might the scientist lack absolute certainty of the truth of his discoveries or hypotheses. On the first day of the *Dialogue*, Salviati asserts that science affords the possibility of objective certainty, yet Galileo's proofs of the Copernican theory seemed far from absolute to the church and to many of his colleagues. There is some evidence, as we have noted, that Galileo himself felt that his proofs in the *Dialogue* did not constitute "necessary demonstrations." Arguably, the grace of insight itself remained for Galileo somewhat unstable, tentative, and illusive.

The anxiety produced by "predestinarian" science might arise not only from uncertainty as to whether one has "grace" (authentic insight into the workings of Nature), but more generally from a new uncertainty about humanity's place in the cosmos. The purpose of Nature, like the intentions of God in radical Protestant theologies, can no longer be taken for granted. Man is no longer at the center of the universe; his function, therefore, is not entirely clear.

One standard theory of Renaissance science is that it destroyed the notion of an anthropocentric cosmos, thereby causing distress to large numbers of people.[51] This anxiety over man's displacement from the center of things does indeed appear in the *Dialogue*, though mainly in certain speeches by Simplicio. On the first day, for example, he points out the implications of Salviati's abandonment of the distinction between the sublunar (mutable and corruptible) world and the supralunar (immutable and eternal) one—a shift prompted in large part by Galileo's telescopic viewings of the moon's rough surface, the sunspots, and other astronomical phenomena. Lunar "generazioni, mutazioni etc."—the forces that influence life on earth—"would be useless and vain," Simplicio says, because they could not possibly be of use to man, and because Nature, after all, does nothing in vain (*D*, pp. 60–61; *Opere*, 7: 85). It is inconceivable to this character that all living creation is not "either directly or indirectly designed for the use, comfort, and benefit of man" (*D*, p. 61).

Though Sagredo and Salviati dismiss this anthropocentrism, it is significant that Galileo included the discussion of lunar life in his *Dialogue*, regardless of whether or not he himself shared Simplicio's anxiety. Galileo was aware of the implications of his own decentering arguments and the anxiety they might cause to those troubled by the apparent diminishment of human power, authority, and purpose. Indeed, seventeenth-century science was greatly preoccupied with precisely this conflict between an impersonal and decentering model of the physical world and people's desire to assert their own importance and relevance in that world.

My point is that the predestinarian elements of the new science, like predestinarian theologies, gave rise to several forms of anxiety. The first involved the scientist's certainty about his own "grace"— that is, the validity of his insight and the "rigorous demonstrations" that proceeded from it. A second and more general form involved the displacement of humans from the center of the universe and, in their own minds, from their place of greatest importance in that universe. Both anxieties involved the limiting of human will, understood either as the desire to know or the desire, shall we say, to matter. Both anxieties also concerned forms of mastery: that of mind over matter, or simply that of *man* over matter by virtue of his supreme place in its order (relative to other life forms in the sphere of the mutable). Just as in the sixteenth century Martin Luther challenged the mastery implied by the works-centered theology of free will, so in the seventeenth century did Galileo challenge other forms of mastery implied by earlier science and theology. The similarity of the challenges posed by these new worldviews should not be underestimated. At the very least, an understanding of how both movements threatened the sense of identity and control of those people they did not otherwise empower helps explain the often violent reactions to them.

Let us turn now to the politically volatile closing statements of the *Dialogue*, which provoked, among other things, the violent reactions of the Inquisition. After presenting on the fourth day a theory of the tides said to prove the movement of the earth, Galileo has Simplicio offer a critique of that theory and of Copernicanism, a critique that had been favored by none other than Pope Urban VIII. Simplicio stresses the uncertainty of Salviati's arguments and of all human endeavors to fathom the mind of God or the workings of the physical world:

I know that if asked whether God in His infinite power and wisdom could have conferred upon the watery element its observed reciprocating motion using some other means than moving its containing vessels, both of you would reply that He could have, and that He would have known how to do this in many ways which are unthinkable to our minds. From this I forthwith conclude that, this being so, it would be excessive boldness for anyone to limit and restrict the Divine power and wisdom to some particular fancy of his own. (D, p. 464)[52]

Simplicio's point is partly that the ways of God do not have to make sense to men (an argument related, certainly, to Luther's notion of the inscrutability of divine justice). The Inquisition felt that because this argument issued from the mouth of Simplicio and was broached in a perfunctory way, it was meant to ridicule the pope and to write off his argument against Copernicanism.[53] Maurice Finocchiaro makes a rather different point, however: he asserts that Galileo himself felt the strength of the argument, because it is in fact a powerful one. Finocchiaro describes the force of this skeptical objection in the seventeenth century, and also in our own; he points out that epistemologists continue to offer a nontheological version of it today through various critiques of the notion of induction. Finocchiaro explains:

Though expressed in what might be called the mythological language of God and divine omnipotence and omniscience, the demythologized version of the argument has become the stock-in-trade of modern epistemologists and methodologists. In modern terminology we might say: no scientific theory is ever conclusively proved since a scientific theory can be proved only relative to a finite amount of data, and for any finite set of data there is always more than one scientific theory about them, whether we view the theory as being inductively inferred from the data or as being an hypothetico-deductive explanation of the data. This is true basically because of the so-called problem of induction, or because of the formal invalidity of affirming the consequent.[54]

Again, it seems appropriate to speak of the Janus face of Galilean rhetoric, which can be read both as an assertion of scientific hubris and as an expression of anxiety caused by the modes of unknowing that the scientist inevitably confronts. In other words, we might read the conclusion of the Dialogue as another manifesto of predestinarian science, the failure or bondage of the will to know, that stresses the impossibility of really knowing what one thinks one knows. If we accept this reading, then we must assume that Salviati's response to Simplicio's argument is straightforward:

An admirable and angelic doctrine, and well in accord with another one, also Divine, which, while it grants to us the right to argue about the constitution of the universe (perhaps in order that the working of the human mind shall not be curtailed or made lazy) adds that we cannot discover the work of His hands. Let us, then, exercise these activities permitted to us and ordained by God, that we may recognize and thereby so much the more admire His greatness, however much less fit we may find ourselves to penetrate the profound depths of His infinite wisdom [quanto meno ci troviamo idonei a penetrare i profondi abissi della Sua infinita sapienza]. (*D*, p. 464; *Opere*, 7: 489)

These are Salviati's last words in the book; Sagredo then suggests that they end their dialogue and go boating. Indeed, after Galileo has contemplated the limitations of his will to know, what else is there for him to say? One can offer an infinity of readings of the text of Nature; one can build powerful arguments that seem to have more force than all others; one can hope to find oneself "idoneo," or "fit," to "penetrate" God's abysses. Still, one can never be fully certain of one's "fitness," the scientific analogue of grace. In an ending that contrasts strikingly with the voluntarism of the beginning of the *Dialogue*, Galileo confesses the limits of will.

Galileo's ambivalence about the scientific paradigm he spells out in his *Dialogue* pertains less to its content than to its implications for his own authority. The statements made by his characters hint at two contradictory possibilities: radical empowerment (a godlike knowledge of necessary truths, such as mathematics), and radical powerlessness (profoundly limited epistemological certainty, and related doubts about one's relevance to the cosmic scheme). The creative power of human discovery, the power to understand perfectly, if to a limited extent, is pitted in the *Dialogue* against something else—the resistance of Nature to human understanding, not to mention the resistance of humans to Galileo's understanding.

The concept of science as mathematical, and therefore as literal and nonrhetorical, is an early modern idea that Galileo helped invent. In attempting to demarcate the border between science and theology, Galileo did not just point out existing disciplinary differences; he constructed them, and he developed a rhetoric of difference out of which "proof" of those distinctions emerged. The study of Galilean rhetoric is tremendously important to an understanding of the origins of the scientific revolution, but even more important, perhaps, to an awareness of how discourses in any culture rise and fall.

In his letter to Cristina, in his 1610 letter to Castelli on the phases of Venus, and in many other writings, Galileo reassembled various materials of his culture into a relatively new discourse. He recycled biblical hermeneutics and put them at the service of a new language, a nonrhetorical and infallible language of geometric shapes. In so doing, Galileo recast the utopian language theories of earlier centuries and adapted them to scientific inquiry. He also reshaped, consciously or unconsciously, the rhetoric of religious discovery, while at the same time putting scientific "conversion" on a presumably more empirical footing. Each of these recastings reveals the complex relation between scientific and theological discourses at the point of their ostensible divergence.

The rhetoric of Renaissance science, like that of any other ideology, necessarily involves the distribution of power. The corollary of universalizing claims to literal truth, access to the "vero assoluto," and mastery of an ideal language is that such claims advance, not coincidentally, the political interests of a particular group. The continued success of such claims hinges on their power to persuade that they are about "reality" rather than about mere "rhetoric," individual interests, and other contingencies. Galileo was one of the first to develop an empowering rhetoric of scientific "reading." By seeming to ransom the will from the abyss of unknowing, this powerful rhetoric continues to obscure its reliance on contingencies even today.

Afterword

◡

In the preceding chapters I have defined Old Mastery in several ways. First, it is a set of ideas about subjecthood critiqued by late-twentieth-century theory, especially by poststructuralism. Second, it is a figure for a group of suspect ideologies concerning individualism, freedom, and personal autonomy, which theorists tend to connect, either directly or indirectly, to an early modern or premodern past. Old Mastery is an idea of the Renaissance, and implicit in contemporary critiques of subjecthood is a dialectical opposition to a shared reading of that past, which is to be mastered and transcended.

In another sense, Old Mastery is a pattern of narrative common to early modern discussions of will and to twentieth-century debates on mastery. That pattern is one of conflict and of conflict overcome—that is, of mastery. Prominent in the narrative is a rhetoric of will that is often thought to characterize early modern discourses, such as humanism, theology, and science. In this sense, Old Mastery is a strategy of self-presentation, a way of depicting one's transcendence of various forms of predestinarian bondage, a transcendence that I call the ransoming of the will. Old Mastery is a strategy in that it is directed above all at persuading oneself and others that such mastery is both possible and deserving of some mark of success—institutional authority, financial reward, or the acclaim of followers, for example. Old Mastery is, above all, a claim to power couched within a certain rhetoric of appeal.

As argued in Chapter 1, every ideology, whether ostensibly voluntarist or determinist, must represent itself as mastery if it is to persuade. We might take this as a corollary of Fredric Jameson's point, much quoted in this book, that the utopian and ergo persuasive component of an ideology lies in the "substantial incentives" it appears to offer. Furthermore, as Michel Foucault has argued, even the most oppressive ideology, the most blatant non-mastery, generates a self-legitimating truth that its "subjects" necessarily experience as "right."

Of course, this double model of ideological appeal itself reflects the conflict over free will and predestination (in early modern terms) or over the status of the subject (in poststructuralist terms). I say this because Jameson's model of ideology, or at least this part of it, seems to accommodate a degree of freedom on the part of the subject, precisely because the rhetoric of "substantial incentives" is the rhetoric of choice (ironically, with certain consumerist overtones). Foucault's model is far more "predestinarian," in that his subject of ideology is comparatively more subjected. Foucault rarely addresses the question of human agency; instead he tends to portray the individual as determined by various social forces. The conflict within the theoretical model of this book is paradigmatic of both early modern and contemporary debates on will. For both between and within various theories of agency and subjecthood one finds a debate on will.

The Jameson/Foucault model of assent presented briefly in Chapter 1 suggests another conclusion about how we represent to ourselves the limitations of our belief systems. Rival systems, competitor ideologies, are likely to be seen as determinisms. But from inside a system, "determinisms," by which I mean real or imagined constraints on the individual or collective exercise of will, are generally represented as having been overcome. Thus one cannot easily inhabit a determinist ideology unless its limitations on will have been ideologically recuperated. To restate an earlier point of this book, even determinist ideologies must be experienced as masteries if they are to persuade.

Still, no system is so perfectly closed or complete that it does not expose the limitations of mastery even as it claims to transcend them, because it is not possible fully to recuperate every form of "predestinarian" bondage. In other words, to represent the bondage of the will, even as that from which one would ransom one's freedom, is to acknowledge the weight of that nonfreedom. Let us review this lack of closure as it occurs in Old Masteries—the humanist, theological, and scientific works analyzed above—before returning to the "non-masteries" of Chapter 1 and to the late-twentieth-century discourse on will.

Old Masters

That paradigmatic humanist and "first modern man," Francis Petrarch, wrote frequently of the unpredictable plays of fortuna and divine Providence. These he opposed to a voluntarist vision of humanist freedom, the possibility of pastoral retreat from the bondage of the marketplace, with its unfortunate patronage requirements for intellectuals like himself. Interestingly, this ideology of intellectual freedom remains influential today, especially, but not exclusively, within academia.

Of course, it was not always possible to transcend either fortuna or Providence, as the Cola di Rienzo debacle tragically demonstrated, and Petrarch also acknowledged the constraints on his dream of freedom. In so doing, he recuperated the actual nonfreedom he experienced in many areas of his life by conveniently invoking a determinism that relieved him of responsibility for certain moral choices. We saw, for example, how Petrarch's letter to his former patron, Cardinal Colonna, obscured the poet's indirect role in the deaths of certain Colonna family members in Rome. We also saw how Petrarch's analysis of nonfreedom (in the *Secretum*, for example) served as a defense and rationalization of the humanist's "predestined" place within the social hierarchy. In various ways, then, Petrarch attempted to convert the bondage of the will into mastery.

A further aspect of Petrarch's sometime rhetoric of mastery was its implicit and explicit claim to difference: to modernity, distance from the dull minds of the recent past, and closeness to the brilliant intellects of the remote past of Greek and Roman antiquity. As suggested in Chapter 3, the rhetoric of conversion also claims difference. Though Martin Luther, Ignatius Loyola, and Teresa of Avila articulated quite different theologies of will, each of them adopted a rhetoric of mastery fundamental to the idea of conversion. They all claimed to have been transformed and to have overcome, to some extent, the errors of their past lives.

Luther's claims to mastery were bolder still; he also claimed to have transcended a millennium of doctrinally degenerate theologizing and to have recovered, among other things, the pristine, predestinarian theology of Saint Augustine. In his 1545 Preface, Luther confronted at least two forms of "bondage" quite distinct from the nonfreedom of the will analyzed in the *De servo arbitrio*. The first was his and his culture's bondage to consuetudo, that is, their historical entanglement with the corrupt Roman church. In the Preface Luther demonstrated the liberating, decentering power of his predestinarian theology by pitting it against centuries of Roman Catholic thought and by insisting on the freedom gained through his theology of justification. The second form of bondage was that imposed on Luther and on his texts by death. The 1545 Preface suggests an anxious and insecure desire on Luther's part to ransom his representation of self-as-master from the encroachments of death and misinterpretation, personified in the Preface as impious readers and malevolent editors of the distant future.

Though inhabiting a theological universe often considered the inverse of Martin Luther's, Ignatius Loyola used a similar rhetoric of will and mastery. The central theme of Loyola's writings was obedience—his own obedience to God's will, and the obedience he hoped to elicit from his followers and the rest of the world. Obedience, paradoxically, was the utopian incentive of Ignatian rhetoric, a freely chosen bondage of the will. Through this right exercise of choice, the obedient servant of God was to experience true liberation.

In Loyola's theology, as in Luther's, the most prominently featured form of bondage of the will was distinct from the form inducing the greatest anxiety in the author—namely, the disorder of the world, with its chaotic lack of obedience and of system. In his *Autobiography* Loyola explored his own condition of uncertainty as the principal locus of that disorder, which he learned to offset by the mantic language of mystical prayer. In this way Loyola's assertions of obedience to God and to his superiors manifested a militant will to power.

In Teresa of Avila's writings, bondage of the will assumed a configuration partly imposed by her gender and her converso heritage. In the *Libro de la vida* these forms of bondage surfaced in another register as the theological description of the loss of will experienced during rapture and other types of mystical prayer. Teresa used a gendered and implicitly raced rhetoric of dismemberment and violation to convey that loss of personal will. Arguably that language expressed the author's ambivalence toward the bondage imposed on her by her own culture. The advantage of her complaints against rapture, interestingly, was that they would be perceived as normative within the misogynistic and violently anti-Semitic culture she inhabited.

However, Teresa did not simply represent the violence of her culture toward her person; she also recuperated it, by insisting on the transformative power of the amorous and paradoxically tender violence of God. This violence authorized Teresa to speak, to write, to correct her confessors, and to circumvent the skeptical interventions of the Inquisition. It was a canonizing violence that sanctified the abased Teresa in the eyes of her contemporaries, as among devotional readers to this day.

If a defining feature of Old Mastery is its authorizing claim of difference and distance from the past, then Galileo's rhetoric of scientific discovery represents a kind of paradigmatic assertion of will. By reconstructing the age-old theory of a nonrhetorical, unfallen language, which he attributed to the geometric book of Nature, Galileo claimed to surpass the hermeneutic limits imposed on merely figural texts, specifically Scripture. Galileo expressed his will to read as the power to transcend the usual boundaries of human knowledge; only mathematical science, he claimed, could afford the human intellect the possibility of absolute certainty.

In defense of the Copernican hypothesis, Galileo spoke of "necessary demonstrations," yet it is not clear that he believed he had discovered such compelling proof of the order of the universe. Most readers of the *Dialogue*, including the condemning panel of inquisitors, have tended to focus on Galileo's language of mastery, overlooking or ignoring the anxiety also characteristic of that work—an anxiety resulting from the "predestinarian" side of Galilean science.

This scientific form of epistemological bondage of the will to interpret evoked grave discomfort in that remarkable reader of the book of Nature.

New Subjects

Old Mastery implies in part a shared reading of the early modern past. One goal of this book is to challenge that reading by showing how recent theory has unwittingly reiterated many strategies of the early modern debate on will, even as it claims, implicitly or explicitly, to have superseded them. The "masterful" discourses of humanism, of theology, and of science cannot be taken at face value, for they are in fact paradigmatic sites of conflict between the desire for mastery and an uneasy acknowledgment of the constraints on that desire, constraints that are recuperated by a strategic kind of rhetoric by which one claims to have ransomed the will. The disjunction between a rhetoric of mastery and "actual" mastery bears pointing out, however, if only because these two categories are quite often confused.

In countless ways (generally acknowledged), deconstructionists and their critical heirs remain both within and without the binary discourse that they claim not to invert, but to dismantle.[1] Theory remains indebted to and embedded in notions of Old Mastery that can be traced back to the Renaissance and even beyond. These connections to the past and its discourses on will and subjecthood can be considered in two registers, the epistemological and the ethical.

The epistemological link between modern and early modern is perhaps most evident in the relation between contemporary theoretical discourses and science. Despite the decentering efforts of radical philosophers, historians, and sociologists of science, the disciplinary distinctions articulated by Galileo are still upheld, especially by those who lay claim to the authority of science. The continued authority of scientific discourse hinges, as I have argued, on the preservation of the distinction between the literal and the figural. Knowledge consists, according to this model, of an access to reality or truth, a truth that admits of no substitutions, defines those substitutions (such as of the particular for the general, or of one term of an analogy for another) as nonproblematic, or, if the substitutions are figures, defines them as "literal" figures admitting of no slippage, no loss, no confusion. Most importantly, these figures of knowledge are different from the "figural" figurality of the less authoritative mediated discourses.

According to this model of knowing, there can be no possibility of an alternative epistemological framework. As Dudley Shapere tellingly writes in his study of Galileo's method: "Whether or not there are kinds of knowledge other than scientific is perhaps only a matter of the breadth of definition we are willing to allow that term; but that science and its method constitute a paradigm case of knowledge and the knowledge acquiring process shall be beyond dispute."[2] Within the framework of this discourse there is only science, which is opposed to the condition of unknowing.

The decentering discourses of the late twentieth century follow a related epistemological model. Deconstruction and its analogues in the social sciences do not succeed completely in understanding knowledge from within an alternative framework. As part of an extended critique of the literal/figural distinction around which disciplines are structured, Paul de Man, after Nietzsche, argued for the contingency of "the most fundamental 'value' of all, the principle of non-contradiction, ground of the identity principle."[3] But even deconstruction, the branch of poststructuralism most scrupulously attentive to the problems of claiming mastery, and to my mind the most interesting of late-twentieth-century discourses on will for that reason, relies on a version of the principle of noncontradiction— namely, the notion of "rigor"—to unsettle the less self-conscious "masters" of philosophical (and, by extension, scientific and political) discourse. Arguably, rigor is only the rhetoric of an admittedly self-deconstructing discourse. Nevertheless, deconstruction remains in this key way akin to philosophy and science (as its advocates freely admit), because its rhetoric functions in virtually the same way.

The decentering arguments of radical social science tend to rely on notions of rigor in a manner less self-conscious than those of deconstruction. Even theorists who abjure the standard quantitative empirical approaches in favor of some less foundational one implicitly share with science a concept of demonstration, which for these theorists just happens to be directed against certain other suppositions of the master discourse. Whether we consider the anthropological critique of science put forward by Bruno Latour and Steve Woolgar, or the discourse analysis advanced by Nigel Gilbert and Michael Mulkay,[4] we see that these different methods depend, like Galileo's theory, on some concept of rigorous demonstration.

Indeed, it is hard to imagine any kind of theory that does not operate within the framework of epistemological demonstration provided by science, and by philosophy and theology before science. There are, of course, "faith" arguments, but these tend to be called upon as a last resort.[5] Late-twentieth-century decentering critiques suggest that all arguments are in some sense faith arguments—for faith is the only way to move from contingency to necessity, despite all assertions to the contrary—but the decentering claims themselves belie their rhetoric against proof or demonstration.

If it is possible to detect a residue of Old Mastery in the rhetorics of rigor and of scientific demonstration within theoretical discourses, another aspect of that cultural inheritance can be detected in the ethical dimension of such theory, especially in post-poststructuralism. The recent critical response to deconstruction and to related theories now perceived as overly determinist and therefore disempowering has been to reconstruct a provisional subject capable of resistance, but itself resistant to the grandiose fictions of traditional bourgeois individualism. Hence the rhetoric of nonessential essentialism, double strategies, third courses, and so forth. Although this particular trend rejects notions of Old Mastery commonly associated with early modern thought, together with those aspects of contemporary capitalist ideologies held to be most worthy of critique or contempt because of their "Pelagian" cast, its strategies for recuperating the agency of the subject are quite distinctly Erasmian. The great irony, of course, is that very similar arguments were rehearsed with great subtlety in the Renaissance, navigating between the Scylla and Charybdis of the under- and overdetermined subject, though the various insights of those debates are now schematized, misrepresented, or ignored. In this fashion theory has, in some ways at least, reinvented the will, though it seems archaic to speak of agency in such terms.

For these reasons it is important to note that ethical criticisms such as feminist, marxist, ethnic, and third-world theory have retained one element of the ideologies of humanist mastery that they critique—namely, a moral and generally pedagogic imperative. In that sense, the radical rhetoric of political progress indicates a humanist origin, as does the rhetoric of tradition, family, and property—although their aims differ drastically. Mastery and morality were permanently joined in the pedagogy that evolved out of Renaissance humanism, and we see in the resurgence of ethical criticism yet another aspect of theory's early modern unconscious.

The predicament of theory—its continuing crisis—revolves around the status of the will. The subject, subjugated or subjected, is of necessity the problem, one that yokes contemporary theory to its monstrous doubles—humanism, individualism, and other forms of Old Mastery. For poststructuralist theory, like early modern discourses on will, is in some sense recuperative—that is, a rhetoric of mastery. Even the branches of theory most clearly predicated on the denial of mastery still operate as insight, whether or not one calls it blind insight, a cloud of unknowing. Theory operates as a ransoming of the will—to read, to know, to have fun, or merely to exist. And therein lies its appeal.

The Will to Theory

One important question posed earlier remains to be answered: Why does it seem to be perpetually necessary to redefine subjecthood, both in relation to determinisms thought to undermine individual choice and responsibility, and in relation to Pelagianism, the perennial fantasy of an autonomous, unified, and hubristic subject? One could argue that theorists—early modern or contemporary—continually reinvent or reconstrain the will because issues of agency remain pressing and require vigilant updating, given that the contexts in which they are experienced are historically variable and volatile. Determinisms are likely to be perceived as anything from annoying to heretical, unless they engender in the mind of the theorist a sense of mastery via their decentering or liberating rhetoric. This is a lesson of deconstruction and, no less, of that great social upheaval known as the Protestant Reformation. Pelagianism evokes the same range of negative responses (unless, of course, one happens to be a Pelagian). The degree of discomfort experienced depends on how much one disapproves of those asserting their will by means of such arguments. Indeed, Pelagianism might be thought of as the authority of whatever group one likes least extended metonymically to the human race; to the critic, it is likely to be experienced and attacked as an ideology of massive presumption.

Though the theoretical debates on subjecthood of the past 25 years are admittedly a small subset of all such conflicts since the Renaissance, they are nevertheless of great significance to the class of intellectuals that has engaged in them. To specify further the historical and institutional contexts of these theoretical struggles helps clarify the participants' stakes. For, like the early modern intellectuals discussed in the preceding chapters, this class has experienced some very pressing constraints on its own identity—both collective and individual—and on its authority. The brief comments that follow must be taken as a prolegomenon to a more elaborate treatment of the political and social conflicts faced by western intellectuals during the late twentieth century.

In the past 50 years, humanist intellectuals have seen a significant decrease in the value of the cultural capital they have traditionally pursued. There are two reasons (at least) for this decrease. First, the ideological buttressing provided to political economies by the ancient discourse of the liberal arts has become increasingly less serviceable to—and therefore less subsidized by—the heavily militarized technocracies that have reigned globally since World War II. Second, in the now-global marketplace of ideas, the western cultural inheritance is no longer the gold standard; rather, this currency has been floating for some time, and, particularly in the West, intellectual speculators are more reluctant to invest.

Certain theoretical determinisms, particularly those of Althusser and Foucault, and even that of Lacan, were flavored with a kind of postwar and postexistentialist pessimism, yet still offered insights into the constructed nature of subjectivity that were recuperative by virtue of their claims to insight and to mastery. It is possible to think of the different currents of determinism that eventually coalesced in deconstruction as symptoms of the changing role of humanists in the postwar political economies of the West. For complicated reasons, many humanists have come to see themselves less as conservators and proprietors of a cultural heritage than as challengers of western culture and/or its political practices. This change might be interpreted—depending, of course, on one's sympathies—as a reconfigured idealism on the part of recent generations of humanists, or as a collective and hardly disinterested effort to bolster the sagging cultural capital of humanism by revaluing its currencies.

Gradually curricula in the disciplines of the liberal arts have come to reflect and to perpetuate this shifting agenda—though not uniformly and not without considerable internal and external resistance by conservative forces. Over time the humanist mission of universities has become more politicized, offering students, faculty, and larger communities ostensibly new ethical self-justifications. The powerful critiques of "centered" subjecthood and of the political and institutional authority it implies have played a significant part in the recasting of the humanist mission—a recasting that is essential, given the presently ambiguous value of traditional humanism as a discourse.

Perhaps the greatest impetus for this recasting during recent years, at least in the United States, was the political climate of Reaganism. It was during the Reagan years that deconstruction was succeeded by the next phase of poststructuralism, the explicitly ethical theory that has come to dominate within the academy. In the quasi-fascist and militaristic climate of the 1980's and early 1990's, the discourses of women's rights, civil rights, gay rights, and human rights were largely confined to colleges and universities, as they increasingly became (or remained) unpopular or heretical elsewhere. Thus it has become more relevant, more pressing, for humanists—particularly those groups who have not until recently held university positions—to challenge the political right outside academia with a rhetoric more effective than that of precursor theories such as deconstruction. Self-undermining and irony were and continue to be perceived by many as less judicious, less direct, and less heartfelt than outrage. It is not yet clear how successful this latest version of the humanist mission will be—for example, in promoting a multicultural agenda outside the university (or even within it), in fostering

grass-roots resistance to imperialism, or in countering savage intol-
erance within the United States. Nevertheless, one can certainly note
the changes with interest and hope.

Because this is a book about Renaissance studies (in relation to
certain contemporary theories of subjecthood), I will close by reflecting on the status of that particular discipline, the supposed epi-
center of humanist discourse. The trajectory of change described
above would apply most readily to a critical avant-garde, who would
appear more slowly in Renaissance studies than in many other fields.
Indeed, this discipline has been a conservative one, in the literal sense
of preserving a cultural inheritance. Its golden age occurred after
World War II, throughout the 1950's and into the 1960's, because it
offered to many an optimistic ideology of reconstruction, which re-
claimed a European history in many ways idealized, while compen-
sating for and even overlooking the devastation of the immediate
past.

However, this comforting vision of the Renaissance and its subjects came to be decentered, both by other types of humanists (who
would eschew that title, along with its implications) and by larger—
indeed, global—political and economic forces that gradually eroded
the disciplinary self-justifications of Renaissance studies. This decentering has accelerated during the past decade, only to be accepted
and absorbed as a new raison d'être by many participants in the reconfigured field of early modern studies.

Some might consider Renaissance / early modern studies to be a
discipline in crisis, unsure of its own direction; a set of conflicting
critical ideologies of indeterminate value in an age of canon reformation. Of course, one can only assess the value of a particular discipline in relation to specific groups. Practitioners, for example, must
ask themselves (as, indeed, they always have) what their own stakes
are in recovering a history and in creating or perpetuating a discourse around it for a contemporary university audience; these stakes
vary considerably, depending on the politics of an epistemic con-
stituency. For example, a feminist's Renaissance will differ from the
Renaissance of a traditional intellectual historian, though the com-
binatory possibilities are themselves worth promoting.

And practitioners of Renaissance studies, like those of any other discipline, must continually revise their sense of purpose by offering "substantial incentives," in Jameson's terms, to those audiences variously removed from the field. Certainly the revisionist scholarship of the past decade has done just that (though it is worth noting that all scholarship is to some degree revisionist). This book, like many others, has made a case for the relevance of discourses of and about the early modern era to other disciplines within the liberal arts, particularly those branches inflected by poststructuralist theory. If indeed early modern debates on subjecthood constitute a kind of unconscious for theory as currently practiced within a host of disciplines, then arguably it is worthwhile to unrepress the contents of this unconscious, to grasp one's critical genealogy, and to think, less individualistically, of one's endeavors as part of a historical continuum. However illusory or problematic one might find such continuities in the wake of poststructuralism, it is probably not useful or even possible to dispense with them completely, any more than with the idea of knowledge itself. That is the seductive quality of history—the notion that it teaches us something important about ourselves—although the desire to refute history, to transcend history, or not to have a history at all is also quite clearly compelling. For behind that desire is the irresistibly Pelagian fantasy of self-creation, a will to generate one's own discourse. That all theory is predicated on the conflicts regarding will and determinism, agency and subjecthood, that are necessarily its content is what I offer as the central paradox and paradigm of this book; the overdetermining weight of history is what one often wills to forget.

Reference Matter

Notes

♋

Introduction

1. See *Dictionary of Cultural Literacy*, in which E. D. Hirsch, Joseph F. Kett, and James Trefil remind the great unwashed of past humanist lessons. They define "Renaissance Man" as "an outstandingly versatile, well-rounded person. The expression alludes to such RENAISSANCE figures as LEONARDO DA VINCI, who performed brilliantly in many different fields" (p. 74).

2. Burckhardt, *Civilization of the Renaissance*, 1: 150, 143, 147.

3. Traditional valuations of Renaissance individualism are still appearing—as, for example, in Duby, ed., *History of Private Life*, a neo-Burckhardtian celebration of selfhood. In a chapter entitled "Toward Intimacy: The Fourteenth and Fifteenth Centuries," Philippe Braunstein writes that "as early as the fourteenth century a new age was dawning, as individuals began to feel the need to perpetuate their image and memory in this world. In the cities of the West a great movement began, which pushed back the limits of the known world and the pillars of Heaven. Around the figure of man an intangible, geometrical space was created, as tears, credulity, and amazement were abandoned to the humble" (2: 630).

However, early modern selfhood has also been judged negatively since the last century; see, e.g., Engels, *Origins of Family*. Not surprisingly, this negative reading of early modern subjecthood has reemerged in poststructuralist histories such as Theweleit's *Male Fantasies*, a feminist history of Germany between the world wars. Theweleit, like Engels, argues that novel and brutal forms of oppression emerged in the early modern age, along with those supposedly liberating notions of individualism. Describing the new sense of identity that arose in early modern Europe, he writes, "The expansion of the European world outward beyond old boundaries found expression in imperialist drives against 'primitive peoples.' I submit that this corresponded to an inner imperialism that took as its territories lands formed from the subjugated nature of female bodies. Just as the external gold was mined from the body of the world's peoples, the *internal* variety (the new male ego with its new freedoms) was extracted from the body of subjugated femaleness. The patriarchal bourgeoisie, arming itself for a new departure toward world domination, depended equally on both forms of subjugation" (1: 323).

Again, despite their differing valuations of the ideology of individualism, critics and historians generally locate the origin of that ideology in the early modern period.

4. *Twilight of Subjectivity*, p. ix.

5. *Renaissance Self-Fashioning*, p. 1. Though Greenblatt, one of the founders of the new historicist movement, rereads the Renaissance in poststructuralist terms, he and "prestructuralist" precursors like Burckhardt share at least one thing: a vision of the Renaissance as the age of burgeoning individualism. This similarity suggests a certain non-divergence of new from old historicism.

6. *Idea of the Renaissance*. Kerrigan and Braden write, "The polemical side of our history lies in its assumption that nothing we know today requires us to close down the Burckhardt tradition, though its major theme, the appearance of a newly ambitious individualism, may of course be described in many vocabularies, some of them less respectful than our own, which is not without uneasiness" (p. xii).

7. Examples of this genre include Petrarch's *Secretum* (ca. 1542–53?), Lorenzo Valla's *De libero arbitrio* (ca. 1435–43), Pietro Pomponazzi's *De fato, de libero arbitrio, et de praedestinatione* (1520), and the noted Erasmus-Luther debate on the freedom or bondage of the will (1524 and after; see Chapter 3 below). For detailed discussions of the problems of will in Italian humanist works, see Cassirer, "Freedom and Necessity in the Philosophy of the Renaissance," in *Individual and the Cosmos*, pp. 73–122, and Charles Trinkaus's remarkable study, *In Our Image and Likeness*.

8. *On the Dignity of Man*, pp. 4–5. Cassirer points out the moral and intellectual tension within this oration, which he takes to be characteristic of Renaissance humanism in general, by explaining the connection between free will and the absolute subjectivity that Pico couples with it: "What is required of man's will and knowledge is that they be completely *turned towards* the world and yet completely *distinguish* themselves from it. Will and knowledge may, or rather, must devote themselves to every part of the universe; for only by going through the entire universe can man traverse the

circle of his own possibilities. But this complete openness towards the world must never signify a *dissolution* in it, a mystical-pantheistic losing of oneself." *Individual and the Cosmos*, p. 86.

9. Martines, *Power and Imagination*, pp. 216–17; Grafton and Jardine, *From Humanism to the Humanities*, pp. 1–28.

10. Wayne Rebhorn has clarified this problem of mastery in *Foxes and Lions*: "Although in the game of life Fortuna holds the cards and people can play only with the hand she gives them, Machiavelli does, admittedly illogically, insist that they can beat her on occasion. He never faces this problem squarely in his works, insisting to the end on Fortuna's omnipotence while still asserting that human beings have the resources to deal with her" (p. 174).

11. The terms "will," "reason," and "appetite" are traditionally treated as separate and distinct mental faculties in medieval and Renaissance psychology, and Galileo himself may have regarded them as separate. Thus to speak of scientific voluntarism is to identify not a discrete theory of will (as opposed to intellect or reason) operating in Galileo's thought, but rather a rhetoric of mastery, within which standard notions of intellect, will, and even appetite are somewhat fused.

12. In "Problem of Free Will," pp. 263–73, Trinkaus explains that Renaissance and Reformation theories of will share a nonmedieval worldview in which everyday economic and political concerns were considered to be separate from spiritual or ethical concerns: "Whereas medieval thought attributed to man the rational capacity both to lead a moral life in the ordinary secular pursuits of this world and to achieve salvation, both the humanists and the reformers denied that man could do both. The humanists took the first step and denied the possibility of subordinating economic to moral ends, but left man the necessary free will to flee contamination by the world and to gain salvation by his own powers, if he so chose. The reformers, particularly Luther, also denied that there was any possibility of morality in business or politics but took the further step of denying man the power of achieving either virtue or justification by his own free will" (p. 268). Thus for Trinkaus the broad attribution of mastery and individualism to the early modern age would be highly reductive. As Kristeller wrote, "The notion that man occupies an exalted place in the universe, and the opposite idea that he is a small and powerless creature at the mercy of far stronger divine, natural, or historical forces, are not only contrary to each other but also complementary. Both of them are too well grounded in obvious facts of human experience and, hence, supply more or less permanent themes for human thought and discourse at any time, in the Renaissance as well as in our own time as we may easily observe." "The Dignity of Man," in *Renaissance Concepts of Man*, p. 20.

13. Marcus notes in "Renaissance / Early Modern Studies" that the phrase "early modern," though now freighted with poststructuralist connotations, can be traced back half a century to the *Annales* school.

14. "Renaissance / Early Modern Studies," p. 43.

15. New historicist and feminist scholars have dramatically changed the terrain of early modern studies. Their revisionary histories and critiques of early modern texts have concentrated for the most part on the issues of gender, race or ethnicity, and class.

The tendency to "reconcile" the Renaissance with poststructuralism attests to a certain "moderno-centrism" in early modern studies. As Marcus has pointed out, "While the boundaries of the Renaissance tend to push toward earlier and earlier chronological beginnings, early modern tends to creep up on the present. Scholars of the early modern period have devoted relatively little energy to the contestation of points of origin, much more to the issue of defining a terminus." "Renaissance / Early Modern Studies," p. 42.

16. Though I use the term "poststructuralism" generically here to denote theoretical trends in Europe and America during the past 25 years, it should be noted that this label encompasses many different and sometimes mutually exclusive positions. In the next chapter, I will spell out some of the differences among these positions, while also identifying their common ground—namely, the views on and against mastery that are virtually omnipresent in the various branches of poststructuralist thought.

17. *Twilight of Subjectivity*, pp. 21–29. Derrida's essay "The Ends of Man," in *Margins of Philosophy*, pp. 109–39, tropes on the double sense of "end"—that is, as aim or purpose, and as finitude or death. "According to Derrida," Dallmayr writes, "what is needed in our time is an effort to shift the weight of the two connotations—which involves a struggle against the metaphysical legacy: 'What is difficult to conceive today is an end of man which is not dominated in advance by the dialectic of truth and purposive negativity and which does not rely on a teleology in the first person plural' " (*Twilight of Subjectivity*, p. 28).

18. *Discerning the Subject*, p. xxvii. On the evolution and contemporary uses of the terms "subject" and "subjective," see Williams, *Keywords*, pp. 308–12.

19. *Hegemony and Socialist Strategy*, p. 115.

20. *Discerning the Subject*, p. xxxi. Smith accounts for his choice of the word "cerned" as follows: "The word 'cerning' conflates and plays simultaneously upon two rarely used English verbs—'to cern' and 'to cerne.' The first means 'to accept an inheritance or a patrimony,' and I use it to suggest that the contemporary intellectual abstraction of the 'subject' from the real conditions of its existence continues—and is perfectly consonant with—a western philosophical heritage in which the 'subject' is construed as the uni-

fied and coherent bearer of consciousness. Simultaneously, I have used the second verb, which means 'to encircle' or 'to enclose,' to indicate the way in which theoretical discourse limits the definition of the human agent in order to be able to call him/her the 'subject.' My project in this book is, then, to be described as an attempt to *dis-cern* the 'subject,' and to argue that the human agent *exceeds* the 'subject' as it is constructed in and by much poststructuralist theory as well as by those discourses against which poststructuralist theory claims to pose itself" (p. xxx).

21. These "determinisms" have been adapted from J. Hillis Miller's discussion of three "grounds" of contemporary theory—the social, the psychological, and the linguistic—in "Search for Grounds in Literary Study."

22. These are the philosophers listed by Manfred Frank in "Subjekt, Person, Individuum," p. 7.

23. In "Transcendence of the Individual," John H. Smith notes the movement in critical theory away from poststructuralist denials of the traditional subject: "The focus in the human sciences has been shifting from denunciations or affirmations of the subject to a 'reconstruction' of the individual in a way that avoids the nostalgia for an undeconstructed self" (p. 82). The negotiation of a theoretical "third course," neither humanist nor completely poststructuralist in its assessment of the subject, will be discussed in the next chapter.

Chapter 1

1. Watchdogs Alan Bloom, E. D. Hirsch, and William Bennett are three prominent examples; they have striven to purge university curricula of nonmasters, the usurpers and pretenders who displace Old Masters as well as real men. See, for example, Bloom's *Closing of the American Mind*; Hirsch, Kett, and Trefil's *Dictionary of Cultural Literacy*; and Bennett's Stanford speech on the traditional canon, published as "Why the West?" See also Dinesh D'Souza's hyperventilating text, *Illiberal Education*.

2. Feyerabend, *Against Method* and *Science in a Free Society*; Latour and Woolgar, *Laboratory Life*; Latour, *Science in Action*; Merchant, *Death of Nature*; Gilbert and Mulkay, *Opening Pandora's Box*; Keller, *Reflections on Gender and Science*; Bourdieu, *Distinction*; Baudrillard, *Pour une critique de l'économie politique du signe*.

3. The use of the masculine pronoun is deliberate here, because the subject as traditionally defined is invariably linked to patriarchal conceptions of selfhood.

4. *American Heritage Dictionary of the English Language*, 1969, s.v. "master."

5. This strategy is also referred to as the "third course." See Intro., n. 23.

6. The point of this radical critique of pedagogy and others like it, how-

ever, is not to do away with teaching, but to undermine the popular fantasy of teacher as master. On the prospect of radical pedagogy as practice, see Shoshana Felman's essay "Psychoanalysis and Education: Teaching Terminable and Interminable," in *Jacques Lacan*, pp. 69–97.

7. De Man uses, after Gérard Genette, the image of the whirligig ("tourniquet") as a figure for rhetorical indeterminacy: "Is it possible to remain, as Genette would have it, *within* an undecidable situation? As anyone who has ever been caught in a revolving door or on a revolving wheel can testify, it is certainly most uncomfortable, and all the more so in this case [of autobiography] since this whirligig is capable of infinite acceleration and is, in fact, not successive but simultaneous." "Autobiography as De-Facement," in *Rhetoric of Romanticism*, p. 70. Benjamin Moss suggested in a conversation with the author in 1992 that a secondary, medical sense of "tourniquet" pits semiology against rhetoric by "staunching" de Man's indeterminacy metaphor.

8. "Semiology and Rhetoric," pp. 138–39.

9. "The Rhetoric of Blindness: Jacques Derrida's Reading of Rousseau," in *Blindness and Insight*, pp. 110–19.

10. The complaints lodged against students of deconstruction are summarized by Jonathan Culler in *On Deconstruction*, pp. 227–28.

11. See, e.g., Bate, "Crisis in English Studies"; Lentricchia, *After the New Criticism*; and Mohanty, "Radical Teaching."

12. Wiener, "Deconstructing de Man." See also Lehman, *Signs of the Times*.

13. Jonathan Culler uses this phrase in a slightly different way. He stresses that Derrida in no way claims to be systematic, unifying, or totalizing—that is, a master—even though his work provides a metacriticism of structuralism. Yet even to speak of Derrida's thought or to formulate its principles is to inscribe Derrida within the framework of Old Mastery. See Culler, "Jacques Derrida," pp. 154–57.

14. Ibid., p. 155.

15. *Modern French Philosophy*, pp. 138–39, 149, 152. On Derrida's adherence to philosophical rigor, see, e.g., Derrida, *Positions*, p. 83.

16. *Positions*, pp. 91, 93.

17. As defined by Kane, *Free Will and Values*, p. 7.

18. Miller defines this linguistic determinism as one of the four "grounds" operating in contemporary theory; the critic working from within the deconstructive framework considers how "language, the more or less hidden rhetorical pressures, or pressures from some torsion within language itself . . . impose themselves on the writer and make it impossible for his work to maintain itself as an absolutely lucid and reasonable account." "Search for Grounds," p. 21.

19. *Political Unconscious*, pp. 286, 287.

20. "Two Lectures," in *Power/Knowledge*, p. 93. Foucault's point in this remarkable statement is at least triple: first, whatever we call "the truth" is contingent on the political economy that produced it (might literally *makes* right); second, truth serves to legitimate whatever power relations are in effect within a culture by appearing to be anterior to those relations; and third, members of a given political economy necessarily experience their reality within that economy as noncontingent, or "true"; they are compelled to be subjugated by this truth. Foucault's contingent "truth" might also be called the "effect of mastery" (ibid.).

21. Foucault's model of power/knowledge does not readily account for change. If every ideology, determinist or otherwise, generates its own compelling "truth," then what makes one truth more compelling than another? Jameson's theory of incentives sheds more light on the rise and fall of ideologies, which it explains by means of a notion of agency—i.e., of human choice. The rhetoric of incentives, in spite of itself, has a certain free-market ring. Compare Barbara Smith's pragmatic account (in *Contingencies of Value* of both personal and communal economies of value, which are contingent upon the exchanges of the "marketplace."

22. "Nothing Fails Like Success," in *World of Difference*, pp. 11–16.

23. *Against Deconstruction*, pp. 98, 112.

24. Ibid., p. 102.

25. *Beyond Deconstruction*, pp. 134, 140.

26. Nowhere, one might add, would this institutional work ethic more likely be felt than at Yale University, home of American deconstruction and the locus of a uniquely Calvinist sensibility dating back to the founding of Connecticut, though now deracinated.

27. "Politics of Chaos," in *Chaos Bound*, p. 232.

28. In "Race for Theory," Barbara Christian denounces the hegemony of deconstruction within the academy and advocates a genuinely political and responsible criticism: "It has begun to occur to me that the literature being produced *is* precisely one of the reasons why this new philosophical-literary-criticism theory of relativity is so prominent. In other words, the literature of black women of South America and Africa, etc., as overtly 'political' literature was being preempted by a new Western concept which proclaimed that reality does not exist, that everything is relative, and that every text is silent about something—which indeed it must necessarily be" (p. 57). For an example of neo-postdeconstruction, see Miller, *Ethics of Reading*.

29. Lacan, "The mirror stage as formative of the function of the I as revealed in psychoanalytic experience," in *Écrits*, p. 2. "This event can take place, as we have known since Baldwin, from the age of six months, and its repetition has often made me reflect upon the startling spectacle of the infant in front of the mirror" (p. 1).

30. Gallop, "Where to Begin?" in *Reading Lacan*, pp. 74–92, 81. Here

I follow Gallop's critique of earlier readers of Lacan, such as Jean Laplanche and Jean-Baptiste Pontalis. Gallop points out that these more Freudian readers attribute too much mastery to the child entering the mirror stage. Gallop suggests, in contrast, that a child's identity not only is fragmented before the mirror stage, but necessarily remains fragmented after that supposed moment of recognition. The mirror stage "is the founding moment of the imaginary mode, the belief in a projected image" (ibid.). For Lacan, this image is the psyche's vulnerable fiction of selfhood.

31. Felman, "The Case of Poe," in *Jacques Lacan*, pp. 49, 57. "As for the theory of psychoanalysis, its originality, for Lacan, consists not so much in Freud's discovery of the unconscious—intuited before him by the poets— as in Freud's unprecedented discovery of the fact that *the unconscious speaks*: that the unconscious has a logic or a signifying structure, that it is structured like a language. This is what constitutes the radicality of the Freudian unconscious, which is not simply *opposed* to consciousness but speaks as something other from within the speech of consciousness, which it subverts." Ibid., p. 57.

32. Marx suggested that with the rise of communism, concrete individuals, free and unalienated, would emerge for the first time in history. On Marx's utopian but vague vision of the postrevolutionary subject, see Paul Smith's discussion in *Discerning the Subject*, pp. 3–23.

33. *Birth of the Clinic, Madness and Civilization*, and all three volumes of *History of Sexuality*.

34. See, to begin with, Lacan's sometimes appalling judgments on Dora's pathology in "Intervention on Transference," in *In Dora's Case*, pp. 92–104.

35. See Derrida's critique of Foucault in "Cogito and the History of Madness," in *Writing and Difference*, pp. 31–63, and his passing critique of Lacan in *Positions*. For a brief summary of Derrida's decenterings of these authors, see Culler, "Jacques Derrida," pp. 174–77.

36. "Unclaimed Experience," p. 181.

37. See de Man on the deconstructive "rhetoric" of mastery in *Blindness and Insight*, pp. 110–19. It could be argued that de Man suggests in that chapter a voluntarism, the possibility of linguistic control (the will to be ironic), that is not necessarily consistent with his determinist view of language. However, such contradictions typify every discourse on will, as I argue below.

38. *Hegemony and Socialist Strategy*, p. 116.

39. P. 148. Smith quotes "one of Gayatri Spivak's interventions at the 1982 MLA meetings in Los Angeles" (p. 171, n. 8).

40. Fuss, *Essentially Speaking*; Frank, *Das Individuelle allgemeine*, *What is Neostructuralism?*, and *Die Unhintergehbarkeit*; Dallmayr, *Twilight of Subjectivity*.

41. "Transcendance of the Individual," pp. 80, 82.

42. Heller, Sosna, and Wellbery, eds., *Reconstructing Individualism*, p. 2.

43. "Transcendance of the Individual," p. 82. Smith argues that critics have succeeded in avoiding the either/or formulation of humanist hubris versus deconstructive abandonment of agency. But notions of "freedom" and "humanism" are fundamental to this new "third course" theory, as well.

44. *Diatribe sive sermo de libero arbitrio* (A diatribe or sermon concerning free will) (1524), in Winter, ed., *Erasmus-Luther*. For an analysis of Luther's determinist theology, see Chapter 3.

45. Ibid., pp. 86–87.

46. Post-poststructuralists generally reject any hint of the Hegelian within their own theory, though arguably the "third course" described above makes use of at least the rhetoric of Hegelian dialectic.

47. *Discerning the Subject*, pp. 133–34. In this passage Smith paraphrases Toril Moi on Julia Kristeva, though Smith's formulation is somewhat more emphatic than Moi's.

Chapter 2

1. Tracing the history of "humanism" and related word forms, Paul Oskar Kristeller has pointed out that the phrase "studia humanitatis [humanities]" was used in Latin antiquity by Cicero and Gellius to denote a "liberal or literary education." In the late fourteenth century that term was revived by various Italian scholars, and by the early fifteenth century it referred to an educational program of certain disciplines, such as grammar, rhetoric, history, poetry, and moral philosophy. In the sixteenth century Italian university students coined the term "humanista" to designate a professor of the humanities, in contrast to the "legista," "jurista," and "canonista" of other disciplines. At the beginning of the nineteenth century, German educator F. J. Niethammer invented the word "Humanismus" for a secondary education curriculum stressing the Greek and Latin canon. Kristeller, "The Humanist Movement," in *Renaissance Thought*, p. 9.

2. A "broader sense of *humanism*, related to post-Enlightenment ideas of HISTORY (q.v.) as human self-development and self-perfection, also became established in C19, and this overlapped with a new use of humanism to represent the developed sense of humanist and the humanities: a particular kind of learning associated with particular attitudes to CULTURE (q.v.) and human development or perfection." Williams, *Keywords*, p. 150.

3. *Classical Heritage*, p. 242. Cf. Intro., n. 3.

4. Bolgar writes, "If [Petrarch] was the first modern man, he was also the first modern—or at any rate, the first Renaissance—scholar." Ibid., p. 253. Cf. Jacob Burckhardt on Petrarch, "one of the first truly modern men." One mark of Petrarch's modernity, Burckhardt claims, was his sensitivity to

natural beauty, as evidenced by the fact that he was possibly the first man since antiquity to climb a mountain for aesthetic enjoyment and write about it. *Civilization of the Renaissance*, 2: 293–97. See also Pierre de Nolhac, *Petrarch and the Ancient World*, p. 5: "Petrarch was the first modern man. No other phrase so well defines him. Individuality, the essential feature of the new man that Italy was fashioning, shines out in him with extraordinary vividness." For similar appraisals of Petrarch's modernity, see also Robinson, *Petrarch*, and Dotti, *Petrarca e la scoperta della coscienza moderna*. And for a recent deconstructive analysis of Petrarch as first modern man, see Ascoli, "Petrarch's Middle Age."

5. *L'Africa*, 9: 453–57; *Petrarch's "Africa,"* p. 239.

6. For a discussion of the inchoate idea of the Renaissance in Petrarch's writings, see Theodor E. Mommsen's classic essay, "Petrarch's Conception of the Dark Ages," and Erwin Panofsky's *Renaissance and Renaissances*, pp. 10–13.

7. Bolgar, *Classical Heritage*, pp. 247–55. "That individualist temper whose first stirrings we have noted among his contemporaries, possessed [Petrarch] in its most fiery and articulate form; and he used the fame won him by his verses to gain public recognition for his personality and his ideas" (p. 247).

8. Hungarian historian Agnes Heller, describing the continuity between the worldviews of Petrarch (as expressed in "The Ascent of Mont Ventoux") and Giordano Bruno, writes: "One of the great achievements of the scientific spirit of the Renaissance was precisely the drawing of a sharp distinction between subject and object. Immediate experience was increasingly evoked by the beauty and harmony of a nature interpreted as an object in itself. Humanity discovered the magnificence, the 'wonders' of its own world." *Renaissance Man*, p. 376.

9. " 'Whan She Translated Was,' " pp. 159, 157.

10. This is not to suggest that all previous historical readings of Petrarch are in some way oblivious to the "concrete historical moment." But the differences between the earlier twentieth-century tradition of Petrarch scholarship and more recent analyses such as Wallace's are the differences between "old" and new historicism. Both relate Petrarch's works to the "concrete historical moment" in which they were produced, but they emphasize quite separate aspects of that moment. So-called old historicism tends to be dominated by a recuperative mood, one that stresses, among other things, historical origins, unities, and coherence. In contrast, new historicism, the field where old historicism and poststructuralism meet, tends to emphasize disjunctions, aporias, etc. In contrast to those of the previous tradition, its thematic foci are generally issues of class, gender, and race.

11. "Contingencies of Value," in *Contingencies of Value*, pp. 47–53, 51.

12. *From Humanism to the Humanities*, p. 219. "The educational ideology contains the rarely articulated beliefs of the community about the functioning of the educational system: why this particular set of aptitudes has been selected for teaching emphasis; how these aptitudes are most effectively taught; and to what and whom the theoreticians believe an education ought to be directed" (ibid.). Cp. related arguments on humanist ideology in Martines, *Power and Imagination*.

13. *From Humanism to the Humanities*, p. xii.

14. The functions of cultural capital and the self-legitimating mechanisms of academia have been analyzed in a more contemporary context by sociologist Pierre Bourdieu. See *Distinction* and *Homo Academicus*.

15. Virtually all of the work of Michel Foucault offers a prime example of the positivist side of poststructuralism, arguing for historical origins and period concepts. Foucault might take Petrarch's own "nonmedieval" insistence that the author's life and mind are the center of any narrative as proof that "the coming into being of the notion of 'author' constitutes the privileged moment of individualization in the history of ideas, knowledge, literature, philosophy, and the sciences." "What is an Author?" p. 141. Indeed, Petrarch's self-absorbed, "individualist" writing brings to mind the conversational hinge: "But enough about me. What about you? What do you think about me?"

16. In the Proem of the *Secretum*, the author represents his "secret book" as autobiographical: "'To avoid the awkward repetition of "he said" and "I said" and to make the conversation as dramatic as possible,' as Cicero says, I have resorted to the simple method of placing the speaker's name before each of their statements." *S*, p. 39.

17. The relative eclipse of Augustinian thought in the European Middle Ages, together with its "rediscovery" by Petrarch and subsequent humanists and theologians, has been discussed by William Bouwsma in "Two Faces of Humanism," pp. 13, 17, 34. John Freccero has also remarked on the renewed interest in Augustine and in confessional autobiography after Petrarch's rediscovery of the Latin church father. "If the modern era is said to begin with the Petrarchan cult of personality, when Cicero and Virgil ceased being *auctores* and became pen pals [here Freccero refers to Petrarch's practice of writing letters to dead Romans], then it may be said that the *Confessions* came to be regarded only in the modern era for what it is: not simply the life of a saint, but also the paradigm for all representations of the self in a retrospective literary structure." "Autobiography and Narrative," p. 17.

18. Liddell and Scott, *Greek-English Lexicon*, s.v. "crisis." See Albert Ascoli's related discussion of crisis in *Ariosto's Bitter Harmony*, pp. 41–42.

19. On the revised dating of the *Secretum*, previously attributed to the

early 1340's, see Rico, *Lectura*, and Baron, *Petrarch's "Secretum."* Rico argues that critics have for decades confused the apparent time of the action in the *Secretum* (1342–43) with the times of its writing (1347, 1349, 1353). *Lectura*, p. 9.

20. In his analysis of Renaissance attitudes toward death and fame, Alberto Tenenti argues that the *Secretum*'s discussion of the value of meditation on death dramatizes two opposing spiritual attitudes that were assuming special importance toward the middle of the fourteenth century: "C'è stato allora un momento in cui la rappresentazione della sorte fisica è divenuta tanto prepotente da erigersi a centro della vita morale. Ma nel contempo un dramma inatteso si è prodotto: mentre gli uni predicavano che soltanto facendo convergere gli occhi sulla sua fine il credente li avrebbe rivolti poi al cielo, gli altri cominciarono ad affermare che la morte non doveva essere temuta da chi viveva secondo virtù." Petrarch belongs to the second category, he contends, and Francis as his spokesman rejects the morbid form of meditation that Augustine recommends. *Il senso della morte*, pp. 48–52.

21. Petrarch follows more or less verbatim *Confessions* 8.8.20, where the historical Augustine describes the state of his will before conversion. However, the *Secretum*'s account of the conversion proper has a Pelagian cast not found in the original. On the predestinarian bent of Augustinian theology, see Augustine, *Select Anti-Pelagian Treatises*. On the theological and philosophical discrepancies between the historical Augustine and Petrarch's quasi-heretical Augustine, see Heitmann, *Fortuna und Virtus* and "L'Insegnamento agostiniano." Charles Trinkaus has suggested either that Francis is meant to be identified with the historical Augustine (by being allied with a theology of grace), or that Petrarch misread or misremembered the *Confessions*. See *In Our Image and Likeness*, 1: 9.

On the partial reconciliation of Stoicism to Augustinian thought in the *Secretum*, see Bouwsma, "Two Faces of Humanism." "The humanism of the earlier Renaissance uneasily blended Stoic and Augustinian impulses which it neither distinguished clearly nor, in many cases, was capable of identifying with their sources. Its Augustinianism consisted of a bundle of personal insights that had, indeed, legitimate affinities with Augustine himself, as Petrarch vaguely sensed; but its Stoicism was singularly confused." However, Petrarch and his successors, Bouwsma argues, made some headway in distinguishing these ideological poles by attempting to "dissolve the identity of ancient philosophy as a whole with a perennial wisdom and thus up to a point with Christianity itself, to sort out one school from another, and so to see every set of ideas, individually identified, as a product of the human mind at work under the limitations of historical circumstance" (pp. 52–53).

22. Heitmann, *Fortuna und Virtus* and "L'Insegnamento agostiniano"; Trinkaus, *In Our Image and Likeness* and *Poet as Philosopher*; Bouwsma, "Two Faces of Humanism"; Marsh, *Quattrocentro Dialogue*; Pelikan, *Reformation of Church and Dogma*, pp. 19–21; Rabil, "Petrarch."

23. Tateo, *Dialogo interiore*.

24. Tonelli, *Petrarca*; Calcaterra, *Nella selva del Petrarca*.

25. *Lectura*, pp. 534–35.

26. *Petrarch's "Secretum,"* pp. 246–48.

27. *Light in Troy*, pp. 104–11.

28. "Figure of the Reader," p. 156.

29. The similarities of Petrarch's treatment of "fortuna" here and in the *De remediis utriusque fortunae* (ca. 1454–57) have been noted by Baron (*Petrarch's "Secretum"*) and several others. It would be intriguing to explore the possible connections or allusions of that text to the ignoble demise of Cola di Rienzo.

30. T. Price Zimmerman has described the development of self-awareness through the highly systematic examination of conscience and the motives of the will in late medieval confessional practices, whence he argues that Renaissance autobiography evolved. He considers the *Secretum* to be one of the earliest such autobiographies. See "Confession and Autobiography." Arnaud Tripet has also written on Augustine's role as confessor in the sacramental sense, as doctor to the soul: "Le confesseur garantit et relaie le bon vouloir et la pénétration du confessé, l'aide à voir clair en lui et à rapporter son jugement aux exigences véridiques que saura lui rappeler ce 'représentant de Jésus-Christ.' " *Pétrarque ou la connaissance de soi*, p. 167.

31. Petrarch champions this same ideal of the reclusive and rustic poet in his verse letter to Horace (*Familiares* 24.10):

> Pronum te viridi cespite, fontium
> Captantem strepitus et volucrum modos,
> Carpentem riguo gramine flosculos,
> Nectentem facili vimine palmites,
> Tendentem tenui pollice barbiton,
> Miscentem numeros pectine candido,
> Mulcentem vario carmine sidera
> Ut vidi, invidiam mens vaga nobilem
> Concepit subito

> When I saw you reclining upon the fresh turf, listening
> to the bubbling of springs and the songs of birds,
> or plucking little flowers from the grassy meadow,
> or binding vine sprouts with pliant hosiers,
> or plucking the lyre with gentle fingers, and
> changing the measures with your white plectrum,

and soothing the stars with varied song; when I beheld
all this, my eager mind suddenly fell prey
to a noble desire

Le Familiari, 4: 251; *Letters on Familiar Matters*, 3: 338.

32. Augustine quotes Virgil's *Georgics* 4, 132–33, a passage that also evokes the ending of the first Eclogue.

33. *Oaten Flute*, pp. 4, 5.

34. *Pastoral and Ideology*, p. 40. In the chapter entitled "Medievalism," Patterson focuses on the reception of Virgil's *Eclogues* by Servius, the fourth-century commentator who viewed them as political and historical allegories, and later by Petrarch, who studied the Servian commentaries and, she argues, accepted and perpetuated that allegorical approach to Virgilian pastoral. Patterson's reading of the *Bucolicum carmen*, Petrarch's imitation of Virgil's *Eclogues*, as pastoral allegory concerning the role of the intellectual can be extended to include the pastoral moments in the *Secretum* and, indeed, figures of pastoral that recur throughout Petrarch's works, as we shall see.

35. See Wilkins, *Petrarch's Eight Years in Milan*; Bishop, *Petrarch and His World*, pp. 320–38; and Wallace, " 'Whan She Translated Was,' " pp. 172–77.

36. *Earthly Paradise*, p. 84. For a completely different view of pastoral, see Williams, *City and the Country*. Williams explores the violence and misery of early agrarian capitalism as obfuscated by generations of English poets and critics.

37. See, e.g., Bouwsma, "Two Faces of Humanism," p. 28.

38. *Contingencies of Value*, p. 131.

39. Siegfried Wenzel has identified the accidia of Francis as an innovative combination of the medieval monastic version of sloth and the Stoic main affects of the soul. *Sin of Sloth*, pp. 155–63.

40. Here Francis quotes Horace, *Carmina* 2.10.5–8, on the golden mean: "auream quisquis mediocritatem / diligit tutus caret obsoleti / sordibus tecti, caret invidenda / sobrius aula" (*OL*, p. 150).

41. See pp. 47–49.

42. Rico, *Lectura*, pp. 7–38; Baron, *Petrarch's "Secretum,"* pp. 1–18. In an earlier work, "Petrarch's Secretum: Was It Revised—and Why?" (in *From Petrarch to Leonardo Bruni*, pp. 51–101), Baron accepted the earlier dating of the *Secretum* (1342–43)—a thesis he later abandoned—and argued that the dialogue had been rewritten in 1347, 1349, and 1353.

Rico and Baron base their redating of the *Secretum* in part on three dates that appear on the Laurentian Library manuscript 26 sin. 9, copied in 1378 by the Franciscan Teodaldo della Casa from Petrarch's autograph. In the margin of the last page of the dialogue appears the following note: "Modo 3. 1353. 1349. 1347." Rico and Baron argue that these dates refer to the final version of 1353, the editorial changes of 1349, and the initial composition of 1347. The dating of the *Secretum* has long been debated. Certain eighteenth- and nineteenth-century critics supposed that the three dates mentioned above referred to the dates of composition of its three books (see Baron, *Petrarch's "Secretum,"* p. 2). But in 1917 Remigio Sabbadini argued that the *Secretum* was originally written in 1342–43, then revised during the three years mentioned in Petrarch's note ("Note filologiche"). Luigi Tonelli, Carlo Calcaterra, and many other critics since Sabbadini's time have held that the *Secretum* was originally occasioned by Petrarch's spiritual crisis of 1342–43. Rico and Baron, in turn, have challenged various assumptions about that supposed spiritual crisis in relation to the *Secretum.*

43. Rico, *Lectura*, p. 8. *OL*, p. 176.

44. Also, in book 2 of the dialogue, Francis talks about his attempt to learn Greek, cut short by the untimely departure of his teacher. Petrarch had undertaken that study under the tutelage of the Greek monk Bernard Barlaam during the summer of 1342. Barlaam had left Avignon on November 12, 1342, to accept a bishopric in Calabria; thus the action of the *Secretum* would seem to take place between November 1342 and April 1343. Rico, *Lectura*, pp. 8–9.

45. Ibid., pp. 9–16. "La crítica moderna, prácticamente con unanimidad, ha arrimado o confundido acción y redacción" (p. 9).

46. Though Petrarch first read the *De vera religione* sometime before June of 1335, Francis claims in book 1 to have just recently read it ("in quem librum nuper incidi" [*OL*, p. 94]). Rico, and Baron after him, argue that Petrarch felt the full impact of that work in 1347, during which time, they contend, he composed both the *De otio religioso* and the *Secretum.* Rico, *Lectura*, pp. 113–22; Baron, *Petrarch's "Secretum,"* pp. 5–6.

47. "The Ascent of Mont Ventoux" (*Familiares* 4.1) is a case in point. It is set in 1336 but was actually written in 1353 or thereabouts (see Billanovich, "Dall' 'Epystolarum mearum,' " pp. 193–207; Baron, *Petrarch's "Secretum,"* pp. 3–6.

48. " 'Whan She Translated Was,' " p. 163. The difficulty of establishing the chronology of Petrarch's works with any certainty has led some critics, such as Umberto Bosco, to dismiss the problem of historical reference altogether. "[Il Petrarca] è senza storia, se lo si considera, come si deve, nel concreto di tutta l'opera sua," Bosco argues. *Francesco Petrarca*, p. 7.

49. In book 2, Francis describes the city he lives in as "the most depressing and turbulent city in the whole world, the narrow and last recep-

tacle of all the filth of the world" (*S,* p. 90). This filthy city has been understood by Rico and others as a reference to Avignon (*Lectura,* p. 230). Baron offers the unorthodox and implausible interpretation, however, that the city is actually Milan, and that Petrarch wrote this part of the accidia section in 1353. *Petrarch's "Secretum,"* pp. 166–80.

50. Dotti, *Vita di Petrarca,* p. 151.

51. *Il sentimento politico del Petrarca,* p. 25.

52. Principal sources for this account of the life of Cola di Rienzo and the Roman populist revolt of 1347 include Wright, ed. and trans., *Life of Cola di Rienzo;* Gabrielli, ed., *Epistolario di Cola di Rienzo;* Burdach and Piur, eds., *Briefwechsel des Cola di Rienzo;* Piur, *Cola di Rienzo;* Cosenza, *Revolution of Cola di Rienzo;* Theseider, *Roma dal comune;* Mollat and Wolff, *Popular Revolutions;* Mazzei, *Cola di Rienzo;* Toppani, "Petrarca"; and the biographies of Petrarch by Wilkins and Bishop.

53. Cosenza, *Revolution of Cola di Rienzo,* pp. 2, 9–10, n. 2.

54. Stefano Colonna, patriarch of the Colonna family, had gone with the militia to Corneto to look for grain. Wright, ed., *Life of Cola di Rienzo,* p. 40.

55. Ibid., pp. 40–45; Mazzei, *Cola di Rienzo,* pp. 64–71.

56. De Mattei, *Il sentimento politico del Petrarca,* pp. 54–55.

57. Wright, ed., *Life of Cola di Rienzo,* p. 73.

58. The example of one Martino de Puorto, a Roman aristocrat who "led the life of a tyrant . . . disgraced his nobility with tyrannies and robberies," and "looked like a lute," was meant to deter the Roman nobility from its usual practices. Puorto was condemned and hanged for having robbed a beached galley. Ibid., pp. 48–50. On the social and moral reforms initiated by Cola, see Theseider, *Roma dal comune,* pp. 551–60.

59. Theseider, *Roma dal comune,* p. 584.

60. In an August 1 letter to Pope Clement VI, the vicar describes his stunned outrage at Cola's actions: "Nicolaus ipse post assumptum honorem milicie infra ipsius misse solempnia, surgens in conspectu populi eique indicto silencio, per quendam Notarium Urbis nomine Egidium Angeli, me inconsulto et protinus inscio, legi et publicari fecit ordinaciones, quas micto presentibus interclusas. Quibus auditis et intellectis obstupui." Burdach and Piur, eds., *Briefwechsel des Cola di Rienzo,* pt. 4, p. 19.

61. On the symbolism of the coronation ceremony and on Clement VI's letter to the cardinal legate, Bertrand de Déaulx, expressing his outrage at Cola's presumptuous rituals, see ibid., pp. 32–41.

62. In mid-September the papacy, by attacking Cola's envoy outside of Avignon, made known to the tribune that he had fallen into serious disfavor. In a September 17 letter to Rinaldo Orsini, the papal notary, Cola com-

plains that the pope's forces smashed his ambassador's wand and letter case on his head. However, Cola says he will refrain from taking legal action because of his reverence for the pope. Gabrielli, *Epistolario di Cola di Rienzo*, pp. 61–67. Petrarch writes of his outrage at the indignity inflicted upon the Roman courier by the papacy in his "Epistolae sine nomine" 2.

63. Wright, ed., *Life of Cola di Rienzo*, pp. 90–91; Theseider, *Roma dal comune*, p. 607.

64. Wright, ed., *Life of Cola di Rienzo*, p. 91; Cosenza, *Revolution of Cola di Rienzo*, p. 151.

65. Theseider, *Roma dal comune*, pp. 525–26. The importance of the request that Roman jubilees be held more frequently (every 50 years, rather than every century) should not be underestimated; jubilee celebrations brought thousands of pilgrims and tourists to the economically blighted city.

66. Ibid., p. 526.

67. Wright, ed., *Life of Cola di Rienzo*, pp. 31–32; Theseider, *Roma dal comune*, p. 528.

68. Theseider, *Roma dal comune*, p. 530; Cosenza, *Revolution of Cola di Rienzo*, p. 4; Bishop, *Petrarch and His World*, pp. 257–58. Petrarch had received the patronage of members of the Colonna family as early as 1330. In that year Cardinal Giovanni Colonna took Petrarch into his service as household chaplain. Petrarch remained in service to the family in various capacities for seventeen years. Wilkins, *Life of Petrarch*, pp. 9–10.

69. According to one tradition, Petrarch's "Epistolae sine nomine" 7 describes the poet's inspiring first meeting with Cola in Avignon in 1343. Petrarch writes that the addressee's eloquent words on the desperate conditions in Rome drive the poet to tears, and he closes with a plea for an end to that suffering. However, Wilkins argues that this letter was written not to Cola, but to Cardinal Niccola Capocci, and that it seems to refer to conditions in Rome in 1351. See "Petrarch and Niccola Capocci," in *Studies in the Life and Works of Petrarch*, pp. 182–92.

70. *Life of Petrarch*, pp. 63–64.

71. *History of the City of Rome*, 6, pt. 1: 262–63.

72. "Epistolae variae" 48, "To Cola di Rienzo and the Roman People," Cosenza, *Revolution of Cola di Rienzo*, pp. 15–16; *Epistolae*, 3: 423.

73. De Mattei argues that Petrarch had nothing against the nobility in principle and was able to reconcile his authoritarian tendencies with his defenses of the people's liberty without contradiction. Indeed, he followed Cicero's example in doing so. "Chi ben guardai, tuttavia, il Petrarca sta, più che per la Signoria, per il Signore, per l'ottimo principe; e qui egli è perfettamente conseguente ai dettami della sua cultura e vocazione classica, che gli fa recercare e venerare i tipi illustri, le vite esemplari, le grandi iniziative.

Il suo ideale è, in fondo, aristocratico: ma che cosa è il Signore se non una copia ridotta dell'Imperatore, funzionando, del resto, da vicario imperiale?" *Il sentimento politico del Petrarca*, p. 73.

74. Cosenza, *Revolution of Cola di Rienzo*, p. 17.

75. Wilkins, *Life of Petrarch*, pp. 13–14; Bishop, *Petrarch and His World*, pp. 114–25.

76. Cosenza, *Revolution of Cola di Rienzo*, pp. 17–18. "The valley of Spoleto claims this one [the Orsini]; the Rhone, or some obscure corner of the world has sent us the next [the Colonna]." Ibid., p. 17.

77. Ibid., p. 23.

78. On the physical condition of medieval Rome, see Krautheimer, *Rome: Profile of a City*.

79. Cosenza, *Revolution of Cola di Rienzo*, p. 25.

80. Ibid., p. 31.

81. *Life of Petrarch*, p. 64.

82. Cosenza, *Revolution of Cola di Rienzo*, p. 32.

83. Weiss, "Barbato da Sulmona," pp. 21, 22. Barbato's 1347 letter suggests that Petrarch serve as theorist and Cola as executive (see Bishop, *Petrarch and His World*, pp. 261–62). In this letter, called "Roma Respublica Urbi Rome" and written as if by the ancient republic to the city of Rome, Barbato writes of Petrarch and of Cola: "Hi namque sunt soli, due lucerne et duo candelabra pro me lucentia, quorum si tu fulgorem eximium aliorumque tuorum civium densissimas tenebras perfecte cognoveris, posthabitis ceteris duobus ipsis totaliter inherebis." Weiss, "Barbato da Sulmona," p. 18. A reference in the letter to Petrarch's return to Italy leads Weiss to believe that Barbato wrote somewhere near the end of November (ibid., p. 17, n. 2).

84. In "Epistolae variae" 38, dating from the end of July 1347, Petrarch claims to have been writing Cola daily to express his anxieties about his friend and about the new Roman state.

85. Gabrielli, *Epistolario* 15, lines 17–19, p. 38; Cosenza, *Revolution of Cola di Rienzo*, pp. 50–51.

86. The first four eclogues were probably written in 1346, and numbers 5 through 8 were written sometime before Petrarch's departure from Avignon in November of 1347. *Petrarch's "Bucolicum Carmen,"* pp. 217, 225, 228, 230, 232. All in-text citations to the *Bucolicum carmen* are to this edition. Eclogue 5, written to Cola and called "Pietas pastoralis," or "Shepherds' piety," features two sons (the Colonna and the Orsini) who argue over who will take care of their mother and her land. While they are debating, news arrives that a third son (Cola) has taken on the job, and that their mother has disowned the other two.

87. Gillias is generally identified as Azzo da Correggio, tyrant of Parma,

who had invited Petrarch to join him at his court. Cosenza, *Revolution of Cola di Rienzo*, pp. 132–33. Bishop, however, leaves open the possibility that Gillias represents Cola. *Petrarch and His World*, p. 245.

88. Bishop, *Petrarch and His World*, p. 245.

89. *Neo-Latin Literature*, p. 94.

90. "Divortium" primarily connotes the separation of man and wife, but it also refers to a point of separation, such as a fork in the road.

91. James M. Saslow has analyzed the popularity of the figure of Ganymede in Renaissance art, especially during the fifteenth and sixteenth centuries. Medieval discussions of the beloved of Jove tended to overlay the classical myths with Christian allegory, and they often ignored or denounced the homoerotic aspects of the Ganymede story. However, both Petrarch and Boccaccio discuss Ganymede "in an essentially antiquarian and encyclopedic spirit, with no moralizing gloss on the original texts." *Ganymede*, pp. 5–6.

92. Virgil's Eclogues 2, 3, and 10, for example, express the homoerotic desires of shepherds.

93. Irigaray, *This Sex Which Is Not One*; Sedgwick, *Between Men*. Irigaray explains:

> The trade that organizes patriarchal societies takes place exclusively among men. Women, signs, goods, currency, all pass from one man to another or— so it is said—suffer the penalty of relapsing into the incestuous and exclusively endogamous ties that would paralyze all commerce. The work force, products, even those of mother-earth, would thus be the object of transactions among men only. This signifies that the very possibility of the sociocultural order would necessitate homosexuality. Homosexuality is the law that regulates the socio-cultural order. . . .
>
> Why then consider masculine homosexuality as an exception, while in fact it is the very basis of the general economy? Why exclude homosexuals, when society postulates homosexuality? Unless it is because the "incest" at work in homosexuality must be kept in the realm of pretense. And so it is, exemplarily so, in father-son relations which assure the genealogy of patriarchal power, its laws, its discourse, its sociality. These relations which are operative everywhere can neither disappear—in the abolition of the family or of monogamic reproduction, for example—nor be displayed openly in their pederastic love, nor be practiced in any other way but in language without provoking a general crisis. A certain symbolic order would come to an end. (p. 107)

94. Bee metaphors abound in Petrarch's oeuvre, particularly regarding the subject of poetic imitation, a process figured as mellification, the bee's production of honey. In this way Petrarch represents his imitations of the works of others as both natural and original. See Greene, *Light in Troy*.

95. "Epistolae variae" 48; *Epistolae*, 3: 426–27. Petrarch's interpretation of Brutus was altogether different from that of Dante and other con-

temporaries. Dante, of course, placed Caesar's assassin in the bottom of Hell.

96. "Epistolae variae" 38; Cosenza, *Revolution of Cola di Rienzo*, p. 54; *Epistolae*, 3: 400–402.

97. "Epistolae variae" 40; Cosenza, *Revolution of Cola di Rienzo*, pp. 64, 65; *Epistolae*, 3: 404–8.

98. As the news from the pope's vicar in Rome reached Avignon, Petrarch found himself very much under fire. He removed to his house in the Vaucluse, where he most probably composed the obscure Eclogue 5 on the future of Rome. This eclogue was so cryptic that Petrarch sent Cola an answer key along with it ("Epistolae variae" 42). Perhaps the poet no longer felt comfortable naming names, since the outcome of Cola's experiment had become even more uncertain. Two other letters, the "Epistolae sine nomine" 2 and 3, dating from early September, express the poet's outrage and fear at Avignon's mobilization against Cola.

99. Bishop, *Petrarch and His World*, p. 264. On Petrarch's diplomatic mission, see Cipolla, "Sui motive del Ritorno."

100. *Familiares* 7.5; Bernardo, *Letters*, 1: 346; Rossi, *Familiari*, 2: 107.

101. *Familiares* 7.6; Bernardo, *Letters*, 1: 347; Rossi, *Familiari*, 2: 108.

102. Since Petrarch appears to have spent much of his adult life in pursuit of major offices—e.g., the archdeaconate of the cathedral of Parma in 1346, and possibly a cardinalate in 1351—this disclaimer seems particularly hypocritical.

103. "Dicitur *mediocritate* non contentis: 'Mendicitatem et divitias ne dederis michi; tribue tantum victui meo necessaria, ne forte satiatus illiciar ad negandum et dicam: quis est Dominus? et egestate complusus furer et periurem nomen Dei mei' [Prov. 3: 8–9]." *De otio religioso*, in *OL*, p. 592 (my emphasis).

104. This manuscript now resides in the Laurentian Library (Plut. 34, 1). It has been described by Pierre de Nolhac in *Pétrarque et l'humanisme*, 1: 181–85. The manuscript contains the *Carmina*, the *Ars poetica*, the *Epodes*, the *Carmen saeculare*, and the *Epistles* and *Sermons*. Petrarch wrote in the front the date of purchase, November 28, and also the note "Liber Francisci Petrarce laureati, qui post obitum eius remaneat penes heredem suum." The rich marginalia of the manuscript may provide more clues to the dating of portions of the *Secretum* dealing with Horatian themes, although thus far my investigation has been inconclusive. Invaluable resources for further analysis of the manuscript are de la Mare, *Handwriting of the Italian Humanists*, and especially Petrucci, *Scrittura de Francesco Petrarca*. In certain of the *Familiares* dating from the early 1340's (3.7, 3.14), Petrarch also writes of "mediocritas." However, as Hans Baron points out in *From Petrarch to Leonardo Bruni*, the letters from that period emphasize

"paupertas" rather than the relatively affluent "mediocritas." For that reason, Baron assumes that the discussions of the golden mean in the *Secretum* date from 1353, when Petrarch was more affluent than he had been a decade earlier (p. 81, n. 82). Baron does not, however, discuss the letter to Socrates (*Familiares* 7.6) in the context of the *Secretum* or of the Cola di Rienzo debacle.

105. *Familiares* 7.7; Bernardo, *Letters*, 1: 350, 351; Rossi, *Familiari*, 2: 110–11.

106. *Letters*, 1: 351.

107. Bishop, *Petrarch and His World*, p. 268.

108. Ibid., pp. 273–74.

109. The four members of the Colonna family killed during this skirmish were Stefano the younger, brother of the cardinal, and Stefano's son Giovanni, plus Pietro and Giovanni Colonna, the cardinal's first cousins.

110. *Familiares* 7.13; Bernardo, *Letters*, 1: 367, 368; Rossi, *Familiari*, 2: 123, 124.

111. Bernardo, *Letters*, 1: 371, 372; Rossi, *Familiari*, 2: 127.

112. After the cardinal died, Petrarch wrote an equally obsequious letter (*Familiares* 8.1) to his father, Stefano Colonna, the aged patriarch who had hosted Petrarch years earlier on the latter's visit to Rome, and who had headed one faction of the baronial opposition to Cola. In that letter, too, Petrarch discusses fate at length, as well as the true Romanness of Stefano Colonna.

113. I have limited the scope of this argument to a consideration of book 2 of the *Secretum* for two reasons. The first is that the portions of that book dedicated to avarice, ambition, and accidia show a thematic and philological relation to Petrarch's other writings of late 1347, as I argue below. The second is that any serious consideration of the dating(s) of book 1 and especially of book 3 would require an investigation much longer than space here permits.

114. Rico, *Lectura*, p. 455.

115. "Naturalmente, esa filosofía que aglutina el diálogo es en gran medida ética y, por ende, también 'teología.'" Ibid., p. 529.

116. Ibid., pp. 534, 532–35 (my translations).

117. Baron, *Petrarch's "Secretum,"* pp. 222, 246–47.

118. Ibid., pp. 30, 159–80.

119. Ibid., pp. 159–80. Rico, significantly, was not persuaded by the earlier form of this argument, made in Baron, *From Petrarch to Leonardo Bruni*.

120. Foster, *Petrarch*, p. 9.

121. Eagleton, *Significance of Theory*, p. 29.

122. Ascoli, "Petrarch's Middle Age," p. 42.

Chapter 3

1. Petrarch's position in the clergy has been discussed by E. H. Wilkins, *Life of Petrarch*, p. 9, and by Morris Bishop, *Petrarch and His World*, p. 60.

2. This unusual honor was bestowed upon Teresa by Pope Paul VI in 1969.

3. On the various views of will, freedom, and grace held by Luther's theological precursors, see, e.g., Pelikan, *Reformation of Church and Dogma*; Ozment, "Luther and the Late Middle Ages" and *Age of Reform*; Oberman, *Harvest of Medieval Theology*; and Harran, *Luther on Conversion*, pp. 43–53. In Luther's view, the most "Pelagian"—i.e., voluntarist—of his predecessors were Duns Scotus, William of Ockham, Pierre d'Ailly, and Gabriel Biel. Cp. Ozment, "Luther and the Late Middle Ages," p. 119.

4. In the fourth century, Pelagius asserted that to will the good, man is not dependent on any directly assisting grace granted by God, and that man does not inherit physical death or any "fault and corruption of nature" as a consequence of Adam's original sin. But for Augustine, these theories were tantamount to a denial of man's fall. Augustine insisted on the reality of original sin, namely, man's inheritance of the guilt and consequences of Adam's transgression in the form of a tainted and disordered nature. Augustine also argued that prevenient grace must be antecedent to man's willing of the good. But his severest assertion against the freedom of will avowed by the Pelagians was his advocacy of what would later be called double predestination—God's willing not only of the salvation of some men, but of the damnation of others. See Bright's introduction to *Select Anti-Pelagian Treatises of St. Augustine*, pp. vii–lxvii; Brown, *Augustine of Hippo*, pp. 340–407; Ozment, *Age of Reform*, pp. 28–29. Actually, Augustine's views of the will varied substantially, depending on whether he was arguing against the Pelagians, who attributed too much power to the will, or the Manichaeans, whose determinism implied that humans bore no responsibility for their actions. Pelikan, *Reformation of Church and Dogma*, pp. 139–41.

5. Lea, *History of Auricular Confession*, 3: 277–84; Ozment, *Age of Reform*, pp. 204–22.

6. Ozment, *Age of Reform*, p. 217; Lea, *History of Auricular Confession*, 1: 227–29.

7. Pelikan, *Reformation of Church and Dogma*, pp. 135–36.

8. In the bull *Unigenitus*, Pope Clement VI declared himself the controller and dispenser of a treasury of merit, a reservoir of good works bestowed by Christ on man through the "copious flood" of his blood. It was against this treasury that letters of indulgence were issued. In 1476 Pope Sixtus IV allowed the living to buy indulgences not only for themselves, but for the dead in Purgatory, thereby greatly increasing possible revenues for

the Vatican. Ozment, *Age of Reform*, p. 217; Lea, *History of Auricular Confession*, 3: 24–25, 345–47.

9. Lea, *History of Auricular Confession*, 3: 379–92; Ozment, *Age of Reform*, p. 251.

10. Pelikan, *Reformation of Church and Dogma*, p. 146. Pelikan adds: "By defining justification as the forgiveness of sins, Luther emphasized even more sharply its gratuitous character. The scholastic doctrine of merit . . . was guilty of 'usurping the right that belongs to Christ alone. Only he delivers from sin and grants righteousness and eternal life' " (Luther, *Commentary on Galatians* [1535], in *WA*, 40, pt. 1: 236–38). Ibid., p. 148. See, too, Althaus, *Ethics of Martin Luther*, pp. 3–24.

11. Luther's critique discredited both the purchaser, vainly hoping to buy God off through papal intercession, and the pope, falsely and presumptuously assuming the authority to intercede with God on behalf of sinners. Pelikan, *Reformation of Church and Dogma*, p. 146.

12. Theses 5 and 6 assert, for example, that:

> The pope neither desires nor is able to remit any penalties except those imposed by his own authority.
>
> The pope cannot remit any guilt, except by declaring and showing that it has been remitted by God; or, to be sure, by remitting guilt in cases reserved to his judgment. If his right to grant remission in these cases were disregarded, the guilt would certainly remain unforgiven. (*LW*, 31: 26)

13. See, e.g., Luther's 1518 *Resolutiones disputationum de indulgentiarum virtute* (Explanations of the ninety-five theses), *WA*, 1: 522–628; *LW*, 31: 77–252. Later Luther would state his view on the limits of papal authority still more forcefully. In his 1520 *Assertio*, for example, Luther abandoned his earlier, more conciliatory formula that "indulgences are a pious fraud practiced upon Christians [indulgentiae sunt piae fraudes fidelium]; they are remissions of good works." In Thesis 18 of the *Assertio*, Luther wrote ironically, "I erred [Erravi]. Therefore I recant and say, 'Indulgences are the most impious frauds and impostures of most wicked popes [Indulgentias esse impiissimas sceleratissimorum pontificum fraudes et imposturas], by which they deceive the souls of the faithful and squander their money' " (*WA*, 7: 125; my translation).

14. Harran, *Luther on Conversion*, p. 167.

15. Victoria Kahn has argued that Erasmus sought to disjoin epistemology, as embodied in human claims to understand the problem of will and grace, from ethics, the ideas of moral responsibility that he wanted to defend. But Luther, Kahn argues, insisted in his critique of Erasmus both that epistemological certainty must be the foundation of any ethical assertion, and that epistemological certainty about the status of the will has been

provided by God's word, the Bible. See "Erasmus: Prudence and Faith," in *Rhetoric, Prudence, and Skepticism*, pp. 89–114.

16. "By means of Scripture, regarded as obscure, nothing definite has ever yet been settled or can be settled concerning free choice" (*LW*, 33: 102).

17. Pelikan, *Reformation of Church and Dogma*, pp. 143–45.

18. On the challenges to institutional authority posed by Lutheran theology, see, e.g., Pelikan, *Spirit vs. Structure*.

19. See, e.g., *The freedom of a Christian*, *LW*, 31: 364–68.

20. Oberman, *Luther: Man Between God and the Devil*, p. 299.

21. In early 1544 Georg Spalatin, minister in Altenburg, and Georg Rörer, Luther's amanuensis, began gathering material for an authoritative edition of Luther's Latin works. In 1545 the first volume of these writings was published in Wittenberg by Hans Lufft, after Luther finally consented to aid in its preparation and added his Preface, which he dated March 5, 1545. *WA*, 54: 179–87; *LW*, 34: 325–38.

22. Stracke, "Luthers groszes Selbstzeugnis 1545," p. 20.

23. Boehmer, *Luther and the Reformation*, p. 32.

24. On the dating and significance of Luther's conversion and hermeneutic breakthough, see Lohse, ed., *Der Durchbruch der reformatorischen Erkenntnis bei Luther*, and Harran, "Luther's Tower Experience," in *Luther on Conversion*, pp. 174–88.

25. On the idea of the Bible's self-evident meaning and the certainty, if not perfect knowledge, that it provides humankind, see the interesting discussions in Kahn, *Rhetoric, Prudence, and Skepticism*, p. 99, and Waswo, *Language and Meaning*, pp. 235–49.

26. *St. Augustine's Confessions*, p. 164; *Confessions*, p. 424.

27. Luther was plagued with scruples in Wittenberg, as Loyola would be in Manresa a few years later: "As soon as he had confessed and turned to the altar, he beckoned again for a priest," Boehmer writes (*Martin Luther*, p. 88).

28. Luther notes that he finds confirmation, albeit inchoate, of his reinterpretation of the righteousness of God in Augustine's *De spiritu et littera* (*LW*, 34: 337; *WA*, 54: 186). Augustine writes: "Sed iustitia Dei, non qua Deus justus est, sed qua induit hominem, cum justificat impium. Haec testificatur per legem et Prophetas: huic quippe testimonium perhibet lex et Prophetae. Lex quidem, hoc ipso, quod jubendo et mirando et neminem justificando satis indicat, dono Dei justificari hominem per adjutorium spiritus: Prophetae autem, quia id quod praedixerunt, Christi implevit adventus. Nam hinc sequitur et adjungit, dicens, *Justitia autem Dei per fidem Jesu Christi*, hoc est, per fidem qua creditur in Jesu Christum" (*De spiritu et littera*, p. 209). Luther's discovery of that precedent assures him that he has done no violence to the text of Scripture; Augustine confirms, that is, the nonsubversiveness of Luther's readings. But more importantly, Luther's in-

terpretation involves no willful disobedience; that is, he does not impose a new (and therefore wrong) sense on the Word, but discovers by God's mercy the meaning that had always been there, though it had been obscured by false interpretations.

In a recent Lacanian interpretation of Luther's conversion, John Zuern points out that "this rupture [in Luther's habitual reading of this text] also establishes a divide between two kinds of paternal power, one terrifying and destructive, the other marked by a passivity that awakens, in the subject subjected to its power, 'a love.' It is with this doubly valenced power that Luther must negotiate a relationship which allows the empowering passivity of God's righteousness to preside over God's threatening—castrating—omnipotence." "Mark of a Subject," p. 21.

29. *Luther on Conversion*, p. 191.

30. *Luther: Man Between God and the Devil*, p. 74.

31. Indeed, the prudent tactic in this and other Luther studies of separating ethics and epistemology, or, in deconstructive terms, the performative and the cognitive, replicates the strategy of Erasmus's *De libero arbitrio* as argued by Victoria Kahn. See n. 15 above.

32. Jedin, *Ecumenical Councils*, p. 161.

33. Jedin, *History of the Council of Trent*, 2: 166–96, 239–316; Pelikan, *Reformation of Church and Dogma*, p. 285.

34. In a three-hour speech on October 26, 1546, Laínez inveighed against the theology of "twofold justice" (Christ's and the believer's) then under discussion. Despite its incorporation of man's will into the process of justification, this theology nevertheless, Laínez argued, owed too much to Luther's theology and undermined the church's teachings on satisfaction, indulgences, and Purgatory. Pelikan, *Reformation of Church and Dogma*, p. 284; Jedin, *History of the Council of Trent*, 2: 256–57; Mitchell, *The Jesuits*, p. 72; Gutiérrez, *Españoles en Trento*, pp. 280–91.

35. "Rules for Thinking with the Church," in *SE*, pp. 140–41; "Para el sentido verdadero que en la Yglesia militante debemos tener, se guarden las reglas siguientes," in *ES*, pp. 410–12. The editors of the variorum edition believe that these rules were probably added to the *Exercises* sometime after 1535 (*ES*, p. 428). Defenders of Ignatian spirituality often stress that this rule alludes to an Erasmian text, the "Supputatio errorem in censuris Beddae" of 1527. There Erasmus writes, "Neque ideo nigrum esset album, si ita pronunciaret Romanus Pontifex, quod illum scio nequam [nunquam] facturum." *Desiderii Erasmi opera omnia*, 9: 517. However, Erasmus's point, that the will of the pope does not make black into white, would seem to be roughly the opposite of Loyola's.

36. *Sade, Fourier, Loyola*, pp. 44, 46. Antonio de Nicolas offers a more sympathetic reading of Loyolan hermeneutics in *Powers of Imagining*.

37. When the Bollandists published the Latin translation of the con-

fession in 1731, they called it the *Acta antiquissima*, after Nadal's provisional title of *Acta quaedam*, which he had written on the manuscript of Coudret's Latin translation (1559–61). The Jesuit editors of the Monumenta Historica Societatis Iesu series entitle their 1943 variorum edition *Acta Patris Ignatii*. However, English, Spanish, and Italian editions of the last 40 years generally carry the title *Autobiography*.

38. Da Câmara tells us that the death of Julius III on March 23, 1555, and that of his successor, Marcellus II, who lasted as pope for less than a month, halted their sessions. Loyola delayed until the election of the Carafa pope Paul IV on May 23, only to claim general business throughout the summer months whenever confronted by his impatient scribe (*A*, pp. 17–18).

39. Da Câmara writes that Loyola finally summoned him on September 22. They had only a few more meetings before their last encounter, which apparently took place on October 20. Da Câmara left on his mission two days later (*A*, pp. 17, 92; *FN*, p. 362, n. 16).

40. The mistake as to Loyola's age when he was wounded is the most noticeable of the historical errors in the text. There is some question as to the date of Loyola's birth, but most agree on the year 1491. Thus, Loyola would have been 30, not 26, when he was injured in 1521. On the possible mutilations of the text, see n. 42 below.

41. Interestingly, da Câmara's complete preface does not exist in the original Spanish. However, the eighteenth-century Latin edition includes an expanded version of that preface (*FN*, p. 348), and this version of the preface is included in most editions today.

42. The *travesuras* of Loyola's youth are summarized thus in the opening of the *Autobiography*: "Until the age of twenty-six he was a man given over to vanities of the world; with a great and vain desire to win fame he delighted especially in the exercise of arms" (*A*, p. 21). Heinrich Boehmer argues that the text of the *Acta* has not come down to us whole, and that information concerning Loyola's youth has been suppressed (*Studien zur Geschichte*, 1: 312–14). The *FN* editors defend da Câmara's overall fidelity (*FN*, p. 325) but also suggest that he did not write down what he had heard, or else did not communicate to others what he had written down (*FN*, pp. 330–31). In the modern Spanish edition of Loyola's works, Cándido de Dalmases writes the following about the scribe: "No cabe otra explicación sino que el respeto y piedad filial le detuvieron de dar publicidad a lo que el Santo con tanta sencillez non había tenido inconveniente en manifestarle." *Obras completas*, p. 74.

43. "Siendo cosa imperfecta no conviene que estorbe o disminuya la fée de lo que más cumplidamente se escribe." See his letter to Nadal of June 29, 1567, quoted in *FN*, pp. 344–45.

44. Ribadeneira's *Vita Patris Ignatii* appeared in 1572, Polanco's *Vita*

latina Patris Ignatii was written in approximately 1574, and Maffei's *Vita Patris Ignatii* was published in 1585 (*FN*, pp. 344, 346). On the changes made in the material of the *Autobiography* by these later biographers, see Boehmer, *Studien zur Geschichte*, pp. 316–17.

45. This process of interpreting providential signs in order to make correct moral choices Loyola formulated as the "Rules for the Discernment of Spirits" ("Reglas para el mismo efecto con mayor discreción de espíritus"), which he appended to the *Spiritual Exercises* (*SE*, pp. 129–34; *ES*, pp. 388–95).

46. Loyola, *Constitutions*, pp. 248–49; *Constitutiones* VI.1.1, in *Obras completas*, p. 531. In his excellent history of the early Society, John W. O'Malley downplays the authoritarian force of Jesuit metaphors of obedience—e.g., that of the corpse, which actually derived from Saint Bonaventure's life of Francis of Assisi (*First Jesuits*, p. 353). O'Malley does, however, stress the importance of the concept of obedience to the developing organization, which was described and understood by its members as "monarchical" (p. 354).

47. "I must have as my aim the end for which I am created, which is the praise of God our Lord and the salvation of my soul. At the same time I must remain indifferent and free from any inordinate attachments so that I am not more inclined or disposed to take the thing proposed than to reject it, nor to relinquish it rather than to accept it. I must rather be like the equalized scales of balance, ready to follow the course which I feel is more for the glory and praise of God our Lord and the salvation of my soul" (*SE*, p. 85).

48. *Ignatius of Loyola*, pp. 234–35.

49. In the early fourteenth century Ludolph of Saxony wrote his *Vita Iesu Christi*, which was translated into Castilian by Fray Ambrose Montesino in 1503 at the commission of Queen Isabella. Loyola also relates that he read *Flos sanctorum* (The golden legend), by Jacopo da Voragine, probably in the translation of Goberto Vagad.

50. Unamuno, "Vida di Don Quixote," pp. 66–67, 71. Unamuno notes' that the *Vida del bien aventurado Padre Ignazio de Loyola* was one of the books in Quixote's library that the village priest decided he should burn (p. 81).

51. Pedro Leturia notes in his influential study that Loyola's solution to the dilemma may have been drawn from books of chivalry. Cervantes's *Don Quixote* alludes in book 1, chapter 4, to this practice of knights-errant. *Iñigo de Loyola*, p. 140.

52. *Vida del Padre Ignacio de Loyola.* Perhaps Loyola's encounter with the Moor was one of the parts of the *Autobiography* considered to "mar or diminish the fidelity of the rest." In his hermeneutic study of Loyola's works,

Antonio de Nicolas writes somewhat defensively of the Moor episode: "This raw interpretation by Ignatius of these early signs already gives us a clue to the direction he is going to take when he becomes more sophisticated. Still, Ignatius seems prone to oversimplifications." *Powers of Imagining*, p. 49.

53. Da Câmara writes: "Thus he decided to watch over his arms all one night, without sitting down or going to bed, but standing a while and kneeling a while, before the altar of Our Lady of Montserrat where he had resolved to leave his clothing and dress himself in the armor of Christ" (*A*, p. 31).

54. *FN*, p. 386, n. 10.

55. Critics such as Juan Creixall, Ignasi Casanovas, and Anselm Albareda contend that the vigil was inspired by certain other religious ceremonies, rather than by the Amadís romance. Their views are described by Leturia in *Iñigo de Loyola*, p. 142.

56. Leturia contends that the romantic vigil of Esplandían definitely served as Loyola's model, but that Loyola, "the Saint of reason and purpose," elevated the pagan version "to spheres of a fecund and *modern* vitality." Ibid., p. 144.

57. De Nicolas, *Powers of Imagining*, p. 50.

58. The *FN* editors suggest that Loyola remembers the story of Saint Andrew the Apostle, who prayed for the pardon of a repentant friend with good results, as related in the *Flos sanctorum* (*FN*, pp. 396–98, n. 12).

59. Cf. Martin Luther: "In qualibet promissione dei duo proponi, verbum et signum, ut verbum intelligamus esse testamentum, signum vero esse sacramentum, ut in Missa verbum Christi est testamentum, panis et vinum sacramentum. Atque ut maior vis sita est in verbo quam signo, ita maior in testamento quam sacramento, Quia potest homo verbum seu testamentum habere et eo uti absque signo seu sacramente." *De captivitate Babalonica ecclesiae praeludium*, WA, 6: 518.

Erasmus's comment on Scripture is highly ironic in light of Loyola's obsession with the footprints of Christ: "Si quis ostendat Christi, quam procumbimus Christiani, quam adoramus? At cur non potius vivam illius & spirantem imaginem in hisce veneramus libris?" *Paraclesis*, in *Desiderii Erasmi opera omnia*, 5: 144.

60. In 1524 Loyola began his study of Latin under Master Ardévol at the University of Barcelona. After two years he proceeded to Alcalá to study the liberal arts. Because of trouble with the Inquisition there, Loyola moved to the University of Salamanca in 1527. Difficulties with the Inquisition also forced him to leave that community, and in 1528 he set out for Paris, where he studied until 1535. *A*, pp. 59–81.

61. *A*, p. 93; *FN*, p. 504. The phrase "di veder Cristo come sole" is translated with difficulty, because "come sole" may be taken to mean not only "as the sun," but "as he was accustomed." Cf. *FN*, p. 505, n. 16.

62. The specific question that preoccupied Loyola during one period of the writing of the *Spiritual Diary* (Feb. 2–Mar. 12, 1544) concerned the degree of poverty that the houses and churches of the Society of Jesus would embrace. Loyola decided finally to allow them a fixed income.

63. What we have of this diary begins on February 2, 1544, and ends on February 27, 1545. For an analysis of this process of meditation and confirmation of decisions, see Guibert, "Mystique ignacienne." On the value of tears as a spiritual gift, see ibid. and Huizinga, *On the Waning of the Middle Ages*, pp. 190–92.

64. "Ay tres maneras de obedecer, una quando me mandan por virtud de obediencia, y es buena. Segunda, quando me ordenan que haga esto, ò aquello, y esta es mejor. Tercera, quando hago esto, ò aquello, sintiendo alguna señal del superior, aunque no me lo mande, ni ordene, y esta es mucho mas perfecta." Ribadeneira, *Vida del Padre Ignacio de Loyola*, 353r. My translation.

65. In *Daughter's Seduction*, Jane Gallop argues that patriarchy is not solely the property of the male psyche. Rather, she says, "if patriarchal culture is that within which the self originally constitutes itself, it is always already there in each subject as subject. Thus how can it be overthrown if it has been necessarily internalized in everybody who could possibly act to overthrow it?" (p. 14).

66. The abundance of Spanish beatas has been well documented. See, e.g., Bainton, *Women of the Reformation*; Imirizaldu, ed., *Monjas y beatas embaucadoras*; and Alison Weber, *Teresa of Avila*, pp. 17–41.

67. For an overview of early modern misogyny, see Maclean, *Renaissance Notion of Woman*, and Fitzmaurice-Kelly, "Women in Sixteenth-Century Spain," which presents an account of patriarchal ideologies in Teresa's Spain. See, too, Jordan, *Renaissance Feminism*.

68. I have elected not to use the most recent translation of the *Vida*, that of Kieran Kavanaugh and Otilio Rodriguez. This translation, though very readable, tends to efface some of the violence of Teresa's language, a violence that might be experienced as unappealing by contemporary devotional readers. I have opted to use the more baroque and somewhat old-fashioned Peers translation precisely because in key places it does preserve the off-putting violence and ambiguity of Teresa's original text.

69. In their introduction to *Rewriting the Renaissance*, Margaret Ferguson, Maureen Quilligan, and Nancy Vickers point out that the Renaissance has largely been described "by educated middle-class men writing for, and frequently about, other educated men." Burckhardt's glorification of that era, they argue, "illustrates the ideologically significant skewing of perspective that occurs when cultural historians focus their attention chiefly on the beliefs and productions of a small elite group" (pp. xv–xvi).

70. In their *Tiempo y vida de Santa Teresa*, Efrén de la Madre de Dios

and Otger Steggink, contemporary editors of Teresa's collected works, write of Teresa's converso origins in a note: "En la I.a edición disimulamos esta condición por mitigar el efecto moral de la noticia en muchos lectores sorprendidos. Pero la noticia tiene una abrumadora mayoría de probabilidades que impiden paliar la realidad de los hechos" (p. 4). They do not mention the fact that the cat had been out of the bag (again) for at least twenty years before the time of their writing.

71. Américo Castro argues that both Islamic and Christian rulers in medieval Spain were fairly tolerant of the small Jewish population—with notable exceptions. See "Spanish Jews," in *Structure of Spanish History*, pp. 466–521. Yitzhak Baer gives a somewhat more pessimistic picture of the situation of medieval Spanish Jewry, whose ever-precarious relations with Christians were characterized both by sometime tolerance and by fanatical oppression, though the latter was relatively less brutal than that of later ages. *History of the Jews*, vol. I.

72. Baer, *History of the Jews*, 2: 95–99.

73. Though the greatly diminished Jewish communities began to recover during the early fifteenth century, Christian hostility was diverted, in part, to the conversos, now free (theoretically) to make their fortunes without discrimination. However, the newly gained freedom of the conversos, many of whom rapidly rose to the top of ecclesiastical and courtly hierarchies, did not fail to inspire hatred among Old Christians; thus anti-Semitism evolved in the century before Teresa's birth from the ostensible hatred of a religion to the hatred of an ethnic group, whose members shared by this time, at least outwardly, the religion of the oppressors.

74. Kamen, *Inquisition and Society*, p. 24.

75. In fact, certain Jews were charged with this crime in Valladolid in 1454, and one confessed under torture. Fortunately, the government interceded at the request of the Jewish community, and the case was transferred to a different jurisdiction. Espina complains bitterly that converso judges on the king's court were able to block the just punishment of the murderers; the case had not been resolved when he wrote his book. See Baer, *History of the Jews*, 2: 287.

76. Baer reports that Espina got his information on the Jewish tradition from a number of texts by converso predecessors, from the thirteenth-century works of Raymond Martini and Abner of Burgos to the writings of fifteenth-century converts, such as Paulus de Sancta Maria and Hieronymus de Sancta Fide. Their texts represent a tradition among conversos of defending their new religion against Judaism with supposedly Christological midrashic homilies (Baer, *History of the Jews*, 1: 150–59, 167–68, 327–54; 2: 284). Some, though not all, of these texts are as hostile to Jews as the polemics of Old Christians. Antonio Domínguez Ortiz claims that almost all anti-Semitic writings of the fifteenth century were produced by conver-

sos, of which Espina was one (see *Los Judeoconversos*, p. 17). Castro also believes that Espina was a converso (*Structure of Spanish History*, p. 540). However, Baer and Kamen believe there is no basis for this theory, especially given that Espina did not know Hebrew (Baer, *History of the Jews*, 2: 284; Kamen, *Inquisition and Society*, p. 24).

77. Lea, *History of the Inquisition*, 1: 150–52.

78. It is worth noting that Ferdinand himself may have had converso ancestors; that certain prominent Jews helped arrange the marriage of Ferdinand and Isabella; that Jews and conversos helped the couple consolidate their power at a time of great anarchy; and that conversos were numbered among the monarchs' most trusted and useful advisors. See Baer, *History of the Jews*, 2: 305–6.

79. Castro, *Structure of Spanish History*, p. 540.

80. Baer describes the notorious trial of several conversos concerning the "Holy Child of La Guardia" as a typical case of anti-Semitic propaganda based on trumped-up confessions extracted by torture. These unfortunate victims of the Inquisition were accused of crucifying a Christian boy on Good Friday, of stealing a host, and of performing on Passover a parodic communion rite with that host and also with the heart of the dead Christian. The point of their ceremony was to kill all Christians by infecting them with rabies. The inquisitors got the idea for the conspiracy from—where else?— the *Fortalitium fidei* and similar anti-Semitic tracts. The accused were executed at an auto-da-fé in Avila in November of 1491. Baer, *History of the Jews*, 2: 398–423. Lea reports that the trial generated a cult of "El santo niño de la Guardia," which has continued into the twentieth century (*History of the Inquisition*, 2: 134).

81. Efrén de la Madre de Dios and Steggink (*Tiempo y vida de Santa Teresa*, pp. 4–5) quote evidence of the 1485 condemnation of Juan Sánchez, which was brought up against the family in a later trial in 1519. Typically, such crimes against the Catholic faith included wearing a clean shirt on Fridays, refusing to eat pork, eating other meat during Lent, and/or washing and shaving corpses in accordance with Mosaic law (see Clissold, *St. Teresa of Avila*, p. 3).

82. Clissold, *St. Teresa of Avila*, pp. 3–4.

83. The "sambenitillo," a long yellow cloak with crosses painted on it, was typically greeted with rocks, spit, and derision when its owner appeared in these penitential processions. Lincoln, *Teresa: A Woman*, pp. 2–3.

84. Kamen, *Inquisition and Society*, pp. 122–23. On the significance of honra, see ibid., pp. 114–24.

85. Clissold, *St. Teresa of Avila*, p. 4.

86. Efrén de la Madre de Dios and Steggink, *Tiempo y vida de Santa Teresa*, p. 6; Bilinkoff, *The Avila of Saint Teresa*, p. 110.

87. Rossi, *Teresa d'Avila*, pp. 9–21, 58; Bilinkoff, *The Avila of Saint*

Teresa, pp. 110, 146–47. The obsession with "stained" or "tainted" blood was addressed by Cardinal Francisco Mendoza y Bobadilla in his book *El Tizón de la nobleza de España* (Blot on the nobility of Spain) (1560). There he defended his own converso origins by pointing out that almost all of the Spanish nobility was afflicted with the stain of alterity—hence, the title of his book. Kamen, *Inquisition and Society*, p. 23.

88. On the more broadly directed persecutions of the sixteenth-century Spanish Inquisition, see the excellent Monter, *Frontiers of Heresy*.

89. Rossi, *Teresa d'Avila*, p. 88.

90. As Henry Kamen notes, there is no doubt "that *converso* blood could be a serious impediment in the antisemitic society of Spain's Golden Age." *Inquisition and Society*, p. 97. Américo Castro (*Teresa la Santa*), Rosa Rossi (*Teresa d'Avila*), Jodi Bilinkoff (*The Avila of Saint Teresa*), Stephen Clissold (*St. Teresa of Avila*), and Victoria Lincoln (*Teresa: A Woman*) all discuss the significance of Teresa's converso origins in the context of sixteenth-century Spanish persecutions.

91. As Rossi and others have observed, the *Vida* falls into four divisions. The first (chapters 1–9) presents Teresa's life up to the time of her second conversion (ca. 1554). In the second (chapters 10–22), Teresa sets forth her mystical theology, explaining the disposition of the will in the soul's progress to union with God. The third (chapters 23–31) narrates Teresa's mystical experiences during the years 1554–61, and the fourth (chapters 32–40) recounts the foundation of the Discalced Carmelite reform, begun by Teresa in 1562. See Rossi, *Esperienza interiore*, p. 21.

92. The request for a written confession was not unusual at that time; Loyola had made a three-day written confession at the abbey at Montserrat.

93. In chapter 23 Teresa alludes to the cases of women purged by the Inquisition for their pseudomysticism: "Yo, como en estos tiempos havían acaecido grandes ilusiones en mujeres y engaños que las había hecho el demonio, comencé a temer" (*LV*, p. 93). One prominent case concerned the Cordovan sister Magdalena de la Cruz. This woman had enjoyed great renown among members of the monarchy and the Inquisition because of her piety and her ability to read the future. Thus, it came as a shock to her admirers when she announced in 1544 that her piety was feigned and that she had acquired her magical powers through a pact with the devil. Hoornaert, *Sainte Thérèse d'Avila*, pp. 16–17. See also Alison Weber, *Teresa of Avila*, pp. 44–45.

94. Consider Luis de Leon's "Prologo al Letor" from *Libros de la B. Madre Teresa de Iesus*, an early edition of the *Vida*: "Cada uno si deve . . . edificarse mucho, siendo que haze una confesion publica, come la hizo S. Augustin, esagerando con tanta humilidad sus peccados, que muestra haver tenido muy grandes, siendo opinion de las personas graves, que trataron toda su consciencia, que a lo que humanamente se puede juzgar, nunca lle-

garon a ser mortales: con todo esso para dar mas entera satisfaction, sepa que el temor grande, que por su mucha humilidad tuvo esta Santa de ser engañada, teniendose por indigna de tan grandes favores."

95. See Llamas Martínez, *Santa Teresa de Jesús.*

96. *Teresa of Avila,* pp. 3–16. The quotations are from pp. 11, 40.

97. Ibid., pp. 45–46, 48, 64. Another version of Teresa's double bind was her "disavowing [of] the privilege to write," which was "of necessity coterminous with the act of claiming the privilege to write" (p. 50).

98. As Caroline Bynum points out, the spirituality of early modern women "owed its intense bodily quality in part to the association of the female with the fleshly made by philosophers and theologians alike." But Bynum also argues that late medieval Christianity, which emphasized the resurrection of the body as well as the soul, tended to conceive of the person as a "somatic unity." "Female Body," p. 162.

99. *Saints and Society,* p. 236.

100. Vives, *De institutione foeminae christianae*; Luis de Leon, *Exposición del Libro de Job*; Teresa, *Libro de las Fundaciones.* Quoted in Fitzmaurice-Kelly, "Women in Sixteenth-Century Spain," 557. My translations. Barbara Johnson has pointed out that the very idea of selfhood from Augustine to Freud is male-identified. Thus it is not surprising that women autobiographers tend to present a vision of female selfhood as in some way monstrous: "The problem for the female autobiographer is, on the one hand, to resist the pressure of masculine autobiography as the only literary genre available for her enterprise, and, on the other, to describe a difficulty in conforming to a female ideal which is largely a fantasy of the masculine, not the feminine, imagination." "My Monster, Myself," in *World of Difference,* pp. 144–54, 154. Domna Stanton further explains the predicament of the woman autobiographer as follows: "Because of women's different status in the symbolic order, autogynography . . . dramatize[s] the fundamental alterity and non-presence of the subject, even as it asserts itself discursively and strives toward an always impossible self-possession." "Autogynography," p. 15. See, however, Alison Weber's reading of the Teresean theory of female weakness: "As much as her repeated references to women's 'flaqueza' suggest an internalization of prevailing misogynistic views, we should note that in most cases Teresa presents women's weakness as primarily physiological rather than moral or spiritual" (*Teresa of Avila,* p. 145).

101. See Laguardia, "St. Teresa," Alison Weber, *Teresa of Avila,* pp. 56–64.

102. Poitrey, *Vocabulario de Santa Teresa,* pp. 633–35.

103. Alison Weber, *Teresa of Avila,* p. 118.

104. *LT,* p. 12; *LV,* p. 39. By "recollection" she refers to the process of concentrating or gathering together the faculties of the soul to prepare the way for prayer. Teresa shows her acquaintance with the Franciscan tradi-

tion of recogimiento, the prayer that unifies the faculties and composes the soul. She would have been familiar with this form of prayer through her reading of Osuna's *Tercer abecedario* and other spiritual treatises. The practice of recogimiento was at that time contrasted with an alternative method of prayer that was also associated with the Franciscan order, known as "dejamiento," or "abandon." This second approach, as well as its advocates, were condemned by the Inquisition on the grounds that they manifested quietist or illuminist tendencies.

105. Teresa explains the distractions of memory and reason with a simple analogy that also seems to serve a defensive purpose. Reason and memory are like doves unhappy with the food that the owner of the dovecote has given them. They go ranging for food but return home when they find none (*LT*, p. 149). The innocuousness of her metaphor, combined with her description of the intense delight granted to the will in union, belies a potentially distressing result of recogimiento—namely, the escape of the will from the usual orbit of the soul's activities, plus the dampening of memory and reason. In Teresa's account, the mystical awareness of divine presence is an affective rather than a cognitive experience; the will experiences what reason and memory cannot.

106. Teresa mentions in the last chapter of the book that after deep "arrobamiento [rapture]" has passed, the soul is sometimes unable to return to itself, and memory and understanding arrive almost at a state of frenzy. This frenzy is likely to occur at the beginning of one's experience of union, she explains, because "no puede sufrir nuestra flaqueza natural tanta fuerza de espíritu y enflaquece la imaginación." She recommends that the troubled person temporarily give up prayer and begin again later on, lest she cause herself serious harm (*LV*, p. 173; *LT*, p. 391).

107. See Poitrey, *Vocabulario de Santa Teresa*, p. 244.

108. The Peers translation reads, "I felt as if I were being ground to powder" (*LT*, p. 191). Here, however, I have rendered the Spanish "ansí quedava hecha pedazos" more literally to emphasize its metaphor of dismemberment.

109. See, e.g., Underhill, *Mysticism*, p. 162, and Alison Weber's discussion of Teresa's *Las moradas del castillo interior*, in *Teresa of Avila*, pp. 109–22. Weber addresses Teresa's description of mystical marriage to Christ, a theme that occurs less often in the *Vida*. However, Teresa's relations to God the Father in her autobiography are in some sense also figured as marriage.

110. Bynum, "Female Body," pp. 174–98; Weinstein and Bell, *Saints and Society*, p. 236.

111. Jane Elizabeth Beckmann has suggested that this vision of hell can be read as "a misogynistic vision of entrapment in the female sex. . . . Hell,

for Teresa, is a womb (or anti-womb) to which she is confined." "Reproduction of the Life of Teresa of Avila," p. 26.

112. *Teresa of Avila*, p. 165.

113. *American Heritage Dictionary of the English Language*, 1978, s.v. "spectacle."

Chapter 4

1. Two of the three characters participating in the *Dialogue*, Filippo Salviati and Giovanfrancesco Sagredo, are modeled after long-dead friends of Galileo. Salviati, the Florentine nobleman and former student of Galileo's, becomes his spokesman in the *Dialogue*. Sagredo, in the text as in life, plays the role of the Venetian gentleman and intelligent layman. Simplicio, the third character, is named after a sixth-century commentator on Aristotle. As his name suggests, he is also a parody of the generic seventeenth-century Aristotelian academic, though he is nevertheless an intelligent and not unsympathetic figure.

2. See, e.g., Burtt (*Metaphysical Foundations of Modern Physical Science*); Husserl (*Crisis of European Sciences*); Hall (*Galileo to Newton*); Koyré (*Études galiléennes*); and Shea (*Galileo's Intellectual Revolution*).

3. Pico's Oration in *De hominis dignitate*, pp. 101–65.

4. At the risk of attributing too much innovation to Galileo, who was, after all, one person among many using similar metaphors of Nature, mathematics, and physics, I will treat Galileo's reading of the book of Nature as the paradigm of a radically new mode of interpretation. It is useful, though, to think of Galileo in terms of the Foucauldian "author function"—i.e., as a figure to whom the nebulous social changes of an era have been attributed.

5. On the theories of will articulated by Italian humanists such as Pico, Valla, Ficino, Salutati, and Pomponazzi, see Charles Trinkaus's superb two-volume work, *In Our Image and Likeness*. On the connections between humanism and the sciences, see Kristeller, "Humanism and Scholasticism in the Italian Renaissance," in *Renaissance Thought*, pp. 92–119, and Trinkaus, "Humanism and Science: Humanist Critiques of Natural Philosophy," in *Scope of Renaissance Humanism*, pp. 140–68.

6. As discussed later in this chapter, historians continue to debate whether Galileo actually thought that he had succeeded in reading the book of Nature by offering necessary proof of the Copernican hypothesis. This issue remains unresolved. We can, however, see in Galileo's writings both the rhetoric of mastery and that of its counterpart, determinism—i.e., the traces of lifelong anxiety over the problems of knowing.

7. The early modern split between theology and science assumes various configurations that are inevitably binary: religion vs. science, authoritarian

dogmatism vs. free intellectual inquiry, bankrupt Aristotelianism vs. mathematicized Platonism, bankrupt Platonism vs. empirical science. It is my intention not to conflate the first terms of these binary oppositions, but to point out their place in the "faith" category—i.e., the space of the discredited knowledge against which science and its correlates operate differentially.

8. E. R. Curtius traces the figure of Nature as book through the Middle Ages; it appears in the writings of Hugo of St. Victor, John of Salisbury, Saint Bonaventure, and Nicholas of Cusa, to name just a few. The metaphor continues to surface in the works of various Renaissance writers, including Paracelsus, Montaigne, Thomas Browne, Donne, Milton, Descartes, and Francis Bacon. *European Literature and the Latin Middle Ages*, pp. 319–26.

Elizabeth L. Eisenstein devotes the second volume of *Printing Press* to "the book of Nature transformed." She argues that the scientific claim to read the text of Nature was dependent on the increased availability of the texts of men. In other words, the printing revolution was the event that made possible a "rereading" of Nature.

Owen Hannaway contrasts the uses of the book of Nature metaphor in the theories of Oswald Croll, a disciple of Paracelsus, and Andreas Libavius, an anti-Paracelsian and defender of "chymia vera." The former's book of Nature is abstruse, alchemical, mystical; the latter's is "the clear-cut, well ordered textbook of the classroom." For Hannaway these two appropriations of the medieval figure signify the split between alchemy and modern chemistry, institutionalized and converted into bourgeois pedagogy in the seventeenth century. See *Chemists and the Word*, p. 113.

Also of note is Michael T. Walton's article, "Hermetic Cabala," on the influence of Jewish mystical theology (the cabalistic book of Nature) on early modern science.

9. *Discoveries and Opinions*, p. 238; *Opere*, 6: 232.

10. On the recurring metaphor of the book of Nature in Galileo's work, see Calvino, "Le Livre de la Nature."

11. See n. 2.

12. Christie, "Introduction," in Benjamin, Cantor, and Christie, eds., *The Figural and the Literal*, p. 3.

13. In February of 1615 Dominican priest Niccolò Lorini sent the Inquisition a copy of Galileo's December 14, 1613, letter written to his protégé Benedetto Castelli. To control the possible damage the letter could cause, Galileo provided an edited and expanded version of it, dedicated to Cristina di Lorena, which was also passed on to the Inquisition. See *Discoveries and Opinions*, pp. 143–71. For a detailed account of the conspiracy against Galileo and the 1616 decree of the Roman Inquisition against Copernicanism, see Santillana, *Crime of Galileo*, pp. 27–144.

14. "This being granted, I think that in discussions of physical prob-

lems we ought to begin not from the authority of scriptural passages, but from sense-experiences and necessary demonstrations; for the holy Bible and the phenomena of nature proceed alike from the divine Word, the former as the dictate of the Holy Ghost and the latter as the observant executrix of God's commands." *Discoveries and Opinions*, p. 182; *Opere*, 5: 316.

15. Ibid.

16. See "Nature and Domain of Sacred Doctrine."

17. "Copernicans and the Churches," p. 87.

18. Galileo was not the only one to offer alternative readings of Scripture regarding matters of natural philosophy. The Neapolitan Carmelite Paolo Antonio Foscarini entered the scripture/science debates of 1615 with the publication of a book that offered Copernican strategies for reading the Bible—that is, ways to circumvent previous "literal" interpretations in order to defend heliocentric astronomy. In this ingenious treatise Foscarini systematically examines six types of problematic scriptural passages or teachings—e.g., those on the motion of the sun and the nonmovement of the earth, and those on the notion of Hell as the lowest point in the universe—and offers alternative (Copernican) interpretations. This book, though condemned with the *De revolutionibus* by the Inquisition, was republished in the second Italian edition of Galileo's *Dialogue*. See "Lettera . . . sopra l'opinione de' Pittagorici, e del Copernico."

19. *Discoveries and Opinions*, pp. 182–83; *Opere*, 5: 316.

20. Martha Fehér describes Galileo's approach to the mathematical characters of Nature in terms not of rhetoric and interpretation, but of scientific and philosophical demonstration: "For Galileo to explain a phenomenon is to find its underlying *rationale* in the form of a mathematical postulate referring to a geometrical system of relations wherein the phenomenon fits, and which exhibits the structure of a deeper level of reality made transparent (but often just confused) by observation and experiments." "Galileo and the Demonstrative Ideal," p. 103.

Fehér's nonlinguistic account of scientific discovery, like those of other philosophers of science who champion Galileo's mathematicizing of natural philosophy, does not acknowledge "slippage" except when rationalized as failed experiment or confused observation. These are precisely the terms of "reading" that Galileo himself established in order to contrast his hermeneutic method with those of faulty—i.e., linguistic—texts.

21. *Discoveries and Opinions*, p. 179; *Opere*, 5: 312.

22. Sizi described three orders of visual error: "nella visione diretta, l'occhio erra e si inganna o col solo senso, o per nozione anticipata, o col sillogismo, ossia, col razioncinio." *Dianoia astronomica*, p. 424. In her intriguing essay "Rhetoric of Optics," Eileen Reeves points out that Galileo

himself subscribed to some notion of reasoning by substitution, as he reveals in his third letter on the sunspots: "Galileo subverts Aristotle's distinction between earthly and thus knowable substances, and those remote
and unknowable, like the sun; he maintains that neither terrestrial nor celestial substances may be fathomed, and that 'until we reach the state of
blessedness' we will have to be content with a frail system of analogy where
elements unknown and unknowable must somehow define each other" (p.
133). But despite his acknowledgment of such reasoning by analogy, Galileo
seems to have remained steadfast in his conviction that the book of Nature
could ultimately be read, as William Shea, among others, has argued
(*Galileo's Intellectual Revolution*, pp. 67–72).

23. "Science and Patronage." Explaining the significance of the discovery of the phases of Venus, Owen Gingerich writes that Castelli remarked
to Galileo that "in the Copernican system Venus should show the entire
range of phases, from a crescent to gibbous to a fully illuminated disk. In
the Ptolemaic system, on the other hand, the epicycle of Venus is locked between the earth and the sun, and Venus therefore has only crescent phases
because it never passes behind the sun." "Galileo's Astronomy," p. 116.

24. *Patterns of Discovery*. Arguing that there is no unmediated sense
perception, Hanson writes: "When language and notation are ignored in
studies of observation, physics is represented as resting on sensation and
low-grade experiment. It is described as repetitious, monotonous concate-
nation of spectacular sensations, and of school-laboratory experiments. But
physical science is not just a systematic exposure of the senses to the world;
it is also a way of thinking about the world, a way of forming conceptions"
(p. 30). Compare the critiques of philosophical figurality offered by deconstruction—for example, that of Jacques Derrida's "White Mythology: Metaphor on the Text of Philosophy," in *Margins of Philosophy*, pp. 207–71.

25. In a different though related vein, Ernan McMullin has written on
Galilean idealization—the way Galileo "reads" the book of Nature by assuming a correspondence between his mathematical constructs and the real
world that they claim to embody. Though clearly Galileo realized that there
were some discrepancies between, for example, his geometrical representations of motion and motion as instantiated in Nature, such discrepancies
did not constitute in his mind a serious impediment to scientific understanding, any more than they do for scientists today. Though he makes a
case for a tentative scientific realism, McMullin argues wryly that "the Book
of Nature is *not* written in the language of mathematics, strictly speaking.
The *syntax* is mathematical, but the *semantics* is not. . . . The Book of Nature, though it employs a mathematical grammar, is written in the *language*
of physics (or chemistry or biology . . .)." "Galilean Idealization," pp.
252–53.

26. Foucault, *Madness and Civilization*.

27. See "Ptolemy, Galileo, and the Scientific Method" and "Reexamining Galileo's *Dialogue*."

28. "Galileo and the Demonstrative Ideal," pp. 90, 105. Nicholas Jardine makes a similar argument concerning Galileo's idea of demonstration in "Galileo's Road to Truth." Explaining how Galileo differs from the sixteenth-century Paduan Averroists, Jardine states: "Galileo was well aware of the contemporary Aristotelian theory of scientific demonstration, had a sure insight into its weakness, rejected it outright, and set up in its place as a crucial part of his propaganda for the union of mathematics and natural philosophy a method of inquiry modelled on a classical account of the quest for proofs in geometry" (p. 310).

29. "Galileo and the Demonstrative Ideal," pp. 99–101.

30. See "Galileo's Science," pp. 161–63, and "Reinterpreting Galileo."

31. See "Rhetoric of Proof" and "Galileo's Letter to Christina."

32. *D*, p. iii; *Opere*, 7: 541. In his Italian note, Galileo draws a tiny circle surrounded by a slightly larger one to designate the sun; here, that drawing has been rendered as "(Sole)."

33. See the reports made by Agostino Oreggi, Melchior Inchofer, and Zaccaria Pasqualigo on the *Dialogue* to the Roman Inquisition on April 17, 1633. In Finocchiaro, ed., "The Later Inquisition Proceedings," in *Galileo Affair*, pp. 262–77. It is also worth noting Pietro Redondi's interpretation of Galileo's trial in *Galileo Heretic*. Redondi argues that Galileo's crime was not his attack on geocentrism, as virtually all have supposed, but rather his implicit critique of the Aristotelian/Thomistic physics of transubstantiation.

34. "Rhetoric of Proof," p. 204.

35. *Against Method*, pp. 29, 81. Maurice Finocchiaro identifies what traditionalists have found so annoying about Feyerabend's approach: "The epistemological factors emphasized by Feyerabend are ones that go against almost every principle held by orthodox philosophers of science; the rhetorical factors seem to violate the ideas of the basic honesty and decency of science, widely held by scientists and laymen alike; the aesthetic factors contradict the alleged gap between the arts and the sciences. Indeed Feyerabend delights in being contrary. His contrariness reaches its highest pitch when he argues that such Galilean procedure is 'perfectly reasonable' in itself . . . and fruitful in other fields. In other words, Feyerabend's *evaluation* of Galileo's method is the orthodox one, it is his descriptive interpretation of the features of that method that is unorthodox." *Galileo and the Art of Reasoning*, pp. 190–91.

36. *Galileo and the Art of Reasoning*, p. 159; see also "Methodical Background," p. 251. Finocchiaro praises Galileo for demonstrating "the expressive ingenuity of the artist and the rhetorical skill of the orator" (*Galileo and the Art of Reasoning*, p. 66), suggesting that rhetoric and reason are ultimately separate but possibly equal aspects of scientific discourse.

However, given the prevalence of words like "rationality," "erudition," and "logic" in the chapter titles of this extraordinarily careful study of Galilean theory and its reception, Finocchiaro undeniably evaluates reason and rhetoric in a hierarchical fashion.

37. In "Knowledge and Salvation in Jesuit Culture" Rivka Feldhay discusses the change in the status of mathematical science from a secondary and inferior discipline in the Middle Ages to a primary one by the sixteenth century. She attributes this change to Jesuit science—in particular that of Christopher Clavius, the leading Jesuit astronomer and influence on Galileo.

38. For a discussion of "rigor" and other gendered rhetoric in the *Dialogue*, see my article, "Gendered Cosmos."

39. The gist of deconstructive theory is precisely such a critique of the "supplemental" relation of a secondary term in a binary opposition to the dominant term—e.g., rhetoric as supplement to philosophy/reason.

40. *Against Method*, pp. 69–108. Finocchiaro takes issue with Feyerabend's assumption that Galileo's reasoning by analogy regarding the question of relative motion is propagandistic and rhetorical, rather than demonstrative or logical. Defending Galileo's use of analogy in this section of the *Dialogue*, Finocchiaro asserts "that a pure analogy argument has *some* force even though the mechanism of the analogy is unknown, i.e., even though we do not know *why* the analogy holds, as long as we are prepared to claim *that* it holds. At any rate, the conclusion is inescapable that interpretations of the rhetorical situation must be grounded on interpretations of the logical situation" (*Galileo and the Art of Reasoning*, p. 199).

41. *Against Method*, pp. 87, 88–89.

42. Ibid., p. 46.

43. Barbara Smith, *Contingencies of Value*; Baudrillard, *Pour une critique de l'économie politique du signe*.

44. Bruno Latour points out in *Science in Action* that even though scientists are highly aware of the contingencies of their own "facts," they show a very different face of science to outsiders. In other words, they understand, at least intuitively, the political power generated by the popular notion of science as objectively true, and they do not want to undermine the authority of their discourse by pointing out its contingencies. See also G. Nigel Gilbert and Michael Mulkay's remarkable deconstruction of the notion of consensus in scientific communities in *Opening Pandora's Box*.

45. Foucault summarizes these utopian theories of the earliest language: "In its original form, when it was given to men by God himself, language was an absolutely certain and transparent sign for things, because it resembled them. The names of things were lodged in the things they designated, just as strength is written in the body of the lion, regality in the eye of the eagle, just as the influence of the planets is marked upon the brows of men: by the form of similitude. This transparency was destroyed at Babel as a

punishment for men. Languages became separated and incompatible with one another only in so far as they had previously lost this original resemblance to the things that had been the prime reason for the existence of language." "The Prose of the World," in *Order of Things*, p. 44. See also Steiner, *After Babel*; Borst, *Der Turmbau von Babel*; and Bono, "Language and Interpretation" and "Science, Discourse, and Literature."

46. *Discoveries and Opinions*, pp. 187, 196; *Opere*, 5: 320, 329.

47. *Political Unconscious*, p. 286.

48. Ibid., p. 290. See also Biagioli, "Social Status of Italian Mathematicians" and "Galileo the Emblem Maker."

49. *Science in Action*, pp. 31–32.

50. In *Protestant Ethic*, Max Weber describes two possible reactions to the doctrine of justification by faith. The first reaction inspires a powerful sense of freedom among those who interpret the doctrine in its most positive light: "The powerful feeling of light-hearted assurance, in which the tremendous pressure of their sense of sin is released, apparently breaks over them with elemental force and destroys every possibility of the belief that this overpowering gift of grace could owe anything to their own co-operation or could be connected with achievements or qualities of their own faith and will." The second reaction, which Weber attributes to late Calvinist thought, is far more negative: "The Father in heaven of the New Testament, so human and understanding . . . is gone. His place has been taken by a transcendental being, beyond the reach of human understanding, who with His quite incomprehensible decrees has decided the fate of every individual and regulated the tiniest details of the cosmos from eternity. God's grace is, since His decrees cannot change, as impossible for those to whom He has granted it to lose as it is unattainable for those to whom He has denied it" (pp. 103–4). Weber words the consequences of this latter worldview in the strongest of language: "In its extreme inhumanity this doctrine must above all have had one consequence for the life of a generation which surrendered to its magnificent consistency. That was a feeling of unprecedented inner loneliness of the single individual" (p. 104). Given the uncompromising nature of Calvinist thought, one was liable to become obsessed with finding proof of one's election.

51. A version of this standard view can be found, for example, in Kagan, Ozment, and Turner, eds., *Western Heritage*, p. 463.

52. See Finocchiaro, *Galileo and the Art of Reasoning*, pp. 3–26.

53. See part 2 of the sixth accusation, which asserts that Galileo puts the medicine of the end in the mouth of a fool and in a section that can be located only with difficulty; the other interlocutor later approves it in a cold manner and only by casually mentioning it without stressing its worth, which is to say, unwillingly (in *Opere*, 19: 326; my paraphrase).

54. *Galileo and the Art of Reasoning*, p. 10.

Afterword

1. This point, now commonplace, has been argued quite eloquently by Vincent Descombes in *Modern French Philosophy*, pp. 136–67.

2. *Galileo*, p. ix.

3. "Rhetoric of Persuasion (Nietzsche)," in *Allegories of Reading*, p. 119.

4. Latour and Woolgar, *Laboratory Life*; Gilbert and Mulkay, *Opening Pandora's Box*.

5. The various reconciliations of deconstruction and religion that were popular several years ago offer a good example of a faith argument: If deconstruction demands the radical suspension of claims to knowledge, then it clears the way for whatever claims of belief or faith that one wishes to maintain.

Bibliography

❧

Althaus, Paul. *The Ethics of Martin Luther*. Trans. Robert C. Schultz. Philadelphia: Fortress Press, 1972.

Althusser, Louis. "Ideology and Ideological State Apparatuses (Notes Towards an Investigation)." In *Lenin and Philosophy and Other Essays*, trans. Ben Brewster, pp. 127–86. New York: Monthly Review Press, 1971.

Aquinas, Thomas. "The Nature and Domain of Sacred Doctrine." In Anton C. Pegis, ed., *Basic Writings of Thomas Aquinas*, vol. 1, pp. 14–17. New York: Random House, 1945.

Ascoli, Albert. *Ariosto's Bitter Harmony: Crisis and Evasion in the Italian Renaissance*. Princeton, N.J.: Princeton University Press, 1987.

———. "Petrarch's Middle Age: Memory, Imagination, and the 'Ascent of Mont Ventoux.' " *Stanford Italian Review* 10, no. 1 (1991): 5–43.

Augustine of Hippo. *Confessions*. Trans. W. Watts. Cambridge, Mass.: Harvard University Press, 1977 [1912].

———. *De spiritu et littera*. In J. P. Migne, ed., *Patrologia latina*, vol. 44, pp. 199–243. Paris, 1841.

———. *St. Augustine's Confessions*. Trans. R. S. Pine-Coffin. New York: Penguin, 1979 [1961].

———. *Select Anti-Pelagian Treatises of St. Augustine and the Acts of the Second Council of Orange*. Ed. William Bright. Oxford: Clarendon Press, 1880.

Baer, Yitzhak. *A History of the Jews in Christian Spain*. 2 vols. Trans. Louis Schoffman. Philadelphia: The Jewish Publication Society of America, 1961.

Bainton, Roland. *Women of the Reformation from Spain to Scandinavia.* Minneapolis: Augsburg Publishing House, 1977.

Baron, Hans. *From Petrarch to Leonardo Bruni: Studies in Humanistic and Political Literature.* Chicago: University of Chicago Press, 1968.

———. *Petrarch's "Secretum": Its Making and Its Meaning.* Medieval Academy Books, no. 94. Cambridge, Mass.: Medieval Academy of America, 1985.

Barthes, Roland. *Sade, Fourier, Loyola.* Trans. Richard Miller. New York: Hill and Wang, 1976 [1971].

Bate, Walter Jackson. "The Crisis in English Studies." *Harvard Magazine* 85, no. 1 (1982): 46–53.

Baudrillard, Jean. *Pour une critique de l'économie politique du signe.* Paris: Gallimard, 1972.

Beckmann, Jane Elizabeth. "The Reproduction of the Life of Teresa of Avila: Mediations of Body and Text." Master's report, University of Texas at Austin, 1990.

Benjamin, Andrew E., Geoffrey N. Cantor, and John R. R. Christie, eds. *The Figural and the Literal: Problems of Language in the History of Science and Philosophy, 1630–1800.* Manchester, Eng.: Manchester University Press, 1987.

Bennett, William. "Why the West?" *National Review* 40, no. 10 (May 27, 1988): 37–39.

Biagioli, Mario. "Galileo the Emblem Maker." *ISIS* 81 (1990): 230–58.

———. "The Social Status of Italian Mathematicians, 1450–1600." *History of Science* 27 (1989): 41–89.

Bilinkoff, Jodi. *The Avila of Saint Teresa: Religious Reform in a Sixteenth-Century City.* Ithaca, N.Y.: Cornell University Press, 1989.

Billanovich, Giuseppe. "Dall' 'Epystolarum mearum ad diversos liber' ai 'Rerum familiarium libri XXIV.' " In *Petrarca letterato,* vol. 1, *Lo scrittoio del Petrarca,* pp. 1–55. Edizioni di "Storia e Letteratura," no. 16. Rome, 1947.

Bishop, Morris. *Petrarch and His World.* Bloomington: Indiana University Press, 1963.

Bloom, Allan. *The Closing of the American Mind: How Higher Education Has Failed Democracy and Impoverished the Souls of Today's Students.* New York: Simon and Schuster, 1987.

Boehmer, Heinrich. *Luther and the Reformation in the Light of Modern Research.* Trans. E. S. G. Potter. London: G. Bell, 1930.

———. *Martin Luther: Road to Reformation.* Trans. John Doberstein and Theodore G. Tappert. New York: Meridian Books, 1957.

———. *Studien zur Geschichte der Gesellschaft Jesu.* Bonn: Verlag von A. Falkenroth, 1914.

Bolgar, R. R. *The Classical Heritage and Its Beneficiaries.* London: Cambridge University Press, 1954.

Bono, James J. "Language and Interpretation in the History of Science: Language Theory and the Scientific Revolution." Unpublished.

———. "Science, Discourse, and Literature: The Role/Rule of Metaphor in Science." In Stuart Peterfreund, ed., *Literature and Science: Theory and Practice*, pp. 59–89. Boston: Northeastern University Press, 1990.

Borst, Arno. *Der Turmbau von Babel: Geschichte der Meinungen über Ursprung und Vielfalt der Sprachen und Völker.* 4 vols. Stuttgart: Anton Hiersemann, 1960.

Bosco, Umberto. *Francesco Petrarca.* Bari: Editori Laterza, 1961 [1946].

Bourdieu, Pierre. *Distinction: A Social Critique of the Judgment of Taste.* Trans. Richard Nice. Cambridge, Mass.: Harvard University Press, 1984 [1979].

———. *Homo Academicus.* Trans. Peter Collier. Stanford, Calif.: Stanford University Press, 1988 [1984].

Bouwsma, William. "The Two Faces of Humanism: Stoicism and Augustinianism in Renaissance Thought." In Heiko Oberman and Thomas Brady, eds., *Itinerarium Italicum: The Profile of the Italian Renaissance in the Mirror of Its European Transformations*, Studies in Medieval and Reformation Thought, no. 14, pp. 3–60. Leiden: Brill, 1975.

Brown, Peter. *Augustine of Hippo: A Biography.* Berkeley: University of California Press, 1969 [1967].

Burckhardt, Jacob. *The Civilization of the Renaissance in Italy.* 2 vols. Trans. S. G. C. Middlemore. New York: Harper and Row, 1958.

Burdach, Konrad, and Paul Piur, eds. *Briefwechsel des Cola di Rienzo.* Vol. 2 of *Vom Mittelalter zur Reformation: Forschungen zur Geschichte der Deutschen Bildung.* Berlin: Weidmann, 1913–29.

Burtt, Edwin A. *The Metaphysical Foundations of Modern Physical Science.* Garden City, N.Y.: Doubleday, 1954 [1924].

Bynum, Caroline Walker. "The Female Body and Religious Practice in the Later Middle Ages." In Michel Feher, Ramona Naddoff, and Nadia Tazi, eds., *Fragments for a History of the Human Body*, vol. 1, pp. 161–219. New York: Zone, 1989.

Calcaterra, Carlo. *Nella selva del Petrarca.* Bologna: Editore Licinio Cappelli, 1942.

Calvino, Italo. "Le Livre de la Nature chez Galilée." In Herman Parret and Hans-George Ruprecht, eds., *Exigences et perspectives de la sémiotique: recueil d'hommages pour Algirdas Julien Greimas*, vol. 2, pp. 683–88. Amsterdam: John Benjamins, 1985.

Caruth, Cathy. "Unclaimed Experience: Trauma and the Possibility of History." *Yale French Studies* 79 (1991): 181–92.

Cassirer, Ernst. *The Individual and the Cosmos in Renaissance Philosophy.* Trans. Mario Domandi. Philadelphia: University of Pennsylvania Press, 1963 [1927].

Castro, Américo. *The Structure of Spanish History.* Trans. Edmund L. King. Princeton, N.J.: Princeton University Press, 1954.

——. *Teresa la Santa y otros ensayos.* Rev. ed. Madrid: Alianza Editorial, 1982 [1929].

Christian, Barbara. "The Race for Theory." *Cultural Critique* 7 (Spring 1987): 51–63.

Cipolla, Carlo. "Sui motive del ritorno di Francesco Petrarca in Italia nel 1347." *Giornale storico della letteratura italiana* 47 (1906): 253–65.

Cixous, Hélène, and Catherine Clément. *The Newly Born Woman.* Trans. Betsy Wing. Theory and History of Literature, no. 24. Minneapolis: University of Minnesota Press, 1986 [1975].

Clissold, Stephen. *St. Teresa of Avila.* London: Sheldon Press, 1979.

Cosenza, Mario E. *The Revolution of Cola di Rienzo.* 2d rev. ed. Ed. Ronald G. Musto. New York: Italica Press, 1986 [1913].

Culler, Jonathan. "Jacques Derrida." In John Sturrock, ed., *Structuralism and Since: From Lévi-Strauss to Derrida,* pp. 154–80. New York: Oxford University Press, 1979.

——. *On Deconstruction: Theory and Criticism After Structuralism.* Ithaca, N.Y.: Cornell University Press, 1982.

Curtius, E. R. *European Literature and the Latin Middle Ages.* Trans. Willard R. Trask. Bollingen Series, no. 36. Princeton, N.J.: Princeton University Press, 1973 [1948].

Dallmayr, Fred R. *Twilight of Subjectivity: Contributions to a Post-Individualist Theory of Politics.* Amherst: University of Massachusetts Press, 1981.

De la Mare, A. C. *The Handwriting of the Italian Humanists* I.1. Oxford: Association Internationale de Bibliophilie, 1973.

De Man, Paul. *Blindness and Insight: Essays in the Rhetoric of Contemporary Criticism.* Ed. Wlad Godzich. Theory and History of Literature, no. 7. Minneapolis: University of Minnesota Press, 1983 [1971].

——. "The Resistance to Theory." *Yale French Studies* 63 (1982): 3–20.

——. "Rhetoric of Persuasion (Nietzsche)." In *Allegories of Reading: Figural Language in Rousseau, Nietzsche, Rilke, and Proust* (New Haven, Conn.: Yale University Press, 1979), pp. 119–31.

——. *The Rhetoric of Romanticism.* New York: Columbia University Press, 1984.

——. "Semiology and Rhetoric." In Josué V. Harari, ed., *Textual Strategies: Perspectives in Post-structuralist Criticism,* pp. 121–40. Ithaca, N.Y.: Cornell University Press, 1979.

De Mattei, Rodolfo. *Il sentimento politico del Petrarca*. Florence: Sansoni, 1944.

De Nicolas, Antonio T. *Powers of Imagining: Ignatius de Loyola*. Albany: State University of New York Press, 1986.

Derrida, Jacques. *Margins of Philosophy*. Trans. Alan Bass. Chicago: University of Chicago Press, 1982 [1972].

————. *Positions*. Trans. Alan Bass. Chicago: Chicago University Press, 1981 [1972].

————. *Writing and Difference*. Trans. Alan Bass. Chicago: University of Chicago Press, 1978 [1967].

Descombes, Vincent. *Modern French Philosophy*. Trans. L. Scott-Fox and J. M. Harding. New York: Cambridge University Press, 1980 [1979].

Domínguez Ortiz, Antonio. *Los Judeoconversos en España y América*. Madrid: Ediciones ISTMO, 1978.

Dotti, Ugo. *Petrarca e la scoperta della coscienza moderna*. Milan: Feltrinelli, 1978.

————. *Vita di Petrarca*. Bari: Editori Laterza, 1987.

Drake, Stillman. "Ptolemy, Galileo, and Scientific Method." *Studies in the History and Philosophy of Science* 9 (1978): 99–115.

————. "Reexamining Galileo's *Dialogue*." In William A. Wallace, ed., *Reinterpreting Galileo*, pp. 155–75.

D'Souza, Dinesh. *Illiberal Education: The Politics of Race and Sex on Campus*. New York: Free Press, 1991.

Duby, Georges, ed. *Revelations of the Medieval World*. Trans. Arthur Goldhammer. Vol. 2 of *A History of Private Life*, ed. Philippe Ariès and Georges Duby. Cambridge, Mass.: Harvard University Press, 1988 [1985].

Eagleton, Terry. *The Significance of Theory*. Oxford: Basil Blackwell, 1990.

Efrén de la Madre de Dios, O.C.D., and Otger Steggink, O. Carm. *Tiempo y vida de Santa Teresa*. Madrid: Católica, 1968.

Eisenstein, Elizabeth L. *The Printing Press as an Agent of Change: Communications and Cultural Transformations in Early Modern Europe*. New York: Cambridge University Press, 1979.

Ellis, John. *Against Deconstruction*. Princeton, N.J.: Princeton University Press, 1989.

Engels, Friedrich. *The Origins of the Family, Private Property, and the State*. New York: Penguin, 1985.

Erasmus, Desiderius. *Desiderii Erasmi opera omnia*. 10 vols. Leiden, 1703–6.

Fehér, Martha. "Galileo and the Demonstrative Ideal of Science." *Studies in the History and Philosophy of Science* 13 (1982): 87–110.

Feldhay, Rivka. "Knowledge and Salvation in Jesuit Culture." *Science in Context* 1, no. 2 (1987): 195–213.

Felman, Shoshana. *Jacques Lacan and the Adventure of Insight: Psychoanalysis in Contemporary Culture.* Cambridge, Mass.: Harvard University Press, 1987.

Felperin, Howard. *Beyond Deconstruction: The Uses and Abuses of Literary Theory.* Oxford: Clarendon Press, 1985.

Ferguson, Margaret, Maureen Quilligan, and Nancy Vickers, eds. *Rewriting the Renaissance: The Discourses of Sexual Difference in Early Modern Europe.* Chicago: University of Chicago Press, 1986.

Feyerabend, Paul. *Against Method: Outline of an Anarchistic Theory of Knowledge.* London: Verso, 1978 [1975].

———. *Science in a Free Society.* London: NLB, 1978.

Finocchiaro, Maurice, ed. and trans. *The Galileo Affair: A Documentary History.* Berkeley: University of California Press, 1989.

———. *Galileo and the Art of Reasoning: Rhetorical Foundations of Logic and Scientific Method.* Boston: Reidel, 1980.

———. "The Methodical Background to Galileo's Trial." In William A. Wallace, ed., *Reinterpreting Galileo,* pp. 241–72.

Fitzmaurice-Kelly, Julia. "Women in Sixteenth-Century Spain." *Revue hispanique* 70 (1927): 557–632.

Foscarini, Paolo Antonio. "Lettera . . . sopra l'opinione de' Pittagorici, e del Copernico. . . . " In *Dialogo di Galileo Galilei Linceo . . . sopra i due massimi Sistemi del Mondo Tolemaico, e Copernicano. . . .* Florence, 1710.

Foster, Kenelm. *Petrarch: Poet and Humanist.* Edinburgh: Edinburgh University Press, 1984.

Foucault, Michel. *The Birth of the Clinic: An Archaeology of Medical Perception.* Trans. A. M. Sheridan Smith. New York: Pantheon, 1973 [1963].

———. *The History of Sexuality.* Trans. Robert Hurley. Vol. 1, *An Introduction.* New York: Pantheon, 1978 [1976]. Vol. 2, *The Use of Pleasure.* New York: Vintage, 1986 [1984]. Vol. 3, *The Care of the Self.* New York: Vintage, 1986 [1984].

———. *Madness and Civilization: A History of Insanity in the Age of Reason.* Trans. Richard Howard. New York: Pantheon, 1965 [1961].

———. *The Order of Things.* Trans. Richard Howard. New York: Pantheon, 1971 [1966].

———. *Power/Knowledge: Selected Interviews and Other Writings, 1972–1977.* Ed. Colin Gordon. New York: Pantheon, 1980.

———. "What Is an Author?" In Josué V. Harari, ed., *Textual Strategies:*

Perspectives in Post-structuralist Criticism, pp. 141–60. Ithaca, N.Y.: Cornell University Press, 1979.

Frank, Manfred. *Das Individuelle allgemeine: Textstrukturierung und -interpretation nach Schleiermacher.* Frankfurt: Suhrkamp, 1977.

———. *Die Unhintergehbarkeit von Individualität.* Frankfurt: Suhrkamp, 1986.

———. "Subjekt, Person, Individuum." In Manfred Frank, Gérard Raulet, and Willem van Reijen, eds., *Die Frage nach dem Subjekt*, pp. 7–28. Frankfurt: Suhrkamp, 1988.

———. *What is Neostructuralism?* Trans. Sabine Wilke and Richard Gray. Theory and History of Literature, no. 45. Minneapolis: University of Minnesota Press, 1989 [1983].

Freccero, John. "Autobiography and Narrative." In Thomas C. Heller, Morton Sosna, and David E. Wellbery, eds., *Reconstructing Individualism: Autonomy, Individuality, and the Self in Western Thought*, pp. 16–29. Stanford, Calif.: Stanford University Press, 1986.

Fuss, Diana. *Essentially Speaking: Feminism, Nature, and Difference.* New York: Routledge, 1989.

Gabrielli, Annibale, ed. *Epistolario di Cola di Rienzo.* Rome, 1890.

Galilei, Galileo. *Dialogue Concerning the Two Chief World Systems.* 2d rev. ed. Ed. and trans. Stillman Drake. Berkeley: University of California Press, 1967 [1953].

———. *Discoveries and Opinions of Galileo.* Ed. and trans. Stillman Drake. Garden City, N.Y.: Doubleday, 1957.

———. *Le Opere di Galileo Galilei.* 20 vols. Ed. Antonio Favaro. Edizione Nazionale. Florence: G. Barbèra Editore, 1933 [1890–99].

Gallop, Jane. *The Daughter's Seduction: Feminism and Psychoanalysis.* Ithaca, N.Y.: Cornell University Press, 1982.

———. *Reading Lacan.* Ithaca, N.Y.: Cornell University Press, 1985.

Giamatti, A. B. *The Earthly Paradise and the Renaissance Epic.* Princeton, N.J.: Princeton University Press, 1966.

Gilbert, G. Nigel, and Michael Mulkay. *Opening Pandora's Box: A Sociological Analysis of Scientists' Discourse.* New York: Cambridge University Press, 1984.

Gingerich, Owen. "Galileo's Astronomy." In William A. Wallace, ed., *Reinterpreting Galileo*, pp. 111–26.

Grafton, Anthony, and Lisa Jardine. *From Humanism to the Humanities: Education and the Liberal Arts in Fifteenth- and Sixteenth-Century Europe.* Cambridge, Mass.: Harvard University Press, 1986.

Grant, W. Leonard. *Neo-Latin Literature and the Pastoral.* Chapel Hill: University of North Carolina Press, 1965.

Greenblatt, Stephen. *Renaissance Self-Fashioning from More to Shakespeare.* Chicago: University of Chicago Press, 1980.

Greene, Thomas. *The Light in Troy: Imitation and Discovery in Renaissance Poetry.* New Haven, Conn.: Yale University Press, 1982.

Gregorovius, Ferdinand. *History of the City of Rome in the Middle Ages.* 8 vols. Trans. Annie Hamilton. London: George Bell, 1894.

Guibert, J. de. "Mystique ignacienne du 'Journal spirituel' de S. Ignace de Loyola." *Revue d'ascetique et de mystique* 19, nos. 73, 74 (1938): 3–22, 113–40.

Gutiérrez, C., S.J. *Españoles en Trento.* Corpus Tridentinum Hispanicum. Valladolid, 1951.

Hall, A. Rupert. *From Galileo to Newton.* New York: Dover, 1981 [1963].

Hannaway, Owen. *The Chemists and the Word: The Didactic Origins of Chemistry.* Baltimore: Johns Hopkins University Press, 1975.

Hanson, Norwood. *Patterns of Discovery.* Cambridge: Cambridge University Press, 1958.

Harran, Marilyn J. *Luther on Conversion: The Early Years.* Ithaca, N.Y.: Cornell University Press, 1983.

Hayles, N. Katherine. *Chaos Bound: Orderly Disorder in Contemporary Literature and Science.* Ithaca, N.Y.: Cornell University Press, 1990.

Heitmann, Klaus. *Fortuna und Virtus: Eine Studie zu Petrarcas Lebensweisheit.* Studi Italiani, no. 1. Cologne: Böhlau Verlag, 1958.

———. "L'Insegnamento agostiniano nel Secretum del Petrarca." *Studi petrarcheschi* 7 (1961): 187–93.

Heller, Agnes. *Renaissance Man.* Trans. Richard E. Allen. London: Routledge and Kegan Paul, 1978 [1967].

Heller, Thomas C., Morton Sosna, and David E. Wellbery, eds. *Reconstructing Individualism: Autonomy, Individuality, and the Self in Western Thought.* Stanford, Calif.: Stanford University Press, 1986.

Hirsch, E. D., Joseph F. Kett, and James Trefil, eds. *Dictionary of Cultural Literacy.* Boston: Houghton Mifflin, 1988.

Hoornaert, Rodolphe. *Sainte Thérèse d'Avila: Sa vie et ce qu'il faut avoir lu de ses écrits.* Bruges, Belgium: Éditions Beyaert, 1951.

Huizinga, Johan. *The Waning of the Middle Ages.* New York: Doubleday, 1954 [1919].

Husserl, Edmund. *The Crisis of European Sciences and Transcendental Phenomenology: An Introduction to Phenomenological Philosophy.* Trans. David Carr. Evanston, Ill.: Northwestern University Press, 1970 [1954].

Imirizaldu, Jesús, ed. *Monjas y beatas embaucadoras.* Madrid: Editora Nacional, 1977.

Irigaray, Luce. "When the Goods Get Together." Trans. Claudia Reeder. In

Elaine Marks and Isabelle de Courtivron, eds., *New French Feminisms.* New York: Schocken, 1981.

Jameson, Fredric. *The Political Unconscious: Narrative as a Socially Symbolic Act.* Ithaca, N.Y.: Cornell University Press, 1981.

Jardine, Nicholas. "Galileo's Road to Truth and the Demonstrative Regress." *Studies in the History and Philosophy of Science* 7 (1976): 277–318.

Jedin, Hubert. *Ecumenical Councils of the Catholic Church: An Historical Outline.* Trans. Ernest Graf, O.S.B. New York: Herder and Herder, 1960.

———. *A History of the Council of Trent.* 4 vols. Trans. Ernest Graf, O.S.B. St. Louis: Herder, 1957–61.

Johnson, Barbara. *A World of Difference.* Baltimore: Johns Hopkins University Press, 1987.

Jordan, Constance. *Renaissance Feminism: Literary Texts and Political Models.* Ithaca, N.Y.: Cornell University Press, 1990.

Kagan, Donald, Steven Ozment, and Frank Turner, eds. *The Western Heritage to 1715.* New York: Macmillan, 1979.

Kahn, Victoria. "The Figure of the Reader in Petrarch's *Secretum.*" *PMLA* 100 (1985): 154–65.

———. *Rhetoric, Prudence, and Skepticism in the Renaissance.* Ithaca, N.Y.: Cornell University Press, 1985.

Kamen, Henry. *Inquisition and Society in Spain in the Sixteenth and Seventeenth Centuries.* London: Weidenfeld and Nicolson, 1985.

Kane, Robert. *Free Will and Values.* Albany: State University of New York Press, 1985.

Keller, Evelyn Fox. *Reflections on Gender and Science.* New Haven, Conn.: Yale University Press, 1985.

Kerrigan, William, and Gordon Braden. *The Idea of the Renaissance.* Baltimore: Johns Hopkins University Press, 1989.

Koyré, Alexandre. *Études galiléennes.* Paris: Hermann, 1966.

Krautheimer, Richard. *Rome: Profile of a City, 312–1308.* Princeton, N.J.: Princeton University Press, 1980.

Kristeller, Paul Oskar. *Renaissance Concepts of Man and Other Essays.* New York: Harper and Row, 1972.

———. *Renaissance Thought: The Classic, Scholastic, and Humanist Strains.* New York: Harper and Row, 1961 [1955].

Kuhn, Thomas. *The Structure of Scientific Revolutions.* Chicago: University of Chicago Press, 1970 [1962].

Lacan, Jacques. *Écrits: A Selection.* Trans. Alan Sheridan. New York: Norton, 1977 [1966].

———. "Intervention on Transference." In Charles Bernheimer and Claire

Kahane, eds., *In Dora's Case: Freud—Hysteria—Feminism*, pp. 92–104. Trans. Jacqueline Rose. New York: Columbia University Press, 1985.

Laclau, Ernesto, and Chantal Mouffe. *Hegemony and Socialist Strategy: Towards a Radical Democratic Politics*. Trans. Winston Moore and Paul Cammack. London: Verso, 1985.

Laguardia, Gari. "St. Teresa and the Problem of Desire." *Hispania* 63 (1980): 523–30.

Langer, Ullrich. *Divine and Poetic Freedom in the Renaissance: Nominalist Theology and Literature in France and Italy*. Princeton, N.J.: Princeton University Press, 1990.

Latour, Bruno. *Science in Action: How to Follow Scientists and Engineers Through Society*. Cambridge, Mass.: Harvard University Press, 1987.

Latour, Bruno, and Steve Woolgar. *Laboratory Life: The Construction of Scientific Facts*. Princeton, N.J.: Princeton University Press, 1986 [1979].

Lea, Henry Charles. *A History of Auricular Confession and Indulgences in the Latin Church*. 3 vols. Philadelphia, 1896.

———. *A History of the Inquisition of Spain*. 4 vols. New York: Macmillan, 1906–7.

Lehman, David. *Signs of the Times: Deconstruction and the Fall of Paul de Man*. New York: Poseidon Press, 1991.

Lentricchia, Frank. *After the New Criticism*. Chicago: University of Chicago Press, 1980.

Leturia, Pedro. *Iñigo de Loyola*. Trans. Aloysius J. Owen, S.J. Chicago: Loyola University Press, 1965 [1949].

Lincoln, Victoria. *Teresa, a Woman: A Biography of Teresa of Avila*. Ed. Elias Rivers and Antonio T. de Nicolas. New York: State University of New York Press, 1984.

Llamas Martínez, E. *Santa Teresa de Jesús y la Inquisición española*. Madrid: Centro Superior de Investigaciones Científicas, 1972.

Lohse, Bernhard, ed. *Der Durchbruch der reformatorischen Erkenntnis bei Luther*. Wege der Forschung, no. 123. Darmstadt: Wissenschaftliche Buchgesellschaft, 1968.

Loyola, Ignatius. *Fontes narrativi de S. Ignatio de Loyola et de Societatis Iesu initiis*. Vol. 1, *Acta Patris Ignatii scripta a P. Lud. Gonzalez de Camara 1553/1555*. Ed. D. F. Zapico, S.J., and C. de Dalmases, S.J., with P. Leturia, S.J. Narrationes scriptae ante annum 1557. Monumenta Historica Societatis Iesu, no. 66. Monumenta Ignatiana, 4th ser., Scripta de S. Ignatio, vol. 1. Rome: Institutum Historicum Societatis Iesu, 1943.

———. *The Autobiography of St. Ignatius Loyola, with Related Documents*. Trans. Joseph F. O'Callaghan. Ed. John C. Olin. New York: Harper and Row, 1974.

———. *The Constitutions of the Society of Jesus.* Trans. George E. Ganss, S.J. St. Louis: Institute of Jesuit Sources, 1970.

———. *Obras completas de San Ignacio de Loyola.* Ed. Ignacio Iparraguirre, S.J., and Cándido de Dalmases, S.J. Madrid: 1952. 2d rev. ed. Católica, 1963.

———. *Sancti Ignatii de Loyola Exercitia Spiritualia.* Ed. Joseph Calveras, S.J., and Candido de Dalmases, S.J. Monumenta Historica Societatis Iesu, no. 100. Monumenta Ignatiana, 2d ser., vol. 1. Rome: Institutum Historicum Societatis Iesu, 1969.

———. *The Spiritual Exercises of St. Ignatius.* Trans. Anthony Mottola. Garden City, N.Y.: Image Books, 1964.

Luther, Martin. *D. Martin Luthers Werke: Kritische Gesamtausgabe.* 65 vols. Weimar: Hermann Böhlaus Nachfolger, 1883–.

———. *Luther's Works.* 55 vols. Ed. Jaroslav Pelikan, vols. 1–30, and Helmut T. Lehmann, vols. 31–55. St. Louis: Concordia Publishing House, and Philadelphia: Fortress Press, 1955–76.

Machiavelli, Niccolò. *Il Principe e Discorsi.* Milan: Feltrinelli, 1960.

———. *The Prince.* Ed. and trans. Harvey C. Mansfield, Jr. Chicago: University of Chicago Press, 1985.

Maclean, Ian. *The Renaissance Notion of Woman: A Study in the Fortunes of Scholasticism and Medical Science in European Intellectual Life.* Cambridge: Cambridge University Press, 1980.

McMullin, Ernan. "Galilean Idealization." *Studies in the History and Philosophy of Science* 16 (1985): 247–73.

Marcus, Leah S. "Renaissance / Early Modern Studies." In Stephen Greenblatt and Giles Gunn, eds., *Redrawing the Boundaries: The Transformation of English and American Literary Studies,* pp. 41–63. New York: MLA, 1992.

Marsh, David. *The Quattrocento Dialogue: Classical Tradition and Humanist Innovations.* Cambridge, Mass.: Harvard University Press, 1980.

Martines, Lauro. *Power and Imagination: City-States in Renaissance Italy.* New York: Knopf, 1979.

Mazzei, Francesco. *Cola di Rienzo: La fantastica vita e l'orribile morte del tribuno del popolo romano.* Milan: Rusconi Libri, 1980.

Meissner, W. W., S.J. *Ignatius of Loyola: The Psychology of a Saint.* New Haven, Conn.: Yale University Press, 1992.

Merchant, Carolyn. *The Death of Nature: Women, Ecology and the Scientific Revolution.* New York: Harper and Row, 1980.

Miller, J. Hillis. *The Ethics of Reading: Kant, de Man, Eliot, Trollope, James, and Benjamin.* New York: Columbia University Press, 1987.

———. "The Search for Grounds in Literary Study." *Genre* 17, no. 1/2 (1984): 19–36.

Mitchell, David. *The Jesuits: A History*. London: Macdonald, 1980.

Mohanty, S. P. "Radical Teaching, Radical Theory: The Ambiguous Politics of Meaning." In Cary Nelson, ed., *Theory in the Classroom*, pp. 149–76. Urbana: University of Illinois Press, 1986.

Mollat, Michel, and Philippe Wolff. *The Popular Revolutions of the Late Middle Ages*. Trans. A. L. Lytton-Sells. London: George Allen and Unwin, 1973.

Mommsen, Theodor E. "Petrarch's Conception of the Dark Ages." *Speculum* 17 (1942): 226–42.

Monter, William E. *Frontiers of Heresy: The Spanish Inquisition from the Basque Lands to Sicily*. New York: Cambridge University Press, 1990.

Moss, Jean Dietz. "Galileo's Letter to Christina: Some Rhetorical Considerations." *Renaissance Quarterly* 36 (1983): 547–76.

———. "The Rhetoric of Proof in Galileo's Writings on the Copernican System." In William A. Wallace, ed., *Reinterpreting Galileo*, pp. 179–204.

Nolhac, Pierre de. *Petrarch and the Ancient World*. Boston: Updike, 1907.

———. *Pétrarque et l'humanisme*. 2 vols. Paris: Librairie Honoré Champion, Éditeur, 1907.

Oberman, Heiko. *The Harvest of Medieval Theology: Gabriel Biel and Late Medieval Nominalism*. Durham, N.C.: Labyrinth Press, 1983.

———. *Luther: Man Between God and the Devil*. Trans. Eileen Walliser-Schwarzbart. New Haven, Conn.: Yale University Press, 1989 [1982].

O'Malley, John W. *The First Jesuits*. Cambridge, Mass.: Harvard University Press, 1993.

Ozment, Stephen. *The Age of Reform, 1250–1550: An Intellectual and Religious History of Late Medieval and Reformation Europe*. New Haven, Conn.: Yale University Press, 1980.

———. "Luther and the Late Middle Ages: The Formation of Reformation Thought." In Robert M. Kingdon, ed., *Transition and Revolution: Problems and Issues of European Renaissance and Reformation History*, pp. 109–29. Minneapolis: Burgess, 1974.

Panofsky, Erwin. *Renaissance and Renaissances in Western Art*. New York: Harper and Row, 1969 [1960].

Patterson, Annabel. *Pastoral and Ideology: Virgil to Valéry*. Berkeley: University of California Press, 1987.

Pelikan, Jaroslav. *Spirit vs. Structure: Luther and the Institutions of the Church*. New York: Harper and Row, 1968.

———. *Reformation of Church and Dogma (1300–1700)*. Vol. 4 of *The Christian Tradition: A History of the Development of Doctrine*. Chicago: University of Chicago Press, 1983.

Petrarca, Francesco. *L'Africa*. Ed. Nicola Festa. Vol. 1 of *Edizione Nazionale delle Opere di Francesco Petrarca*. Florence: Sansoni, 1926.

———. *Epistolae de rebus familiaribus et variae.* 3 vols. Ed. Giuseppe Fra-
cassetti. Florence, 1863.
———. *Le Familiari.* 4 vols. Ed. Vittorio Rossi, vols. 1–3, and Umberto
Bosco, vol. 4. Vols. 10–13 of *Edizione Nazionale delle Opere di
Francesco Petrarca.* Florence: Sansoni, 1933–42.
———. *Letters on Familiar Matters, Rerum familiarium libri.* 3 vols. Trans.
Aldo S. Bernardo. Vol. 1, Albany: State University of New York Press,
1975. Vols. 2 and 3, Baltimore: Johns Hopkins University Press, 1982–85.
———. *Opere latine di Francesco Petrarca.* 2 vols. Ed. Antonietta Bufano.
Turin: UTET, 1975.
———. *Petrarch's "Africa."* Ed. and trans. Thomas Bergin and Alice Wil-
son. New Haven: Yale University Press, 1977.
———. *Petrarch's "Bucolicum Carmen."* Trans. and annot. Thomas G.
Bergin. New Haven: Yale University Press, 1974.
———. *Petrarch's "Secretum" with Introduction, Notes, and Critical An-
thology.* Ed. Davy Carozza. Ed. and trans. H. James Shey. American
University Studies, no. 17. Classical Languages and Literature, no. 7.
New York: Peter Lang, 1989.
Petrucci, Armando. *La Scrittura de Francesco Petrarca.* Studi e Testi, no.
248. Citta del Vaticano: Biblioteca Apostolica Vaticana, 1967.
Pico della Mirandola, Giovanni. *De hominis dignitate, Heptaplus, De ente
et uno.* Ed. Eugenio Garin. Edizione Nazionale dei Classici del Pensiero
Italiano, no. 1. Florence: Vallecchi Editore, 1942.
———. *On the Dignity of Man, On Being and the One, Heptaplus.* Trans.
Charles Glen Wallis. Library of Liberal Arts. New York: Macmillan,
1965.
Piur, Paul. *Cola di Rienzo.* Trans. Jeanne Chabod Rohr. Milan: Fratelli
Treves Editori, 1934 [1931].
Poggioli, Renato. *The Oaten Flute: Essays on Pastoral Poetry and the Pas-
toral Ideal.* Cambridge, Mass.: Harvard University Press, 1975.
Poitrey, Jeannine. *Vocabulario de Santa Teresa.* Madrid: Universidad Pon-
tificia de Salamanca, 1983.
Pomponazzi, Pietro. *Libri quinque de fato, de libero arbitrio, et de praedes-
tinatione.* Ed. Richard Lemay. Lucca: Aedes Thesauri Mundi, 1957.
Rabil, Albert, Jr. "Petrarch, Augustine, and Classical Christian Tradition."
In *Renaissance Humanism: Foundations, Forms, and Legacy,* vol. 1, pp.
95–114. Philadelphia: University of Pennsylvania Press, 1988.
Rebhorn, Wayne. *Foxes and Lions: Machiavelli's Confidence Men.* Ithaca,
N.Y.: Cornell University Press, 1988.
Redondi, Pietro. *Galileo Heretic.* Trans. Raymond Rosenthal. Princeton,
N.J.: Princeton University Press, 1987 [1983].
Reeves, Eileen. "The Rhetoric of Optics: Perspectives on Galileo and
Tesauro." *Stanford Italian Review* 7 (1987): 129–45.

Ribadeneira, Pedro de, S.J. *Vida del padre Ignacio de Loyola, fundador de la religion de la Compañia de Iesus.* Madrid, 1586.

Rico, Francisco. *Lectura del "Secretum."* Vol. 1 of *Vida u obra de Petrarca.* North Carolina Studies in the Romance Languages and Literatures, no. 33. Chapel Hill: University of North Carolina Department of Romance Languages, 1974.

Robinson, James Harvey. *Petrarch: The First Modern Scholar and Man of Letters.* New York: Greenwood Press, 1969 [1914].

Rossi, Rosa. *Esperienza interiore e storia nell' autobiografia de Teresa d'Avila.* Biblioteca de Critica e Letteratura, no. 14. Bari: Adriatica Editrice, 1977.

———. *Teresa d'Avila: Biografia di una scrittrice.* Rome: Editori Reuniti, 1983.

Sabbadini, Remigio. "Note filologiche sul *Secretum* del Petrarca." *Rivista di Filologia e di Istruzione Classica* 45 (1917): 24–37.

Santillana, Giorgio de. *The Crime of Galileo.* Chicago: University of Chicago Press, 1955; reprint, Midway, 1976.

Saslow, James M. *Ganymede in the Renaissance: Homosexuality in Art and Society.* New Haven, Conn.: Yale University Press, 1986.

Sedgwick, Eve Kosofsky. *Between Men: English Literature and Male Homosocial Desire.* New York: Columbia University Press, 1985.

Shakespeare, William. *The Riverside Shakespeare.* Ed. G. Blakemore Evans et al. Boston: Houghton Mifflin, 1974.

Shapere, Dudley. *Galileo: A Philosophical Study.* Chicago: University of Chicago Press, 1974.

Shea, William R. *Galileo's Intellectual Revolution.* New York: Macmillan, 1972.

Sidney, Sir Philip. *A Defence of Poetry.* Ed. J. A. Van Dorsten. New York: Oxford University Press, 1971.

Sizi, Francesco. *Dianoia astronomica, optica, physica.* In Vasco Ronchi, ed., *Scritti di ottica.* Milan: Edizioni Il Polifilo, 1968.

Smith, Barbara Herrnstein. *Contingencies of Value: Alternative Perspectives for Critical Theory.* Cambridge, Mass.: Harvard University Press, 1988.

Smith, John H. "The Transcendence of the Individual." *Diacritics* 19, no. 2 (1989): 80–98.

Smith, Paul. *Discerning the Subject.* Theory and History of Literature, no. 55. Minneapolis: University of Minnesota Press, 1988.

Stanton, Domna. "Autogynography: Is the Subject Different?" In *The Female Autograph: Theory and Practice of Autobiography from the Tenth to the Twentieth Century,* pp. 3–20. Chicago: University of Chicago Press, 1987.

Steiner, George. *After Babel: Aspects of Language and Translation.* New York: Oxford University Press, 1975.

Stracke, Ernst. *Luthers groszes Selbstzeugnis 1545 über seine Entwicklung zum Reformator historisch/kritisch untersucht.* Schriften des Vereins für Reformationsgeschichte, no. 44 (1926).

Tateo, Francesco. *Dialogo interiore e polemica ideologica nel "Secretum" del Petrarca.* Florence: Le Monnier, 1965.

Tenenti, Alberto. *Il senso della morte e l'amore della vita nel Rinascimento.* Turin: Einaudi, 1957.

Teresa of Avila. *The Book of Her Life: Collected Works of St. Teresa of Avila.* 2 vols. Trans. Kieran Kavanaugh, O.C.D., and Otilio Rodriguez, O.C.D. Washington, D.C.: Institute of Carmelite Studies, 1976.

———. *Libros de la B. Madre Teresa de Iesus, fundadora de los monasterios de Monjas, y Frayles Carmelitas descalzos de la primitiva Regla.* Ed. Luis de Leon. Naples, 1604.

———. *The Life of Teresa of Jesus.* Ed. and trans. E. Allison Peers. Garden City, N.Y.: Image Books, 1960 [1944].

———. *Obras completas.* Ed. Efrén de la Madre de Dios, O.C.D., and Otger Steggink, O. Carm. Madrid: Católica, 1962.

Theseider, E. Duprè. *Roma dal comune di popolo alla signoria pontifica (1252–1377).* Storia di Roma, no. 11. Bologna: Licinio Cappelli Editore, 1952.

Theweleit, Klaus. *Women Floods Bodies History.* Vol. 1 of *Male Fantasies,* trans. Stephen Conway, with Erica Carter and Chris Turner. Theory and History of Literature, no. 22. Minneapolis: University of Minnesota Press, 1987 [1977].

Tonelli, Luigi. *Petrarca.* Milan: Edizioni "Corbaccio," 1930.

Toppani, Innocente. "Petrarca, Cola di Rienzo e il mito di Roma." In *Atti dell'Instituto Veneto di Scienze, Lettere ed Arti,* no. 135, pp. 155–72. Venice: Instituto Veneto di Scienze, Lettere ed Arti, 1977.

Trinkaus, Charles. *In Our Image and Likeness: Humanity and Divinity in Italian Humanist Thought.* 2 vols. Chicago: University of Chicago Press, 1970.

———. *The Poet as Philosopher: Petrarch and the Formation of Renaissance Consciousness.* New Haven, Conn.: Yale University Press, 1979.

———. "The Problem of Free Will in the Renaissance and the Reformation." In *The Scope of Renaissance Humanism,* pp. 263–73. Ann Arbor: University of Michigan Press, 1984.

Tripet, Arnaud. *Pétrarque ou la connaissance de soi.* Travaux d'humanisme et renaissance, no. 91. Geneva: Librairie Droz, 1967.

Unamuno, Miguel de. "Vida di Don Quixote y Sancho." In *Obras completas,* vol. 3, pp. 49–256. Madrid: Escelicer, 1968.

Underhill, Evelyn. *Mysticism: A Study in the Nature and Development of Man's Spiritual Consciousness.* London: Methuen, 1977 [1911].

Valla, Lorenzo. *De libero arbitrio.* Trans. Charles Trinkaus. In Ernst Cassirer, Paul Oskar Kristeller, and John Herman Randall, Jr., eds., *The Renaissance Philosophy of Man*, pp. 147–82. Chicago: University of Chicago Press, 1948.

Wallace, David. "'Whan She Translated Was': A Chaucerian Critique of the Petrarchan Academy." In Lee Patterson, ed., *Literary Practice and Social Change in Britain, 1380–1530*, pp. 156–215. Berkeley: University of California Press, 1990.

Wallace, William A. "Galileo's Science and the Trial of 1633." *Wilson Quarterly* 7 (1983): 154–64.

———. "Reinterpreting Galileo on the Basis of His Latin Manuscripts." In *Reinterpreting Galileo*, pp. 3–28.

———, ed. *Reinterpreting Galileo*. Washington, D.C.: Catholic University of America Press, 1986.

Walton, Michael T. "Hermetic Cabala in the *Monas Hieroglyphica* and the *Mosaicall Philosophy*." *Essentia* (Summer 1981): 7–18.

Waswo, Richard. *Language and Meaning in the Renaissance*. Princeton, N.J.: Princeton University Press, 1987.

Weber, Alison. *Teresa of Avila and the Rhetoric of Femininity*. Princeton, N.J.: Princeton University Press, 1990.

Weber, Max. *The Protestant Ethic and the Spirit of Capitalism*. Trans. Talcott Parsons. London: Unwin, 1985.

Weinstein, Donald, and Rudolph M. Bell. *Saints and Society: The Two Worlds of Western Christendom, 1000–1700*. Chicago: University of Chicago Press, 1982.

Weiss, Roberto. "Barbato da Sulmona, il Petrarca e la rivoluzione di Cola di Rienzo." *Studi petrarcheschi* 3 (1950): 13–22.

Wenzel, Siegfried. *The Sin of Sloth: Acedia in Medieval Thought and Literature*. Chapel Hill: University of North Carolina Press, 1967.

Westfall, Richard. "Science and Patronage: Galileo and the Telescope." *Isis* 76 (1985): 11–30.

Westman, Robert S. "The Copernicans and the Churches." In David C. Lindberg and Ronald L. Numbers, eds., *God and Nature: Historical Essays on the Encounter Between Christianity and Science*, pp. 77–113. Berkeley: University of California Press, 1986.

Wiener, John. "Deconstructing de Man." *The Nation*, Jan. 9, 1988, 22–24.

Wilkins, E. H. *Life of Petrarch*. Chicago: University of Chicago Press, 1961.

———. *Petrarch's Eight Years in Milan*. Cambridge, Mass.: Medieval Academy of America, 1958.

———. *Studies in the Life and Works of Petrarch*. Cambridge, Mass.: Medieval Academy of America, 1955.

Williams, Raymond. *The City and the Country*. New York: Oxford University Press, 1973.

————. *Keywords: A Vocabulary of Culture and Society.* New York: Oxford University Press, 1983 [1976].

Winter, Ernst F., ed. and trans. *Erasmus-Luther: Discourse on Free Will.* New York: Ungar, 1961.

Wojciehowski, Dolora A. "Galileo's Two Chief Word Systems." *Stanford Italian Review* 10, no. 1 (1991): 61–80.

————. "A Gendered Cosmos: Galileo, Mother Earth, and the 'Sink of Uncleanliness.' " In Laura Benedetti, Julia Hairston, and Silvia Ross, eds., *Gendered Contexts: New Directions in Italian Cultural Studies.* New York: Peter Lang, forthcoming.

Wright, James, ed. and trans. *The Life of Cola di Rienzo.* Toronto: Pontifical Institute of Medieval Studies, 1975.

Zimmerman, T. Price. "Confession and Autobiography in the Early Renaissance." In A. Mohlo and J. A. Tedeschi, eds., *Renaissance Studies in Honor of Hans Baron*, pp. 119–40. De Kalb: Northern Illinois University Press, 1971.

Zuern, John. "The Mark of a Subject: Luther and the Language of Conversion." Master's report, University of Texas at Austin, 1990.

Index

In this index an "f" after a number indicates a separate reference on the next page, and an "ff" indicates separate references on the next two pages. A continuous discussion over two or more pages is indicated by a span of page numbers, e.g., "57–59." *Passim* is used for a cluster of references in close but not consecutive sequence.

DATE DUE